SCALE OF MILES
1" = APPROX. 20 MI.
MAP BY C. EGGERT.

0 5 10   20   40

N

UTAH

ARIZONA

ABAJO MTS.

WHITE CANYON

ANDERSON'S BOTTOM

CATARACT

HITE

SAN JUAN RIVER

NAVAJO MT.

RAINBOW BRIDGE

GUARDIAN POOL

MARBLE CANYON

ESCALANTE RIVER

HIDDEN PASSAGE

LEES FERRY

ECHO CLIFFS

COLORADO RIVER

LITTLE COLORADO RIVER

VERMILION CLIFFS

MARBLE

RIVER

COLORADO

GRAND WASH CLIFFS

LAKE MEAD

traveler in the **WILDERNESS**

by Cid Ricketts Sumner

traveler
in the
WILDERNESS

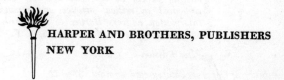

by Cid Ricketts Sumner

HARPER AND BROTHERS, PUBLISHERS
NEW YORK

TRAVELER IN THE WILDERNESS

traveler in the **WILDERNESS**

chapter

wwwwwwwwwwwwwwwwwwwwwwwwwwwwwwwwwwwwwwwwwwwwwwwwwwwwwwwwwwwwwwwwwwwwwwwwwwwwwwwwwwwwwwwwwwww

1

How did a woman of my age and sedentary habit come to be involved in so curious, not to say unseemly, an adventure? It was really quite simple. I read an ad in the personals column of the *Saturday Review*, and if I must defend myself, surely there is no more impeccable instigator of ideas than that magazine. The ad read as follows: "EXPLORE WITH TOP BOATMEN and renowned wilderness photographer down Green and Colorado Rivers. Expedition leaves Green River, Wyoming June 10 on 60-day journey to Lake Mead through fabulous canyons including Grand Canyon. Re-live voyage Major Powell made in 1869. Requirement: ruggedness! Inquire Charles Eggert, Barrytown, New York."

Now before the fish will take the bait he must be not only somewhat bored with his regular daily diet but hungry enough to risk something new. I was in such a state. I wanted to escape from the confusion and clamor of headlines and newscasters, from lectures on the implications of the atomic age, from the telephone, TV, the laundryman and all the regular routine, and if this escape involved a certain amount of risk, had I not often expressed the idea that age, since it had little to lose, is the time of life when risks should be freely taken? Youth is the time for caution. For surely just being young is full enough of jeopardy, growing up a hazardous affair, marriage a battle—for self-control and consideration of others—the bearing of children a vast, indeed if one listens to the psychologists, an ominous enterprise, making a living high adventure, and coming to know one-

1

self and other people a ticklish business. So I had evolved my
little theory that age should hold not only contemplation but
danger, adventure. And I do believe in theories. Right or wrong
they provide a slight stay against the confusions of existence.

At the moment when I read the ad, I had furthermore the
feeling that I needed to withdraw and consider, that somehow I
should renew a sense of wonder at the world around me, achieve
a fresh kinship with the old elementals of earth and air and sky
and water to which in the natural course of events I would before
too many years be returned; that I would like to be reduced,
by hardship and danger if need be, to my own essential parts,
perhaps even created anew.

There were also more intimate and personal reasons for wanting to get away, for when one meets with a situation which no
human power may remedy, when there is nothing to do about it,
then surely is the moment to plunge into activity so great that
there is no time for thought or grieving. But the obvious truth
is that, since I was now in my sixties, I was at that period of life
when one is too young for the chimney corner, too old to be
at the center of things, is rather poised on the periphery ready
to take off at any tangent that promises distraction, excitement,
fun. And on the latter, youth has no monopoly. That is one of
the pleasant surprises of age.

So I was ripe to rise to such bait as the ad offered. I marked
it with a black penciled circle and laid it in my desk drawer,
less with any idea of actually following it up than from fear
that some child or grandchild might come upon it, think me in
my dotage for even noting such a wild expedition and take steps
toward confining me in an institution. The third day, April 27,
I wrote what used to be a penny postal: "Dear Mr. Eggert,
Please send information about your excursion—cost, equipment,
lodging en route etc. How rugged must one be? I am not very.
I am old but intrepid. Yours truly etc."

That *intrepid* was a bare-faced lie. I am often scared to death.

However I must add that I am tougher than I look, as indeed are all the gentle, delicate-seeming Southern ladies such as I who give the impression that we are far too fragile to support anything more rigorous than what that devilishly shrewd observer David L. Cohn calls "those agreeable fatigues incident to an excess of male gallantry."

In due time several mimeographed sheets arrived. From these I learned that the primary object of the Expedition was to make a documentary film of the canyons, many of which would soon be lost forever if certain proposed dams were built. Like most Easterners and Southerners I knew little or nothing and cared less about the controversy raging over those dams, and if I now have quite a violent opinion it is a personal one, the result of my own observation.

The Expedition, I further discovered from the prospectus, would be conducted with more than ample precautions *"because of the film."* The italics are mine but, even without them, the phrase seemed to me to show a fine nonchalance toward the human lives involved. This would not be an "armchair" tour; each member of the party would be expected to take his part on the portages and at the oars on this journey through the most hazardous canyon country in North America. The head boatman was quoted as saying, "This trip will take all we have." A tough hide was also recommended. In rubber boats fourteen rugged men with only maps to guide them and no human help within call were to travel 1,030 river miles, a feat which only about ten other parties had matched, the first in 1869, the last in 1940. Fourteen rugged men, I repeated, and cried with Lady Macbeth, "Come, you spirits that tend on mortal thoughts, unsex me here!" I got no results from this appeal to the spirits, and had I done so there was still the little matter of age. Was resignation then to be my lot?

When M. C. M., a friend and contemporary came to tea, I told her about my wonderful short-lived dream, for many years ago she had paddled down the Mississippi and camped along-shore. We both sighed and regretfully agreed that there had come a time when we had to recognize our limitations. But after a morning at the dentist's—a form of minor torture which always fills me with rage against the ravages of time and decay, and after a noontime glass of sherry (strictly medicinal), I wrote again to the Eggert-Hatch Expedition. "Dear sirs," I said, "I thank you for the folder recently received. I see that I am nothing that you ask for, being a woman, over sixty who can offer nothing more than ballast, a good spirit and some skill as a cook." Then, the sherry having gone to my fluency, I continued in somewhat disjointed manner, "My life is of little real importance. I would try not to be a nuisance. I have been a medical student. I am old enough not to be disturbed in the company of men (no matter what may be their physiological necessities). My children are of age and independent. No one is in actual need of my presence. I am at that place in life when I can feel altogether reckless, adventurous, ripe for whatever fun can be wrung from existence. Do not imagine that I am trying to commit suicide via your expedition. I love life and people and shall to my last gasp. When I go abroad I carry a note saying, 'Just bury me where I fall and no to-do about it. Notify John Cutler, Duxbury, Mass.' This would apply to your Expedition. I would like to write up the voyage from the point of view of one woman—to fourteen men. If at the last moment you need my fare and are willing to take a chance on me, let me know, will you? I'll fly out to Green River. I like your spirit. Sincerely yours etc."

Having thus had my little fling on the typewriter instead of the river, I forgot about the whole affair. So much so that a letter postmarked Barrytown, New York, made me wonder for a moment who could be writing me from there. I tore it open and read, "Dear Mrs. S., My young man Kip (short for Christopher) is sort of musically inclined—at least at nine he plays the piano better than his father does, age thirty-seven. On Sunday mornings we have a little musicale here in which a very good buddy of his named Tino (short for what, I don't know) joins him, playing the recorder. Tino's mother joins in too—"

Here I looked across the room to Ida Mowry who was spending the day with me. "Ida," I said, "I am in correspondence with a madman."

She gave me an uneasy glance. "I hope it is a long-distance affair."

"Barrytown, New York."

"Barrytown? But that's where Peggy and Buzz live."

"Oh—" I'd known her daughter Peg for years, Buzz too. "Did you ever hear them speak of anyone there named Charles Eggert?"

"Of course. They're neighbors and good friends."

"Is he sane?"

"Very much so."

Reassured, I read on, ". . . Peg, the mother of Tino, asked me how the river trip was coming on. . . . And she knows you."

This small coincidence seemed like the finger of fate pointing the way. Not that I am superstitious. My feeling about those things is like that of the old countrywoman down in Mississippi who said, "No ma'm, I don't believe in signs and such. I just don't like to go contrarywise." I, too, prefer to take a hint when all signs point.

Well, Charles Eggert went on to say that he liked *my* spirit, that the seven or eight men who had signed up needed someone along to watch out for, that they would need ballast in a psychological as well as physical way, that they would need a sort of go-between and smoother-outer, a broad shoulder to cry upon. (I had neglected to tell him that I weigh only 130 pounds and that while well-proportioned, my shoulder is not broad enough to accommodate eight or even seven men.) He said he really wanted me to come along, and other nice things. I read on, waiting for the big BUT which usually follows such amiable pleasantries. It did—

"But I am uncertain about you because I am uncertain about what we are getting into ourselves. We can depend only on the accounts of others who have made this trip. Do they exaggerate its terrors? Perhaps to make heroes out of themselves? Do they describe them as so fierce in order that they alone will hold the record? Perhaps it is even worse than they say and being sadists they want others to suffer as they have. I know some of the canyons myself. There are rapids that *must* be run, the worst in America, where canyon walls rise sheer from the river's edge and there is no other way out. The river can be terrifying. There are undercurrents that pull you down. There are rocks to bang against. They will chew you to hamburg if you can't recover yourself quickly. We have good boats but they can tip over if an error in judgment is made or an oar broken in the hard pull. What would be your chances if you were dumped in the river? . . . If you should come with us through my decision and should you get dumped and drowned . . . I am not sure I am big enough to carry that responsibility. . . . Let me talk with Don Hatch, my head man. . . . What do you mean, you are not needed? A world so lacking in spirit and gaiety needs a gal like you around. . . ."

"Gal" indeed! But like most older people accustomed to being treated with respect, I rather relished this touch of sauciness. In fact I was quite charmed with his attitude. I therefore replied at once, telling him so. I added that there would be no hard feelings if he turned me down and I said also, regarding the sense of responsibility: "You have none. It is all mine. I assumed it when I first wrote you a letter of inquiry. . . . However, though I have just had a complete physical examination and been pronounced sound, I must tell you that I cannot carry heavy loads. I cannot swim against a fierce current. But if dumped in the river, I can float, unless made into instant hamburg. My name Cid is short for Placid. I would love to be watched out for and cherished by all those men, for though I live in New England, I am Southern born. Sincerely yours etc."

After this it was settled that I might go "sectionally"—not in pieces, myself—leave that to the rocks—but taking the voyage in five parts, at the end of any one of which I might give up if I found it all too much for me. About this time I began to tell my children and friends that I thought I would go west this summer since I had never been west of Chicago and surely it was high time I was going, if ever. Incidentally, I said, I might see something of the canyon country, visit my old friends Bess and B. W. Stiles in Denver and of course go on to California to see my son Jacques. It all sounded quite sane and reasonable. "How nice," everybody said. People don't really care much what one does, as long as it is sufficiently conventional and commonplace.

But after another letter from Charles Eggert listing equipment I had to get, suggesting anti-tick and tetanus shots—thus involving visits to the doctor and long sessions at the Army and Navy Surplus Store, where friends discovered me trying out an army cot in the main aisle of the place, after my hints to Ted and Sarah that I'd like to borrow a sleeping bag, appeals to Ed to give me any shirts he was about to abandon, after borrowing Bobbie's old green flannel jumper and snatching some of Deedy's wool socks, after retrieving from Lucy Palfrey a short jacket I'd swapped her for a light blue coat, and after I had taken out insurance from a neighbor for everything from broken limbs to total disability, suspicions began to grow, odd rumors began to circulate. I remember there was quite a little stir in the drugstore when I asked for a rattlesnake kit. It is hard to keep a secret in a village the size of Duxbury. My own children began to ask leading questions. To them I retorted, "Can't I have any private life of my own?" thus achieving a small long-delayed revenge by quoting their favorite teen-age response to my motherly inquiries.

Green River, Wyoming, was to be our meeting place. Wyoming! A name that had always fascinated me, warmed me like a draught of new wine. Years ago in church our summer-supply minister, a desiccated, godly old man, announced, "Next Sunday the pulpit will be occupied by the Bishop of Wyoming." Instantly I seemed to see him as in a vision, full of life and vigor and color, riding a milk-white charger (related perhaps to Hi-O Silver), red robes billowing around him as he came, blown in on the wind of vast open spaces to more than fill the chaste white pulpit of St. John's church in Duxbury. That was about as substantial as my knowledge of Wyoming. Of course I was familiar with a few stereotyped phrases such as "The land of rugged individualism" and "The romantic frontier" which I in common with many others of equal ignorance was accustomed to apply indiscriminately to a region which comprises at least 40 per cent of the United States. No wonder the government in Washington has blundered and still blunders in its approach to the problems of the West.

In the rush of getting ready I found time for a little preparatory reading and was lucky enough to find in the Plymouth library Powell's *First Through the Grand Canyon,* a fascinating and thoroughly scientific account of his voyage of 1869. I read how the Indians had warned Powell not to enter the canyons. There was a legend of a chief who mourned for his wife till one of the gods made a trail for him through the mountains and led him by this canyon path to see the happy land where his wife now was. And having seen, he returned to his desert home to mourn no more. Then the god sent a raging river through the gorge, a river that would engulf any who tried to pass through it. Indeed the wrath of the gods would be upon the heads of any who entered there. One Indian had tried it and a fellow tribesman told Powell about it. He said, "The rocks heap heap high," and lifted his arms straight up to illustrate how the walls of the canyon rose. "The water go h-oowoogh, h-oowoogh; water pony heap buck; water catch 'em; no see 'em any more."

Powell's boats had fared not much better than the Indian's "water pony," and I read his account of each day's happenings with intense excitement augmented by increasing uneasiness. Would we duplicate not only his route but his disasters? The very names he gave to points along the way were frightening—Flaming Gorge, Hell's Half Mile, with its hundred-foot descent in that half mile; Whirlpool, Dirty Devil River, Sockdologer Rapid, S O B, Disaster Falls, Split Mountain, Desolation Canyon. For the first time I began to see what I was getting into.

I know I had been warned by Charles Eggert, but now it all became vivid and immediate as I read of Powell's difficulties—of how he lost a boat that crashed to pieces in the cruel rapids, how they all tipped over and supplies were lost, men nearly drowned. I read how they had to line the boats down over the falls, I read of cold and heat and rain and blowing sand, of rattlers, isolation, broken oars, moldy flour, difficult portages over great rocks and crevasses where they had to climb far up the cliff in order to get any passage at all. Frankly, I quailed. What really gave me pause more than anything else, I think, was the account of how Powell was trapped—rimrocked is the correct term—three hundred feet above the river, caught in such a position that he could move neither up nor down. He was saved only because a companion, higher up on a ledge, was quick-witted enough to strip off his long balbriggan underwear and lower one leg of it down to him. I asked myself what chance I would have in a similar situation with these modern "briefs" I am told that men wear nowadays! The courage of ignorance which had so far sustained me began to waver. But I had an oft-pronounced theory about age and danger, didn't I? I had to live up to that or feel like a fraud. Besides I was by now committed.

On the fifth of June, therefore, I made the flight to Denver, a journey impressive to me only for its speed and the glimpses I got of the country when I leaned across the Vassar girl who sat beside me and looked out the window. I got a new appreciation of the size of the Western states and of the farms, the green and purple-plowed fields so vast that houses and barns were dwarfed almost to invisibility.

Denver then, in the afternoon, and good friends to meet me. I breathed with delight the thin electric air of that mile-high city. It was like the air of Capri in February, it was like the wind off icebergs when one makes a northern crossing of the Atlantic in the month of May. It seemed to aerate not only the lungs but the very bones. I was so invigorated by it that, in order to get a better look at the Rockies, I took bus instead of plane to Vernal, Utah, where it had been agreed that I was to meet Charles Eggert to drive with him up to Wyoming.

This bus trip would have been a tiring one but for the magnificence of the scenery and the excitement of the heights, still splashed with snow, and the way we hairpinned up and down them. It reminded me of the bus trip from Sorrento to Amalfi, only there we had at least a low wall between us and eternity. After we had crossed the Great Divide and come down to less dramatic scenes, I found myself still exhilarated beyond fatigue. It is a curious fact that when one is entertained and interested one does not tire.

This was the day when I saw sagebrush for the first time. Close by the roadside, windswept and distorted, it looks like a miniature forest fit for the wee folk. Not the green gay fairies of Ireland but for some wizened, desiccated species of leprechaun, brittle as dried butterflies. In the distance it takes on a subtle gray-green color and in texture reminds one of the stretches of heather of northern Scotland. The afternoon passed slowly, the mountains blued off into the sky. I talked with the couple behind me, bound for Salt Lake City after a visit with grown children in Denver. We spoke of the slow passage of the pioneers across the crisp dry land, of how they must have known each grain of sand under the reluctant wagon wheels, each sprig of sage, and how they must have treasured each rare red or golden cactus flower or bit of blue delphinium blooming then as now.

The woman said, "My husband's mother took sick and died on the way. They put her best silk dress on her and buried her beside the trail and planted sage on the dug earth so the Indians would not find her." I could almost hear the creak of the wagon as she talked of those days. And I shall always be grateful to her for insisting to the bus driver that there was another passenger not yet aboard after the "rest stop" in Craig. I have met with many such kindnesses in my travels. It may be that the small hazards involved in being out of one's familiar surroundings bring people closer together, make them feel more generous and helpful. It would be cheering if we could hope that the larger dangers of the age in which we live might bring us all into better relationship.

At last Vernal signs began to appear along the roadside— motels, cafés, garages advertised in such large letters that I was driven to picture the place as consisting of nothing else. It turned out to be a very pleasant small town. Don Hatch, head boatman of the expedition, came to the bus station to meet me. I was appalled at sight of him, so slim and young. How could such a man be physically capable of swinging an oar against the rapids, how could one so gay and lighthearted seeming, so casual in manner, bear the responsibilities of such a journey as ours was to be? I should have known better by the way he shouldered my two heavy duffel bags, by the way he instantly took charge of me and all my affairs, saying, "I'll just run you over to my father's house and let you rest a bit while I phone round and see which motel Charles arranged for you to stop at."

The back seat of the car was still piled high with luggage and the debris of a day's trip. He had just driven in from Salt Lake City an hour ago with his wife and children, he said, for his school had not closed till yesterday. He tossed a woolly brown bear out of my way and helped me in.

I have always found a man's manner of driving a car rather revealing, artists in my experience being the worst drivers and

schoolteachers a close second, so now I watched Don with some
trepidation. He sat slumped and at ease behind the wheel,
seemed to give little attention to what he was doing, yet as we
passed one car, slowed behind a truck, I relaxed. He was all
right, and if he did as well on the river, I need not worry. "You
seem to know your way around this town," I said.

"Ought to. I was born here, lived here till I went to Salt Lake
City to high school and the university."

"Do you know the river as well?"

"Some of it. I've spent all my vacations taking parties out
on the river."

We turned a corner and drew up before a tree-shaded house.
Don left me in the cool living room, went to a telephone in the
hall and I heard him calling a motel—the wrong one, for they
had no reservation. Before he could call another, the phone rang.
I picked up a magazine, then sat motionless listening, for I
gathered at once that it must be Charles Eggert on the line.

"Yes, yes, I've seen to that . . . that's okay. . . . She's right
here. . . . On the bus . . . What's she like? Wait and I'll look."
He popped his head round the doorway like a roguish jack-in-the-
box, gave me a wide-eyed quick inspection as if he had not
noticed me before and said into the phone in an astonished tone,
"Why, she's lovely!"

I laughed. "Better say I look healthy and good-natured." But
he had already disappeared and their talk was of more important
matters.

Charles had been delayed by car trouble, Don told me as we
drove to my motel a little later, but he would arrive tomorrow
and we would all get off in good time. Meanwhile he advised
me to have a good night's rest and see the sights of the town
next morning.

chapter

2

The main street of Vernal is very wide, giving the place a pleasant look of spaciousness. There was not much traffic when I went out to breakfast the next morning, and when I paused on the curb to let a car go by I was astounded to have it stop and wait for me to cross. As I passed in front of it, I expressed my appreciation by a small bow and a wave of the hand. Later, somewhat to my disappointment—for I had liked to believe this was a sample of the fabled courtesy of the West—I learned that there is a state law saying a motorist must stop for a pedestrian. Even so, what a contrast to the East! Once driving in New York City I paused to let an apparently endless stream of people pass and a policeman shouted, "What are you waiting for, lady? Come on, come on, get a move on."

It may be that all courtesy has to be imposed by authority—think of all the mothers saying, "Tell the lady thank you," and "Say excuse me, please," till that wonderful day when the child spontaneously makes the proper response. In any case I am all for it.

I was pleased too here in Vernal when I asked a passerby if he could tell me the way to the museum, to have him reply, "Yes, ma'm." That little ma'm adds something to even so brief an encounter, lends a special flavor that is more than just a reminder to me of my native Mississippi. It gives a woman something to live up to, makes her want to be worthy of it. A "yeah," or "sure" may be prompted by just as kindly a spirit, but it is not inspiring.

I ate in a small café down the street and watched the people passing on the sidewalk and those who sat at the tables around me. They seemed quite beautiful to me, the girls tall and healthy-looking, the men of superb physique. And so many of them! Indeed this is something I noticed wherever I went in the West. That section of the country seems aswarm with giants broad-shouldered, ruddy, tanned and full of vigor. Maybe the geographer Ellsworth Huntington was right in his theory that those people who survived the rigors of climate and transcontinental migration were truly the most fit, the weakest being all weeded out, so that here in the West their descendants to this day form our sturdiest stock.

I had time in my day of waiting in Vernal to read in the Book of Mormon which I found in my motel room as one finds the Gideon Bible in the East. I read that many "simple and precious things" had been lost from the record, that they were to be found here in this book. I shall look again for them sometime. In this hasty skimming I found mostly battles and begats. However, since I had always wondered how the "plates" got across the ocean to that place in New York State where Joseph Smith found them, I was much interested by the chapter describing a boat built at the Lord's command, a boat that was to be "tight as a dish." Of course, being tight as a dish, there was only darkness in the hold, and the people complained, whereupon the Lord caused a rock on the mountain to shine and give forth light. This rock, placed in the hold, made it bright as day. Then the winds began to blow, the waves to rise, and the ship with all its passengers and records was driven across the ocean to this hemisphere. All this I learned while waiting in Vernal.

Next day there was a knock at my door. "Are you there?" someone called in a tone that said, if I were, that was good news. Charles Eggert, blond, young, with a twinkle and an infectious laugh, had arrived at last. Even now, weary from the long drive and car trouble on the way, he was full of enthusiasm, concerned for my comfort. Had I had lunch? Well, come along and at least have a cup of coffee and keep him company while he had his. Would I like to drive out to the Dinosaur National Monument? Yes, I'd like to, I said, and then having gotten the word only by ear and not being as familiar with it as I later became, I said, "What? Is there really a national monument to Dinah Shore?"

That drive was my introduction not only to the hospitality of the Park Service people, here represented by the Robinsons, but to the awful sight of my first canyon. We stopped by the roadside not far from where the earth seemed to fall away into nothingness. Charles went ahead to stand on the very brink, outlined against vacancy, his close-cropped hair gold in the sunlight. "We'll be coming along here in about a week," he said. I took one hasty look and stepped back. I simply could not look. It was too much for me. My eyes refused to see, my mind to comprehend, and my memory of that gorge is even now as vague and blurry as an over-exposed film. I could not get back to the car fast enough. It was quite a little while before I got back my breath.

But I was not yet through with this preview of what lay ahead. Charles was following a narrow road that led right down into the canyon—one of the rare places where such an entrance is possible. I had not the courage to say, "No, no, I cannot bear any more of this." Sometimes it takes courage to be cowardly. The walls grew higher and higher as we descended. I could feel them bearing in upon me. When we reached the very bottom, we got out of the car and I stood on a spit of sand between a cave and the noisy tumbling river, arms folded tight across my breast to keep my heart in it. The river itself did not dismay me; I am accustomed to sailing in a small boat in rough water. But the canyon! Digging into the sand with my toes, I forced my gaze upward to where the sky, no longer a familiar sheltering dome, lay like a jagged blue lid clamped across the top of the canyon walls. I could not have been more overwhelmed had I been of a sudden translated to a valley of the moon. The rocky sides were all colors—red, yellow, orange, with streaks of purple and black like streamers hanging down, and there were terraced sections draped with a thin veil of green too distant to be identified as any earthly growth.

It was not so much these details that astounded me, as the fact that there could be this ghastly breach in the solid ground I had always depended upon. The very existence of such a place was more fantastic and incredible than that of those creatures, the dinosaurs, whose bones were being dug from the stone back at the museum. Indeed, if this fearful canyon could exist, then a dinosaur was nothing to wonder at. Anything could be. And I was not only physically displaced from all familiar things, I was thrust backward in time by these exposed inward layers of the earth, laid down so many eons ago. I myself was reduced to a mere dot, and a diaphanous one at that, against a backdrop of eternity. I know, safe at home in Duxbury, I had told myself that I wanted to be reduced to my essential parts. But I had not realized they would be so small. It was not until I was back again in my small motel room in Vernal that I was able to gather myself once more into some sort of entity. Indeed I am not yet sure that I got all the parts of me in the proper places.

The next day I was to see a still more amazing canyon. We left by jeep, Charles and I, in mid-afternoon for the drive from Vernal, Utah, to Green River, Wyoming. Don Hatch and the two boatmen, Les and Bruce, were to follow in a truck with supplies and the two boats.

I felt as we drove together through the sun-struck hours that I had known Charles for years. Somehow we had gone at once deeper than external circumstances and I already knew the essential person without the help of any of the conventional trappings of fact. It was a curious reversal of the usual course of friendship. Yet I have met with it before in my life. I remember a kilted gentleman I suddenly found myself knowing quite well as we talked, leaning on the rail of a small boat off the coast of Scotland, and later when I lunched with him in London and saw him in city garb, I realized that I did not know any of the superficial details of his life—whether he had a family or where he had lived or how he made a living in the world. I think too of a European met by chance, of one New Englander many years my senior, and there was a young woman first encountered on a bus. This quick knowing of a stranger has little to do with sex or age. It is rather a kinship in one's essential outlook on life, or most of all, perhaps, a kink or quirk of mind in common which makes one laugh at the same sort of thing. For the quality of humor is as varied as character and a likeness in it makes a kind of secret fraternity for which the password is laughter. Old friends, too, come into this category—not all of them, but those we meet, as I had recently met my Denver friends to find after many years that our feeling for each other is independent of time and space. Yeats says, "And say my glory was I had such friends." It is true. They are the richness, the real glory of life.

And here beside me was Charles. With him of course I had become somewhat acquainted through our sprightly correspondence. Now I sensed that this strange country held some special, perhaps even spiritual significance for him, that here he might have found some emotional release which he in his young life had needed. And here I too, toward the end of a longer one, had come seeking something, I did not yet know what. Also I wondered if his desire to photograph these canyons and to see them preserved did not arise out of a wish to share with others the good which he himself had gained from them. This was a purpose with which I already felt the greatest sympathy.

Almost as if he had read my thoughts, he now began to tell me how he had gotten the idea for this Expedition. He had rather gone from one thing to another when he got home from the Navy, he said, studying music at the Juilliard School, doing pho-

tography for a magazine that folded, making hi-fi recordings.
He had come west and somehow that straightened him out, gave
him a purpose.

I said, quoting Thoreau, "In wildness is the preservation of
the world."

He nodded. "It was mine, all right. So I made the Dinosaur
documentary, met Don—the best boatman on the river. And
what we're heading into now grew out of all that. If they put
through those dams, there will at least be a photographic record
of what is destroyed. And it even might be that when people
see my film they'll shift the dam sites elsewhere. There are no
other canyons in the world like those we'll be seeing."

There was such real feeling in his tones that now for the
first time I felt as if this were more than a personal search and
adventure. There was a larger purpose and a truly worthy one.

The road grew steadily worse. I remembered the advice given
me in Denver by B. W. "Now when you come to the rapids," he
said, "just relax. Don't fight them, go with them." It was good
advice for taking anything unavoidable. Therefore now amid
these bumps and jolts of the road I applied it, and let myself
bounce around on the seat like a half-filled sack of meal.

We stopped at Windy Point for the sweeping view that
stretches away over lower rounding hills and valleys, sharp
cliffs, green fields, to the snow-capped Uintas. The marker there
said we were looking at 200,000,000 years of time, at rock
formations from the beginning of the world, and I could well
believe it. Charles took pictures and I was nearly blown away
by the wind. The jeep trembled, sitting there.

Later we stopped again to look down into Red Canyon. We had
to leap across bottomless crevasses to reach the brink. Charles
said, "You must always step on a rock this way, on the side that
lies flush with the ground. The other edge with a small cave
beneath is too good a place for rattlers." I stepped gingerly and
looked where I would land before I leaped a crevasse.

This time, on the very edge of the world, I was able to look, to see the gorge that was a mile wide here; and fifteen hundred feet down, the little pea-soup river that had made the big canyon. I even noted below us far to the left a cathedral-like formation of rock and said, "I'll watch for that as we come along the river." The sun was lower now, the opposite side was in shadow, the red rock purpling there; the cedars that topped it were black. Far away on the horizon a mountain peak held a drift of snow that shone like a fallen white sun. I moved to the very edge and peered over. There was no downward slope visible, only a ledge some five hundred feet below. The rock we stood on, flat as a table here, was hollowed out, concave, and that last crevasse we had jumped across needed to widen but a little more to send this great hunk of wall crashing downward.

In the face of immensity it may be that the mind, to preserve its sanity, seeks relief in something small and comprehensible. It was while we were standing there that I was struck by two things insignificant in themselves and worth remembering only because of the effect they had on me. One was a small bird, slight and swift, of the swallow family perhaps. It flew among the pines that stood behind us. Then, with the utmost daring, it went on, on, out over space. Of course I knew that the air was the same there as above solid ground, I knew it was quite unreasonable of me to feel such admiration. But later when I too, in an ancient shaky cub plane, was flying along the brink of an even deeper canyon and back and forth across it, I remembered that small bird and took courage.

The other thing that struck me was a nosegay of what looked to be ground phlox. It grew just over the edge of the gorge out of no more than a spoonful of soil lodged on solid rock, with not even a small crevice to support it. Pure white, all blossom, with no visible green. I pointed it out to Charles. He looked at me a moment, puzzled, then he nodded and took a picture of it. He was good at quick understanding.

We drove on through "parks," that is, open level ground and wooded stretches. There were ridgepole pines and great forest pines. Now and then we came upon a clump of twinkling aspens, surely the most spiritual of trees, white-bodied, virginal and showered now in early June with a delicate snowfall of yellow-green leaves. Rosettes of prostrate yew circled darkly at their feet. A white-tailed doe sprang across the road ahead of us, another bounded lightly through the woods. A dead porcupine lay on the roadbank, there was a series of beaver dams on a steep rushing stream and in a level spot I saw a beaver humping himself along, trying to make his fat body as flat as his tail. Always there was the clean pungent smell of pine needles and sage.

Then we dropped down into Sheep Creek Canyon. On the right a cream-colored cliff jagged its way upward, growing, growing as we descended till it was a fantastic cardboard cutout, two-dimensional and utterly unreal against the sky. Ahead was a swooping incline of red and yellow layered rock, a giant rosette on the mighty breast of the canyon wall, thrust upward by some violent cataclysm of the earth and forever fixed there like a topsy-turvy monument to madness. Like a "statue" from the childhood game, here it had been flung in a frenzy and frozen so. We got out of the car to stand and stare at this visible evidence of forces that were too great for human beings to tamper with. And I shuddered, thinking of the violence being unleashed at Los Alamos and elsewhere in the world today. Men who order such things and we who permit it should be brought here and made to stand and look.

As we returned to the car, Charles said he sometimes played with the notion that if one dug deeper yet in such a spot as this one might come upon the remains of a previous civilization like ours, with even another Empire State Building down below there somewhere and a United Nations all in crumbled ruin, a civilization which had gone on a few steps beyond us, to blow itself to annihilation. This set me to thinking of mankind as moving forever in cycles of disaster, arriving always at destruction, only to begin again. I dwelt gloomily on this idea as we drove on beside the narrow creek that roared between its banks.

Then we came upon a slight widening of the canyon. Here in its curve on our left was a small neat cottage set against the red rock wall, a purple lilac in full bloom beside it, trained vines across the porch, apple trees, half blossom, half green leaf, a vegetable garden laid out in orderly rows. Peace, love of earth and of mankind—it was a reassuring sight.

We mounted a winding narrow road, came up and out of the canyon into a sane green, gently rolling land that slowly flattened out. At Manila we stopped for gas. From there we headed into the largest and most lasting sunset I have ever seen, the long straight road through the South Pass seeming to go on forever toward it. With each alteration of color—from pink to red to salmon and mauve and purple and back to red again—I thought that now at last it would surely fade to gray. But it hung on.

With dusk the even range of hills on each side drew back yet farther in a velvet roll against the horizon, the flat sage-covered plain melted into a pool, a lighter darkness, and the sky stretched itself wider and wider. One star, then another, was hung up to show how big the sky was. There were no earthly lights, there was no sign that man existed on the face of the planet. We drove in silence, the new jeep humming softly over the paved road.

Then abruptly on the right, hugging the earth like sparsely scattered glowworms, there lay the lights of Green River, a place born out of nothingness, out of darkness, space and silence. After Sheep Creek Canyon and the vast distances of sky and plain, it was rather a jolt to come upon this flat human town, rimmed with bare low cliffs, just faintly visible by the lonely street lights and swept by a ceaseless wind. We did not stop long now, only paused at the Star Motel to engage four rooms and then dash on in search of the Rock Springs airport. For we had to meet the 9:10 plane that was bringing in two more of our party. These were Tony, a college student who was to serve as Charles's assistant, and Fred, fiftyish, I was told, and the owner of some bookshops in Connecticut. It was a search in the dark. "You can't miss it," the motel man had said. But it has been my invariable experience that, when people tell you that, you are fated to go astray. The phrase puts a curse on you.

We overshot the turn by some fifteen miles of black empty road with not a soul to ask, so when we at last reached the airport the plane had been in for over half an hour. Fred and Tony were standing with their duffel bags under the one dim light at the corner of the building, looking as desolate and neglected as they were no doubt feeling. They climbed into the back of the jeep and Fred reached over the seat to give me a hearty hand-shake. "I'm certainly glad to see you here," he said, his glasses gleaming in the semi-darkness. I think he felt reassured to see someone definitely older than himself, of equally bookish habit and just as much out of place as he on this wild expedition. I thought he looked as if he belonged in a bookshop.

When we were back in town, seated around a small table for our long-delayed supper, I asked, "How did you ever come to get into all this?"

"I saw the ad in the *Saturday Review*. Just as you did." For he had met Charles in New York and had been told all about me. "Besides," he added, "the West has always been rather a hobby of mine."

Just wait, brother, I thought. Wait till you see these canyons. They're no man's hobby. They're a great terrible beautiful monstrous marvelous joke the gods of the Indians left as a warning to the rest of mankind. But I said nothing and continued to speculate about him as the conversation went on around me. A man with a book in his hand and a dream in his head, I thought. Now he was entering into that dream. Like many people whose greatest activity has always been of the mind, the imagination, he was perhaps eager to test himself against some greater reality. I do not mean that there is nothing real in a quiet, intellectual, orderly, conventional life. But there must be, rightly or wrongly, some sense of incompletion in such a life, a feeling that not all of one's capacities are being used to the utmost. Without some stretching of oneself, life may seem diminished, may even fill up with frustration. Of course there are some, and I have known them, who in the middle years look at their quiet lives and accept the limitations, saying, "No, I'll never set the North River afire." And seeing this, they get to work consciously to dig deeper where they are, finding the needed challenge and richness in the limited space, through generosity and kindness and sympathy in all their human relationships. But these are the rare ones.

In any case, I wished Fred well in his search, if search it was, and looked across to Tony. He seemed to be youth personified. I saw regular, almost classic features, a clear, unfrightened gaze, eagerness with a hint of hesitancy—like a thoroughbred setter on his first field trial. Before such youth one falls silent, feeling both tender and sad, finding there a momentary reminder of one's own early, untouched and vulnerable self, seeing too the hurts and bewilderments that lie ahead. Tony, like Fred, I decided, wanted to widen his world and, in a different way, to prove himself.

Maybe we were all seeking something. I, too. But what was it? What was it that I really wanted? I asked myself in this small smoke-filled café at midnight in Wyoming. Something beyond possessions, beyond all material things. So much I knew. And I felt myself already rich in friends, in warm human relationships. What I really sought, I thought now, was a still quiet place somewhere, perhaps just within myself, where I might withdraw in times of stress, in moments of dismay such as must come to all of us as long as we are alive, a place where I might find peace and strength and courage to be both wise and kind. Would I find such a place in this part of the world that was so strange to me, in this adventure deep in the chasms of of the earth amid the rocky teeth of the canyons and the white water of rapids? It did not seem likely.

"Come," said Charles, tapping me on the arm, "you're half asleep already, and we have a busy day tomorrow."

Fred picked up the check.

Next morning I awoke too soon. In the gray light of my motel room I lay and thought of home, of how pleasant it was to rise, no matter what the hour, start the coffee, take a shower, get into my old red dressing gown and come back to the chaise longue in my snug little kitchen and sit there sipping the first delicious cup of the day—a brew of my own, half Sanka, half regular grind so I can have as much as I like without getting the coffee jitters. To me the height of luxury is a comfortable chair in the kitchen where one may begin the busiest day with a sense of leisure while the bubbling of the coffeepot gives the illusion that work has already begun.

But when I leave home, I kiss comfort good-by. If I find it elsewhere, good enough and welcome, but I do not expect or demand it. So now I got dressed and went round to the office. Sometimes a solitary woman traveler, looking wan and hungry, can wring a home-cooked breakfast from the most reluctant host. This one, a long, lanky man, sad-voiced as if contact with the world on wheels had depressed him, hollow-eyed as if his business kept him up too late and woke him too soon in the morning, just shook his head. "No way to make you so much as a cup of coffee here, lady. Nothin' but rooms and you can't eat them."

"Then where—?"

He led me to the door and pointed toward the low-lying gray buildings that bordered the silent street, deserted in the dawn. "Might be a café open down yonder." Then he jerked a thumb the other way. "Or there's Husky—never closes." Husky's seemed to hang on the edge of flat, unending distance, the last outpost of man.

"Which is nearer?"

"Six of one—ain't much choice."

I let the wind decide me. At home on stormy winter days when I walked the beach, I always go into the wind. Then I am sure to be blown back safe, unfrozen. But even a nor'easter seldom blows as hard as the Wyoming wind I fought this morning. It had gathered power as it swept unopposed over the great South Pass to come tearing down this empty road, twisting my skirt around my knees, thrusting under my coat to belly it in and out like a luffing sail. I leaned into the wind, bent almost double, struggled against it. I caught it in my arms like Jacob wrestling with the Angel at the breaking of the day. And like Jacob I prevailed against it and said, "I will not let thee go, except thou bless me." So the wind blessed me and I let it go and turned in at the door of Husky's Truck Spot.

A man in dingy shirt and faded blue jeans was sweeping up last night's cigarette stubs. The place smelled of beer. "With or without?" the man behind the counter asked. He looked sleepy. It must have been the last hour before the arrival of the morning's relief.

"Without if it's canned," I said.

"It's canned, lady."

It was a queer color, I thought, as I carried my cup to a small table and sat down. It might have been weak tea by the looks of it, and it tasted like nothing. Maybe it was made with some strange alkali water—or more likely it was the last of the night's brew. At least it was hot.

A truck stopped at the door and two men came in. They wore wide-brimmed hats that were rolled up at the sides in cowboy fashion but they did not wear cowboy boots. They had a dusty look, big men in khaki, red-necked, sun-bronzed. They sat at the counter and talked in low tones. Now and then I caught a word or two—"stake it out . . . the hell we can't . . ." And something about getting the drillers in next week. I stared at their broad backs in wonder—the forty-niners come to life, history made visible! And what would they do if they really found uranium? How would it change their lives? Or did anyone ever change, essentially?

One of them left his high stool, sauntered past me to the juke box against the wall. I heard the click of a nickel in the slot and as he came back to the counter the machine began to grind out something like this—

> All the time
> I'm a-sighin,
> All the time
> I'm a-crying—

The voice was a hoarse whine, something born of a banshee out of a nutmeg grater. Another of those weepy songs, I thought. You can't turn on the radio nowadays day or night without hearing somebody count the teardrops as they fall. This juke-box singer went on relentlessly —

> Won't you please come home, baby,
> Papa's got a present for you.
> Say bye-bye to the butcher, the baker,
> Pay no mind to the candlestick maker,
> Papa's got a great big present for you!

The accompaniment was more explicit than the words, having a sort of pseudo-jungle tom-tom, tomcat beat. What a pity, I thought as I ordered toast, marmalade and another cup of coffee-by-courtesy, that the admirably arranged and—if I may venture to say so—one of the more agreeable physiological functions of the human body, should be so distorted, indeed degraded, by such imitations. True vulgarity of the earthy sort has a certain wholesomeness about it, being closer to reality.

The forty-niners had sung songs, I remembered. But not like
this one. Powell's "Old Shady," Andy Hall sang—

> When he put his arm around her
> She bustified like a forty-pounder
> Lookaway, lookaway, Dixie-land—

Was she a Southerner? She probably did more than bustify (was
it a pun?) in the next stanza which, alas, has been lost from
the record. I paid my bill and went out into the wind and found
that the sun had climbed up to pour a waterfall of warmth and
brightness over the long level gray butte that edged the road.

Charles, Fred and Tony, thinking me still asleep, had gone
off to breakfast. I wished them better luck than I had had and
occupied myself with taking off my traveling suit and repacking
my duffel so as to put it down in the very bottom out of the
way. I would not need it again till the trip was over. Or would
I ever need it again? I wondered rather grimly. But I cheered
up when I was dressed in river clothes and saw myself in the
long mirror on the bathroom door. Yellow sweater, visored
cotton cap from J. C. Penney's and the tan jodhpurs—very good-
looking, really—that I had bought in Covent Gardens so I
could ride along Rotten Row, all gave me a jaunty, adventurous
air. I'd go down gaily, anyway, I thought.

Those next two days merge one into the other in my recollection so that now I cannot separate them accurately. I know
we spent most of the first morning riding around in the jeep
looking down side streets and alleys, searching for the truck
with boats and boatmen. Had they had an accident on that rough
road we had traveled? Where could they be? Anyone else would
have been in a frenzy of impatience and anxiety, but Charles,
if he fretted inwardly, gave no sign of it. This was to be char-
acteristic of him throughout the whole journey and to me at
least it gave a pleasant feeling of leisure and irresponsibility.
We drove down to the river's edge and looked both ways in

vain. The river lay wide and peaceful, bordered by cottonwoods, innocent of boat or of violence. What was there about such a stream to strike terror in the hearts of the early explorers? I wondered. Then I saw the current on the far side. It moved with fearful swiftness, as if it knew it had work to do lower down, a mountain range to cut through, a million rocks to rush around. It was a river with a purpose, a mission to fulfill. "Oh, come on, let's forget about them and have lunch," Charles said at last. "They'll turn up some time."

As we parked by the Teton Café, Don came strolling down the street. "Where on earth have you been?" both he and Charles cried at the same time.

"And the boats?" Charles demanded, after explanations.

"Down the river a mile or so," Don said. "Les is standing guard. They're all blown up."

Blown up? I puzzled as I went through the door Fred was holding open for me. But I said nothing—I had revealed sufficient ignorance in the matter of my "Dinah Shore" Monument.

We sat at a circular table and had a good meal, at the end of which Charles brought out papers for us to sign. Bruce, one of the boatmen, joined us about this time and ordered a large ice-cream mixture topped with whipped cream, nuts and a cherry. I looked across the table at him with interest. Bronzed by the sun, his close-cropped hair, eyes and skin seemed all the same color, and he was magnificently built, broad-shouldered, muscular. A fine upstanding country boy accustomed to hard physical labor on the farm, well able to handle a plow or an oar.

I got out my pencil to sign the papers but the point was broken, so while I waited to borrow someone else's I talked with Bruce. As I had guessed, he had grown up on a ranch, in Wyoming, though he had lived in Montana and South Dakota and on Ski Patrol had come to know the skiing areas in that part of the country. I was relieved to hear that he had been used to boats all his life and knew how to take care of skiers with broken bones. "I'll know whom to come to if I break a few arms and legs on this expedition," I said.

Bruce grinned. "I'll do my best."

He had mentioned Cody as one of the places where he had lived so I asked if it was named for Buffalo Bill.

"Yes." Bruce downed a cherry, poked around in his tall glass for another and added, "He was my great-great-uncle."

At once I remembered my one glimpse of Buffalo Bill riding round the ring in the Wild West Show I had been taken to when I was about ten, and now looking at Bruce I thought, "Well, give him a few years and a goatee and he'll probably look quite a bit like his famous relative." Certainly he would sit a horse with the same superb air of ease and authority.

He had taken up the paper Charles had laid at his elbow and now said rather ruefully, "I can't sign this."

"Why not?" Charles demanded.

"It says here, 'I hereby warrant that I am of full age and have every right to contract in my own name.' And I—I am just seventeen."

I was astounded—he looked much older. Charles gave him paper and envelope so he could at once write to his mother asking her to fill out and sign for him. Fred silently passed me his pencil, and, thanking him, I remembered how he had held the door open for me as we entered the café and how without a word he had picked up the check that first night, and I thought how quickly and unconsciously a man reveals himself and his background. "Gentleman" is an old-fashioned word quite out of style in the casual world we live in, yet looking back over my life it seems to me that in all the really vital situations I have found truly trustworthy only those men who either through their upbringing or through innate kindness and gentleness were deserving of that name.

One of the legal statements I now examined absolved the

Eggert-Hatch Expedition of all responsibility for broken bones, death by misadventure and any other disaster due either to an error of man or an act of God. I signed without a qualm. After all, I had taken out life insurance. The other statement was headed MOTION PICTURE RELEASE. What? Was I—yes, I was going to be in a movie, I would be captured for time and eternity, for better for worse against a backdrop of wild river scenes. Or more likely, I would be the backdrop. Anyway, what fun! So I signed away rights to picture, likeness, photograph and voice, handing them over to Charles Eggert Productions and all affiliated companies and successors, assigns, agents and licensees—I love legal language, it has such a momentous sound—now and forever for the sum of one dollar—which Charles promptly demanded back for some sort of permit we had to have. No matter, we were going to be in a movie and we were in no mood to haggle. Was it childish of me to be so "pleased with a rattle"? No, I think not. For surely one of the noblest "toys of age" must be the ability to find delight in small affairs.

Then in the midst of our talk and laughter and a second cup of coffee all around, I remembered one haunted evening years ago in Ithaca, New York. We had gone to see the film made by an expedition to Ethiopia. And again, remembering, I felt that stab of grief, that shiver that was like the fingers of death along the spine when I saw Louis Fuertes, our good gay friend and neighbor, moving lifelike across the screen—he had been killed in an accident right after his return from Africa.

At once now, my mind leaping ahead, I could see how it might be—the documentary film being shown in Boston or somewhere, my children—heavens! I gave myself a shake. What a nuisance an imagination was!

Charles said, "I've got to get a shot of the bridge. Want to come along?" So I went and sat for what seemed like hours on angular rocks by the river below the railroad bridge waiting for a passenger train to come from the East. Later I toughened, acquiring calluses in strategic places, but this afternoon I could do nothing but shift my weight about and change rocks from time to time. They were all hard.

This picture from below the bridge was important for Charles's film because it was on this very spot that Major Powell and his party camped in May of 1869. Here they got ready for their journey into the unknown. Here they watched the first transcontinental train cross the Green River. I thought of them as I sat in the warm sunshine with Fred perched on the bank above me and Charles and Tony working at their cameras, getting all ready to start shooting when the train came. They too, were a chance collection of people brought together by some curious concatenation of circumstance—William Dunn and J. C. Sumner. Yes, I found his name in the Sumner genealogy, a ninth-generation descendant of that William Sumner who settled in Dorchester, Massachusetts, in 1636 and who already in the year 1879 had provided the genealogy of that date with 636 other descendants among whom is my children's grandfather. There were also Powell himself and his brother, Bradley and Hawkins fresh from the Civil War, O. G. and Seneca Howland, Goodman and Andy Hall—two more than were to compose our party. They had to take rations for ten months, for they planned to lie over when winter came and go on in the spring. We would go less heavily loaded, as there were now places where we could touch civilization and get fresh supplies.

I thought too of the changes in the world since the year of their adventure, and I marveled at the way time had verified so many of Powell's ideas about the management of the West and its development. He had gotten those ideas by first-hand scientific study, they were shaped by concern for the general good—and he took the long view of things, unwarped by personal greed or selfishness. I wondered if there were any such men today in Washington.

Meanwhile, here was the river running now as then, swift and brown, green-fringed under the hot sun. Its waters had come down from the snow-capped peaks of Doubletop and Mt. Sheep that towered ten thousand feet and more, from Gannett and mountains that even yet have been given no names; from New Fork, from Willow, from Boulder and Half Moon and from a hundred other cold green lakes that cup the melted snow and yet send it forever down, down the rocky slopes to reach the Green by Big and Middle Piney Creeks, by way of La Barge and Sandy and Cottonwood and many another creek as well—to pass here before my eyes on the ninth day of June in the year of 1955.

Beyond a mudbank and a cluster of cottonwoods, it rounded a bend and was lost to my sight. But anything that curves away into the unknown is an enticement, a mystery, luring one on. I was impatient to get under way—as Powell's party must have been. I wanted to see what came next.

All at once the rails began to hum. Charles and Tony sprang into position behind their cameras. But this was only a freight train of endless boxcars. It rounded the curve, spread itself across the bridge, grinding slower and slower to a stop. It blocked all possible view and there it sat, panting and graceless, while the through train from the East, the passenger train for which we had waited so long—having mistaken the hour—overtook and passed it by. "That's photography for you," Charles said, and we took off for the railroad station to meet Bob, the doctor from California, our last fellow voyager. Fred and I were dropped at the station to do the honors while Charles and Tony went on to attend to some of the many details that had to be seen to before we could begin our journey.

Bob came swinging along the platform, swaying a little under the weight of his duffel, fishing poles projecting at odd angles like inquisitive antennae. He was a big man physically, and mentally too, I soon observed, an Easterner gone West and fairly outdoing the West in vigor and heartiness. As we sat on the hard bench of the station waiting to be picked up, his enthusiastic laugh made people turn and look at us with interest and perhaps a trace of envy. We were so evidently holiday bent. Bob could be with us only one week, he said. He could spare no more time than that from his jobs as Director of Laboratories and Interne Training for a California hospital; I believe he was also superintendent of some hospital as well—in any case a formidable array of responsibilities. But this was his week of freedom and it was immediately apparent that he was going to make the most of it, and that he would be quite an addition to our party. He was not unlike many of the men I have known in the scientific world—hard-working, hard-playing and presenting to all of us who are uncertain, who fumble, who wonder, an almost discouraging air of competence. He and Fred had long known each other, indeed they had married sisters, and I think his presence rather bucked Fred up—he seemed so utterly ready for anything. I am sure I felt more at ease knowing that expert medical aid would be at hand through at least the first section of the journey.

Later in the afternoon Charles gathered us up and drove us to the Powell monument so as to get a picture there beside the river under the cottonwoods. We read the inscription on the stone and I perched on the iron railing that surrounded it, popping a button off my jodhpurs as I climbed up and being unable to find it in the tall grass. Luckily the zipper held, and I had a sewing kit in my duffel.

It was here that Charles made two announcements—first, that we would not sleep that night at the motel but would go down the river to where the boats were tied and camp there. This was greeted with general approval. Then he said there was so much to do, supplies still to be laid in, that we might not get off before the next afternoon. We did not mind. We would be camping out. And I was glad that I could have a small amount of practice on my equipment before the journey was actually begun. I had told no one but never before in all my life had I slept outdoors in a tent and I was a little uneasy about how I was to manage.

We gathered up our duffel—which left little space for human cargo in the jeep—drove out of town and turned off on a dirt road. Gray-brown buttes rose to jagged peaks on our left as we bounced over a railroad spur and followed a winding trail, for it was scarcely a road now. The low sun was touching the peaks with a rosy light. Beyond the sparse tall grass that grew in the sandy soil we came upon the river, now turning to gold. On the other side of it tall brown reeds, green-tipped, were waving in the wind and beyond them a pale brown lift of rock studded with sage was like a giant step up to a yet higher level that lay bleak and bare against the bright sky. We stopped here in a grove of lively young willows where yet more luggage was strewn about in helter-skelter fashion. Below the bank I saw for the first time the boats in which we were to travel.

I went right down to have a look. I had never before seen anything like them—one was about twenty-six or -seven feet long, the other about half that size, both made of inflated rubber. They looked like great black sausages, two parallel links to a boat and curved at the ends to join together forming rounded bow and stern. EGGERT-HATCH RIVER EXPEDITION was painted along the side, and BRONTOSAUR in big letters was the big boat's name. A man was working in the stern of the latter, fitting a wooden platform across from one side to the other. "Has it any bottom?" I asked, imagining us hanging on as if to great oval life preservers, swinging by the ropes that laced the sides.

"Come aboard and see." He seemed to me a giant of a man as he rose and came limping along the bouncy rolled gunwale to meet me and help me across. He had a faintly battered look— his nose must have been broken at some time, a finger joint was missing from the hand he gave me—but he had an altogether indomitable air as he stood there, feet well apart, cap at a jaunty angle, his size exaggerated by jacket and trousers made of that stiff waterproofed mottled material that was used during the war for camouflage purposes. "Les Jones, isn't it?" I said.

"That's me," he said, smiling.

I looked down into the boat. There was a bottom, of course, of black rubber. "Will it hold me?"

"Try it."

I stepped down and had it not been that I had resolved to let no feminine shrieks of dismay issue from my lips on this expedition, one would have escaped me now. The rubber floor of the boat gave under my weight in most disconcerting fashion; it went up and down in bouncy waves under my feet as I moved. "Well," I said, "now I know how Peter felt when he walked on the waters of Galilee—and I don't wonder he cried out for help. What are we going to sit on?"

Les looked as if so small a matter as that had never occurred to him. "This platform is for the tripods and cameras." He looked over to the shore where all our duffel and some eight or ten big boxes were scattered about. "There'll be plenty to sit on."

I was still studying the boat. "You really think this thing will carry us through?"

Les laughed. "Sure it will. After all, I made it in a canoe, all alone, too." I must have looked my amazement for he added, "I come away to the river every chance I get. I'm really a bridge engineer—work for the state—on vacation now."

I said I was glad he was with us and mounted to the gunwale. The sunlight was leaving the clouds, they were fast turning from pink to gray and the wind was growing colder every minute. The boat seemed farther out than when I had stepped aboard, for the current had swung it round, and I saw that Don, standing amid the luggage, was watching me with an expression that was both intent and uneasy. And all in a flash I understood that he felt uncertain about me and what I would be able to take, that he was the one of all the party in whose eyes I must establish myself. Not that he seemed to be disliking me or resenting my presence on the expedition but rather that, feeling the responsibility of his position as head boatman, he was worried lest I add to its hazards.

Les was moving nearer, offering me his hand, but I said quite boldly, "No, thank you, I can make it," and gathering all my strength took a flying leap over the widening stretch of water. Luckily I landed on the shore and in a fairly upright position. So without giving myself the pleasure of a triumphant glance in Don's direction, I set about finding my luggage.

I untied my duffel bags and began a search for sewing kit and the small box of toilet articles I had allowed myself. I discovered at once that there is no object invented by man that is more frustrating than a duffel bag. I know now why the soldiers in *From Here to Eternity* had to use such dreadful language. It is one thing to ask our boys to give their lives for their country and quite another to expect them to endure such things as duffel bags, I thought, as I dug down savagely, breaking fingernails and jabbing my fingers on sharp objects. I know that nowadays there are such conveniences as side zippers—indeed from the corner of my eye I could see Bob opening his that way—yet he was having to search just the same. There should be little pockets, shoe-bag fashion on the inside. I gave up my search for the sewing kit and for anything but the barest necessities. I unstrapped my tent and air mattress.

Charles was prowling about uneasily studying the heaps of luggage. "Too much of this," I heard him say. "We'll have to give up everything that is not absolutely essential." His eyes rested at this moment on my folded army cot.

Well, I decided, I could just sleep on my air mattress—nobody else had a cot and I had early resolved that I was not to be pampered just because I was a woman. So I left it tied up and dragged the rest of my stuff over to the level sandy ground under the shelter of a small willow tree. There I opened up the tent and studied it with mounting dismay.

I can lay out a fairly complicated dress pattern, cut and fit and sew together the parts without too great difficulty. But this tent had no resemblance to any human form. It bulged in strange places, came to peaks in others, was equipped with little dangling loops, and no matter which way I turned it there was no rhyme or reason to it. All at once I was conscious of someone standing beside me. I don't know how long Charles had been there.

"This one time," he said in that tone of quiet authority which he had to use only a few times during the entire journey, "this one time I will show you how to set it up."

I watched with desperate concentration, for it was not yet too late for him to say, "Sorry, but we just can't be bothered with you." He gave the thing a quick flip this way and that, he jerked out the rope which I had started running through the loops rather after the manner of a ribbon through the beading on a 1910 corset cover. Deftly he tied one peak to a willow branch, propped the other up on a jointed pole I had not yet noticed and staked the sides down and there it was. I thanked him humbly and added with more assurance than I felt that I would need no help hereafter.

All my life I have been spoiled by men. For so many years I had only to look helpless and someone would come to my rescue. But now, I thought, now I was a white-haired old woman and strictly on my own. Then all at once I remembered something my oldest brother Rob had said long ago—and it is strange how sometimes a chance word idly spoken will come back at the right time to give one encouragement. He had said, "I notice that when there are people around and a mouse comes in, my little sister is on top of the table squealing with the rest of the girls. But when she is by herself she quietly copes with it."

Well, I was by myself now, the time was upon me at last and

I was determined to cope. I unrolled my sleeping bag and mattress. But what good was a mattress without air? After I had blown myself hollow with no visible results, I cast a quick glance around. Everyone was busy. Fred and Bob were setting up the tent they were to share, Bruce had lighted the Coleman stove and was getting out cans of food from the boxes, Don and Les were down by the boats with Charles. But Tony was working some kind of foot pedal up and down—yes, inflating a mattress. I carried mine over and, when he had finished, tried to fit my tube to the valve. Mechanical things like this have always resisted me, indeed they seem to take a malicious delight in defeating me. Once I was actually attacked by a washing machine—but that is another story. I'm still nervous about such things.

Fred had come over with his mattress and was waiting his turn. He said, "Could I help you with that?" Looking back, it seems to me that Fred was always coming to my rescue. He was like that. But this time it was to no avail; these parts were too alien to each other, if not actually hostile, made by rival manufacturers, perhaps. So Fred used his own lung power, and after a few mighty blows the thing began to fill out. I said I would get another attachment before the next night and, feeling as if I had a live body over my shoulder, I carried it back to my tent. I wondered how it would be to sleep with. But when I had laid it down and spread my sleeping bag on top, it seemed quite proper and subdued, indeed rather cozy and inviting.

We had a good supper around the campfire that Tony had built. Full dark came and we sat on enjoying the crackle of the burning logs, the subdued ripple of the river, the sound of the wind in the willows and, most of all, the knowledge that we were fairly launched on our adventure. Charles came to me with paper and pencil and asked for help in composing a long telegram to Lowell Thomas, who had asked for information about the Expedition so he might describe it in one of his broadcasts.

Already Lowell Thomas and all the rest of the world seemed far away and of no consequence, but with some help from everyone we got the message ready to send off in the morning.

The wind grew colder, and one by one we slipped away to our tents and sleeping bags, leaving Tony writing a letter to his girl by the light of the dying fire. I found my tent not much more inconvenient for undressing than a lower berth in a Pullman, though considerably more airy. The mattress felt bouncy enough and my only difficulty was staying on top of it. And why did they have to make sleeping bags so narrow? Oh well, I would get used to it in time, I thought.

Suddenly from nearby came laughter—a shout from Fred and one peal after another from Bob. There was something so contagious about it that one after the other we all began to join in from down on the river's edge and back among the trees till the whole camp sounded like a congregation of hyenas. "What's it all about?" someone shouted. "Bob's red underwear," Fred called back. "He looks like the devil." We settled down at last.

I wished for some red underwear myself—"duofold" had been on the list Charles sent me and I had just skipped that. It would have felt very comfortable indeed this first night, for the wind grew wilder and colder every minute. I found my blanket—by a miracle—and was just composing myself for sleep when a faint sizzing sound began right under my ear. Slowly and irretrievably Fred's breath, so generously given, was oozing out. And as it went the ground and innumerable small sticks and stones came up to jab me.

And yet strange to say, the next morning found me little the worse for the sleepless night. It must have been the crisp invigorating Wyoming air that kept me going, for I felt no fatigue the next day, an almost endless one, spent in Green River City. We made the Teton Café our headquarters, for the proprietor and the waitresses made us feel welcome even when we were not ordering something to eat. Surely this is the test of true hospitality

in any place where food is sold. We came and went as we
remembered odds and ends of things we had better get while we
were still within reach of supplies. Wandering through one of
the stores I saw on the bargain counter a remnant of white nylon.
Surely it must have been the hand of the Lord pointing it out to
me, the voice of my guardian angel saying, "Buy that." For more
than once in the next few weeks I honestly believe it saved my
life. I tried to find something to mend my mattress with but alas
it was made of plastic and everywhere I went I was offered
nothing but rubber patches, which even the kindest of men at the
Texaco filling station could not induce to stick. I was much
relieved when Charles said, never mind, I could take the army
cot instead. He had come back to the café, weary from marketing, to have a mid-morning cup of coffee. All at once he leaned
toward me and began sniffing.

"What, drinking this early in the day?"

Then I remembered that when getting my duffel repacked
right after breakfast I had let fall the small bottle of whiskey
that F. A. R. back in Duxbury had given me for emergencies. It
was one of those tiny things that sit on the counter in a basket
like samples, only they are not free. It had fallen and struck
one of the stones I had slept on top of, and most of it had spilled
over me as I tried to snatch it up quickly. I explained all this to
Charles, the others choking back their laughter all the while, but
the more I explained the less credit I got for sobriety. It was
thus innocently that I acquired the reputation as a hard drinker
which I bore throughout the rest of our practically liquorless
journey. "We'll know where to find her if she gets lost today,"
one of them told another. "Yeah, the White Owl, that's where
she'll be." "Or in the Black Cat," another suggested.

I presume these were drinking places. I came near to telling
them that if I were missing I would not be found in saloons.
For after sixteen hours with only the bushes I was simply fascinated by the rest rooms of Green River City. I haunted them in

pure delight regardless of need and shall always remember them as the noblest work of man. But I said nothing of all this and let them have what fun they liked while I went on raveling the edge of my square of white nylon.

Finally one of the waitresses came over and asked me what I was planning to do with it. "We've been watching you and wondering," she said.

"I'll wear it like a veil," I told her, "to keep off the mosquitoes and the sun." There was something at once bridal and nunlike about it, I thought, suggesting as it did tremulous expectation coupled with the serenity of one withdrawn from the troubles of this world—and thus it reflected the emotions predominant in me at the moment. Moreover, it rather tickled my fancy to crown my Wild West costume with a hint of the elegant nineties.

"What! Do you mean that you are going down the river, too?"

"Yes," I said and looked up in time to catch her expression of amazement and that certain little gleam—is it envy?—which I have seen in the eye of every woman, old or young, who has heard about my journey down the rivers. It comes when they exclaim, "You mean you were the only woman with all those MEN?" It is not just envy; there is a speculative glint to it which at my age I find very flattering.

After this, word must have spread around the small compass of the business section of Green River City. For as I went about the streets a little later searching for a plastic bag in which to carry certain small things I did not want to bury in the depths of my duffel bags, looking for a tin cup with a handle such as I noticed the others had, I saw people turning to look at me. So as I wandered about on these last shopping errands, I began to swagger a little, putting on a kind of elderly Annie Oakley air. All I lacked was a pistol in a holster on my hip, the one I used to wear in Mississippi when I took long lonely drives into the back country.

It was nearly six in the evening by the time all supplies were loaded on the truck and headed out toward camp. We followed, feeling we had had enough of Green River City. And there had been so many false starts when we had said good-by forever to the Teton Café that I think in the end we left without so much as a wave of the hand.

I suppose we must have had supper around the campfire again, indeed I think this was the night we had those wonderful T-bone steaks, but I have little recollection of it. Now at last I began to be overcome by sleep and I went off to my tent before darkness had actually closed in around us. I had my army cot this time and how delightfully comfortable it seemed after the stony ground. All comfort is comparative, perhaps, and maybe it was a good thing that I had had tough preparation for this cot which, compared to my own big wide four-poster at home, was— well, quite a change. Just before I fell asleep I heard Tony playing taps on his horn. As the last note was still echoing from the bluff across the river, the engine on the spur of tracks we had passed on our way to camp let out a single derisive answering blast. So I went to sleep to the sound of laughter.

Next morning after breakfast of pancakes, bacon and eggs and powdered coffee, the seemingly impossible task of stowing away supplies and duffel was accomplished. The boats were heavily laden yet did not sink appreciably lower in the water. Don took a last look around our campsite to make sure we had everything and we climbed aboard, Bob and Fred going in the small boat with him. My position was in the middle of the big boat, where I was perched on top of a heap of baggage, one item of which—the box of medical supplies—must have left, I am convinced, a lasting imprint upon my ribs, to the confusion of any X-ray diagnosticians who may examine them at some future date. Charles and Tony with the cameras were on the platform, Les and Bruce at the oars.

It was nearly ten o'clock, June 11, a sunny morning, when we pushed off, a day later than planned. But we had already acquired a feeling that all the time in the world was ahead of us, so why worry about being a mere twenty-four hours late? Indeed, one of the strange effects of this Expedition—and a peculiarly relaxing one—was this almost instantaneous alteration in our attitude. Even with the small boat towing us, the blue Evinrude seven-and-a-half horse-power motor tugging and chugging away, the current in our favor, we were making not much more than seven or eight miles an hour. Yet no one pointed out that this was only a tenth of the speed we might easily be achieving on a new highway with almost any reasonably efficient automobile. We had become emancipated from the fetters of space and time.

Or rather, in this new freedom we felt them as elastic, stretchable, instead of fixed by milepost and ticking moment. I wondered as we floated on down the river at this leisurely pace whether, dropped into the midst of eternity, we might not be able to welcome with equal composure that contraction of time which would make a thousand years as a watch in the night. It seemed highly probable.

The boatmen had no rowing to do this morning. Now and then Les put in an oar to straighten us out and swing our bigger boat into line when we had been caught by a crosscurrent. Bruce whittled on a spare oar he had started carving out the night before. Don alone was constantly on the alert, one hand on the rudder of the small boat as he watched the river, looking out for rocky shoals or sandbars, crossing slantwise to gain advantage of a swifter current and back again as the river shifted its course. From time to time, Les, who was seated in front of me on the crossboard of the wooden framework that ran along the gunwales and supported the oarlocks, would read aloud from Powell's *First Through the Grand Canyon*.

By the time Powell's party had come this far they had run aground once, had lost an oar trying to avoid a rock, and two other oars had been dropped overboard and retrieved with difficulty. I could see no rocks and it seemed to me that the current was far from being as swift and rough as he had described it. But Les said the height of the water made a great difference and what was true at one time might not be at all so at another season. I was amazed by his knowledge of the river. He knew it not only from personal experience—indeed on this journey alone in a canoe he had kept accurate notes and maps—but he knew it from a historical point of view, having studied carefully all accounts of expeditions from the earliest right up to recent years.

Gradually the scene around us altered. The buttes on one side rose higher and more color came into them—red and buff

mixed with the gray brown. Some were ribboned masses topped
now and then with a small nipple, reminding me of the Paps of
Jura. At times these formations were close to the riverside,
again they were set back beyond a level stretch of green woods
and grasses or a bleak expanse of shale. Then, as the buttes
grew higher, turreted castles appeared. What manner of crea-
ures might dwell in these stony habitations, I wondered. Would
they be some sort of Stone Age men armored in shale, scaly as
dragons and strong enough to clank aside a cliff to make a door
and pull it to behind them at the alien sound of our motor? Or
would they be creatures delicate as a cloud, diaphanous, made
of mist, having their exists and entrances by some mysterious
process of osmosis?

While I was speculating along these lines I suddenly became
aware of a click and a buzz—the cameras were at work. Ahead
Bob and Fred were frantically trying to get one of theirs going
in time to catch this scene—apparently it had jammed. Don
was steadying the rudder with his knee while he turned his lens
slowly from side to side. Tony was involved with tripods which
did not stay as firmly upright on the platform as Charles had
hoped, and Charles himself was cranking the handle of his big
camera. Bruce was the most saving of his film, Les the most
reckless. Indeed at times I suspected Les of merely buzzing his
movie camera for effect long after the roll was used up. I was
the only member of the expedition who was not a camera
fiend—I had not so much as brought one along.

At noon we stopped for lunch. Don had suggested that we
eat in the boats, but Charles wisely decided that we needed a
rest and a change and a chance to stretch our legs. Many people
have asked me in that particular lowered tone of voice, "How
did you manage?" I managed very well indeed, thank you. I
simply put a roll of t. p. under my arm and walked off into
the woods and bushes. One can accomplish anything by the use
of proper dignity.

This time our stop was at a historic spot—across from the site of Powell's first night's camp, at the foot of overhanging cliffs. They gave back an echo of as many as four notes of Tony's horn and a reverberating repetition of our shouts. Powell gives an account of how he climbed up here and got a fine view of the Green River badlands. It was a scene of barren desolation, he said, yet with the changing shadows as the sun went down, he had found that the varied colors and fantastic carven rocks possessed a certain beauty of their own. Les read bits of this description aloud to us while we ate and, as he rolled forth with relish the rather florid phrases such as were the fashion in the literature of the 1860's, I thought that Les himself perhaps rather belonged back in such a time as that. For he was physically equal to the challenges of that day—truly a modern Paul Bunyan —and he had the soul of an uninhibited poet in his appreciation of the river and all its wild scenery. His reading of this description of Powell's gave us more than ever a feeling of remoteness from the world. For now as then there was no human habitation in all those miles on miles of barren rock.

We made no fire at lunchtime but had our sandwiches of cheese and peanut butter, lettuce and canned meat and fruit juice, sitting in a circle on the shore. Les, while reading to us, had gotten a bit behind with his eating and now with some amazement I watched while he took a green cabbage, cut it in half with his hunting knife, heaped it up with some rather soft cheese till the half became almost full circle again. Then lifting it to his mouth he bit into it with the greatest ease, indeed with the apparent skill of long habit, and crunched away with relish. Not being one ever to do things by halves, he then took the rest of the cabbage and treated it in the same manner, muttering as he scooped cheese from the jar—"This plastic stuff—"

It was about this time, and apropos of this sort of combination of food, that Les and Bob got into a discussion of diet which was continued at intervals throughout the whole of the time that Bob was with us. Les had his own ideas on the subject and he was not in the least overawed by Bob's medical degrees, his laboratory and hospital experience. They never did settle the question.

In the afternoon of this day we ran out of the butte country and the scenery was less exciting, though there was always the border of willow and box elder along the river's edge and its watery green reflection, the shifting clouds overhead, a beaver diving out of sight, or a few cows that lifted their heads and turned them, watching us in wonder. The wind died down and the heat of the sun began to make itself felt. I was rather dismayed to find it settling down upon us so early in the voyage, for heat is one thing I do not take very well. I found little relief even when Don added the spare engine to the one already in use so that the small boat in which he and Fred and Bob were riding could pull us a bit faster. The sound of the engines beat on my ears, heat and glare assailed me from all sides. Conversation which might have distracted my mind from these discomforts became impossible.

Luckily I remembered my white nylon veil. This I trailed over the side till it was soaking wet, then I arranged it over my cap, fastening it securely with a pin I had dropped in my bag just on the chance that it might come in handy. It was one I had been given in Scotland and was designed to fasten together the skirt of a kilt. In shape it was no different from an ordinary safety pin but in size it looked as if designed to fasten the diaper of some infant Hercules. With this holding the veil in place, the visor of my cap pulled down low over dark glasses and the length of the veil draped around my shoulders, crossed under my chin, I caused considerable amusement among my companions. I daresay the total effect was rather odd, especially when I took off my shoes and sat on the side dangling my feet in the water.

In spite of these little arrangements and would-be alleviations, the afternoon was to me one of pure endurance. There are often such periods in the ordinary course of living, uneventful, rather dull times. Yet if one day out of such days were offered us for the reliving, at the last gasp, say, or even just after a long passage of years, wouldn't it seem wonderful, just being alive, just being young? Dullness, boredom, even discomfort would drain away and here would be all the richness and excitement of life. So it was that now the novelty of my surroundings, the fact that I was present and launched on such a strange adventure gave me a similar perspective and I felt neither regret nor impatience, nor was I conscious of weariness.

The sun was still high when Don stood up and pointed ahead to a wooded island on our left. Charles nodded his approval and the small boat headed in, came around and, as the engines died, Bob sprang out, rope in hand, braced himself on the high mud bank and held us against the current. With a stroke of the oar Bruce brought our boat in line alongshore. I stood up rather stiffly and made the leap to the bank, landing on all fours and scrambling up with the aid of a few scrubby bushes to hang on to. The others followed with duffel and the great waterproof boxes that held our supplies. I was thankful I did not have to shoulder my share. Bruce located my things and brought them ashore. "Where will you have them?" I pointed to the thin shade of a bush close by the bank. The least I could do was to settle near at hand and save him from any further lugging. But after I had studied the situation more carefully, I decided I was too much in the pathway, so I dragged my stuff farther downshore. There, achieving a small measure of privacy by flinging a blanket over a low branch of a cottonwood tree, I got into my bathing suit.

Not that anyone was paying any attention to me—at the moment there was nothing but confusion around the campsite, no one knowing quite what he was supposed to do and everyone running about from one thing to another. As for me, I offered no help—I felt I could not survive another moment without getting cooled off. The air was breathless, the sun, sloping into the west, shone on the river and by reflection redoubled its power. I flung a towel round my shoulders and went back to where the boats were tied. There I let myself down into the water, hanging on by one of the ropes. It was icy cold, delicious. I did not try to swim, just stood there up to my chin with the soft mud of the bottom oozing up between my toes.

As I returned at last to my spot downshore, I saw that Les had taken the platform from the boat and was fitting short metal legs to it for a table—a most ingenious arrangement. Bruce was building a fire, Don opening the boxes of food, rummaging through them for his list of menus, all carefully made out in advance. Tony had wandered off in the woods and the sound of his horn came rather plaintively from downstream. Bob and Fred were setting up their tent back under a great cottonwood—and I knew I should be doing the same.

It was not so difficult as I had feared; I had learned my lesson well and, while my tent did not have the truly professional air Charles had given it, at least it stayed up. As soon as I was dressed I went to join the others. Don had everything ready for our evening meal. But now Bob, Fred and Bruce in bathing trunks and life preservers were in the water. I walked upstream to watch them dive into the current there and float down past the boats, climb out and come back alongshore to repeat the performance again and again. I wished then that I had waited for my dip in the river. This seemed like great fun—though I was not sure I would have had the nerve to try it. They shot by with terrifying rapidity once they were caught by the current.

At last we were all seated round the table. The great question was whether to stretch one's legs out under it or double them up, knees under chin. I tried both methods without achieving any great comfort, but that was perhaps due to the state my muscles were in by this time. Bob still had some rye whiskey, and since my soaking had left me alarmingly limp I was thankful to have a good swig of it undiluted by ice—of which we had none—or by water, of which we had plenty. This gave me strength to get through dinner, but as soon as it was over I slipped away to my tent. There I just managed to get off my shoes and crawl in on top of my sleeping bag. And lying there alone I had a few moments of panic. How was I going to manage if I kept on being this tired? Had I for once in my life bit off more than I could chew? Every muscle in my body ached. I was tired right down to the marrow of my bones. Suddenly I remembered Charles's quotation from Bernard DeVoto when he was invited to join this expedition. "No thanks," he had said in that tone of finality of which he was a master. "I'm too old." Why, he was not as old as I! Just had more sense, I thought bitterly. Then sleep hit me and I knew no more.

Sometime in the night when the air grew colder, as it always did with the going down of the sun and the cooling off of the rocks, I must have roused up enough to pull off my jodhpurs and get inside the sleeping bag, but I have no recollection of it. Anyway I awoke refreshed and ready for the day, ashamed of having felt so jittery the night before. Maybe after all I was going to be able to make it. In any case I could not turn back now. Once launched on the river, one was irrevocably committed. It was like getting born. Or dying, maybe—I haven't tried that yet.

There was some delay in getting off this morning because Charles and Don had withdrawn to sit on a log with pencil and a sheet of paper and seemed to be engaged in some private literary effort. When they rejoined us we found out what it was. "There's just been too much confusion and running around without getting anything done," Charles announced. "Don and I have made out a schedule of tasks, assigning something to each one of us."

After the way I had felt the night before I thought I would do well just to accomplish the task of surviving, but I said nothing and when my name was called was much relieved to discover that I had been giving nothing more difficult than setting table and getting out food. And Fred was to be my partner in these tasks. I knew he would take over for me any time I fell by the wayside.

The morning's run was not spectacular as to scenery, but

the air was comparatively cool. Then too, since Charles had moved to the small boat for the day, I took his and the cameras' place on the platform in the stern. This was more comfortable, as there was room for some of the duffel to be piled up behind me, making a sort of back rest. Tony sat beside me. "I brought one book along," he said.

"So did I. Now we can settle for all time that old question of what book one would take to a desert island. I'll tell if you will." People are always arguing about what book they should take along to a desert island. Why does the question plague them so? Few of us ever get there—the chance must be about one in a trillion or so, I thought, while Tony was rummaging in his duffel. But we are all headed where we can take nothing with us—nothing tangible, anyway. Maybe now and then we should stop and speculate on what intangibles would be most valuable and long-wearing for eternity. Kindness? Honesty? And courage is never out of place.

Tony brought forth his book with a flourish.

"*Moby Dick*. Very good," I said.

"What's yours?"

I reached down in the Cellophane bag I carried on my arm and fished out a tiny volume wrapped in a Kleenex. It was one of those miniature editions, two inches by one-and-a-half perhaps, and I had to confess that I chose it not so much because I could not live without *Twelfth Night* forever at my side, as because I thought it would take up little room. If I had had more space I would have brought along the *Practical Cogitator* (Curtis and Greenslet), that anthology which has accompanied me on many a journey.

Tony admired the red leather binding and read the inscription on the front page—I suppose it sounded to him as if it had been written in the dark ages—"Wishing Miss Ricketts a very happy Christmas—John Rogers, 1905."

"It belonged to my Aunt Lucy," I said. "I think one of her

pupils must have given it to her. She taught long ago in Memphis, Tennessee." Now that was an odd thing for me to say. It was the truth, of course. But certainly by the year 1905 I was well able to read this play; indeed I was old enough to appreciate it. Why should I so defensively disclaim its ownership at that date? I was quite annoyed with myself. If there is anything I cannot abide, it is women always making themselves out to be younger than they are.

"We might put on some dramatics," Tony said.

"At least we have some good backdrops for the coast scenes. Are you interested in that sort of thing?"

This set him off on his dramatic career—he had been in plays ever since he could remember, for his father had once been at the Westport theater, then had taught drama at various colleges. From this we went on to talk about writing. Tony hoped to write someday and he wanted to know how I had gotten started. He put his questions with such flattering eagerness that I was quite led on. That was one of the charming things about Tony—his eagerness to know. I wondered if he was just born that way or if this was one of the good results of his education which had been for the most part in the so-called progressive schools. As soon as I could, I got the conversation round to that subject.

Tony was a good talker, indeed often a brilliant one, and I enjoyed listening as we sat there in the stern of the boat on the heaped-up duffel, my eyes on the green moving border along the river's edge and noting now and then how the view had widened, the buttes leveled away in the distance. Tony's command of words was extraordinary, I thought, and bore the influence of what I have often privately dubbed the little-magazine vocabulary.

I do not mean to imply that Tony was pedantic or precious in his speech, only that he slung highly specialized words around after that rather *avant-garde* fashion as he spoke of the courses that interested him, of the other students at the college and some of the problems they were concerned with.

And as he talked I began to find at least one explanation of that inner tension which I had early noted in him and which I have found in many young people of his generation and background. It is something more than a normal reaction to the hazards of the atomic age in which we are all living, it is something more profound and vital than the rather simple unease which must necessarily arise from constant threat of physical danger or even annihilation. After all, the human race has had that sort of thing hanging over its head ever since the ideas of fire, brimstone, the last trump and the day of judgment were first presented. The only difference between that threat and the more modern one being that then we could still hope for a little leniency from the Lord, whereas we know there would be little meted out to us by a mortal enemy.

No, the tension I was thinking about was something which people of my generation and upbringing did not have to suffer under. We moved in a world in which most things had been decided—rightly or wrongly. There were many ideas which it simply did not occur to us to question. I do not say that this was a superior state of affairs, especially if carried to an extreme of docility and acceptance—that would mean an end of progress. And certainly we of my generation argued about religion, philosophy, human conduct, science, psychology, such things. But the point is that the basic fundamental principles of conduct were at that time settled for us. The moral code was there, ever present, accepted without question as existing. Whether or not we subscribed to it fully or lived up to it—that was another matter. But the mere acknowledgment of the existence of what was then considered the wisdom of the ages in the business of human behavior gave a great measure of stability and serenity to the young mind.

As for Tony and many of his contemporaries, it seems to

me that they have been thrust as it were naked into the world, have been given no garment of protection in the melee of existence, that for them nothing is really settled or stable. They are asked to consider, to decide for themselves all the innumerable problems of complicated modern living. Some of them come out all right—as Tony gives every indication of doing—but it seems to me that this is too much to ask of the young, to ask that every human being begin all over again out of nothing, create his own standards, set up his own rules. There used to be an idea current—I have not heard so much about it lately—that the child growing up had to go through all the ages of man, all his stages of civilization from savagery up. But this notion did not keep us from trying to help him safely through. We now have shifted this idea over to the moral and spiritual realm and seem to have adopted a hands-off attitude. Maybe it is the psychologists with their complex-and-fixation-haunted chamber of horrors that have paralyzed us. In any case, no wonder there is little serenity of spirit in these young people, no basic calm with which to meet the more and more overwhelming complexities of existence.

While I was considering all these things, Tony had opened his book and begun to read, and now my eyes came to rest on Bruce. Or rather, I became conscious that I had been watching him all the while. He had been practically standing on his head over the side, repainting the letters there that spelled out EGGERT-HATCH EXPEDITION. At the moment he was cleaning his brush. There was no waste motion in anything he did, just quiet concentration on the task at hand. Now and then under his breath he sang a snatch of song—"Born on a mountaintop in Tennessee—" There was in his pose, in his every gesture, even in this fragment of song unconsciously escaping his lips, a great ease and relaxation. Serenity! That was it. The very quality which I had missed in young people of Tony's environment. Why? Was it not because for Bruce here in the West,

traveler in the WILDERNESS 57

among what we sometimes with a slight feeling of superiority call "country folks," there had been as for me in an earlier generation, a stability of background? He was so quiet, so forever busy at something, that one tended rather to overlook him. But I began to see now that he was not a person to be overlooked.

At this moment there was a shout from the forward boat. Don was standing up, pointing ahead. "White water! White water!" Quickly he cut off the engine and tilted it up out of harm's way. Fred, who all this time had been perched on duffel in the bow of the big boat writing his diary-letter home, caught the tow rope and coiled it. Les and Bruce manned the oars. Ahead was the rapid. Compared to what we encountered later, it was nothing much, but it was our first and we were all excitement. In the sunlight, still distant, it was like a many-ruffled white petticoat laid on the brown surface of the river. I took a good hold of the duffel bags and braced my feet on the platform.

Bruce let out a Wild West whoop as we struck the foaming water. The boat undulated with both a forward and side motion, it danced like a hula-hula girl, delicately, gracefully giving itself with voluptuous acquiescence to the motion. We were all exhilarated. "Wonderful!" Tony shouted, his voice high-pitched over the roar of the waves. I shouted back, "I'm a mermaid on a dolphin's back—whoopee!" That last being the closest I could come to a Rebel yell.

All too soon it was over. Don attached the engine again and we chugged on through tranquil water. After lunch which we had at the mouth of a dry wash—the Western name for a dry creek bed—clouds began to gather. The wind rose, blowing as always up the river so we had to move against it. Les and Bruce pulled hard on the oars to help the motor and Bob in the forward boat did his share there. Off to the left beyond a fairly level green park we began to get glimpses of the Uinta Moun-

tains, that great east-west running range that the Green River
cuts through. There is a theory that this range was lifted slowly
from the plain so the Green had time to keep up with the rise
and wear away its bed while that leisurely elevation took place.
I myself, having no scientific knowledge—or geological reputation in the balance—prefer to believe that the Green simply
went where it wanted to go, regardless. This is a more credible
theory to any who know the power of the current.

The river moved for a while now at right angles to the
mountains that lay blue, and farther away purple-blue on the
horizon, crowned with snow. They had a velvet-soft, gentle look.
It was the sky that held the greater menace now, for above the
mountaintops it had taken on a queer greenish color and higher
yet the clouds were a deep thunder-blue and moving toward us
at high speed. In an incredibly short time they had spread over
all the sky. Great drops began to fall, pockmarking the water,
noisy on duffel and deck, heavy as hail. I turned up the big
collar of my jacket and swathed myself in a poncho, black oil-
skin hat pulled down over cap and veil and tied under my chin
with straps. The poncho whipped up and down like a live thing.
I tried to sit on the corners but I could not keep that cold wind
out.

Nor could the boats make any progress against it. After a
little Don pulled in to the bank in a curve of the river and we
battened ourselves down to sit it out. Almost at once the rain
stopped, though the wind was still high. The motor was running
out of fuel. More had to be mixed and strained. I did not follow
the process very carefully, nor when the need arose to filter the
gas did I offer my precious nylon veil. I felt rather mean about
that. But suppose I forgot and lighted a match while it was still
soaked with gasoline! Charles finally volunteered to sacrifice the
orange silk scarf he used to wrap his best camera in.

I went ashore while all this was going on and walked up and
down, watching the clouds scurry across the sky, enjoying the

wide view of level green that stretched away to the foothills of the mountains. Bob, Charles and Fred, leaving the others to struggle with the motor, set out to have a look at a small tumble-down cabin that clung, gray and lonely against the first rise of the hills. Who had once lived there, I wondered, who had chosen this God-forsaken, this man-forsaken spot for his home? And what disaster, what discouragment had caused him to abandon it? I was about to take off to see for myself if he had left any sign, any word of his life there, when it occurred to me that the men might be merely in search of a moment's privacy. So I let them go on alone.

All aboard again, the sky cleared quickly save for a few white clouds, and for a while owing to the tortuous course of the river, the wind was with us and we made good speed. Ahead from time to time we could see the red cliffs that marked the entrance to Flaming Gorge. At last we were coming into real canyon country. Three geese flew high overhead and one lone gray heron rose from a marshy strip at the river's edge and led the way for us, settling and then rising again as we approached. Les turned his camera on it each time, buzzing away at the most impossible angles and distances as if he felt that human determination alone could overcome the limitations of mechanical things.

Powell, in his account, says that the entrance to Flaming Gorge may be seen from a score of miles away. We had not seen it so long in advance, perhaps because, unlike him, we were not forever climbing up as high as possible to look the landscape over. But now it was in plain view and we could feel the river gathering speed to move into the narrowed channel. The color of the stone walls rather than their height impressed me. Orange red, they were, with tufts of gray-green sage and sparsely scattered cedars darkly set on ledges here and there. Cameras buzzed and clicked. I only sat and looked and wondered.

Flaming Gorge is a short canyon and before long we began

to run out of it. First one wall leveled downward, then the other and we were passing through another park. These alternations of park and gorge are said to be due to the variations in the resistant quality of the rock. The soft rock goes, worn down by wind and water till it is almost level, and here vegetation comes. The harder rock—sandstone or massive limestone—holds till the river, eating away at underlying beds of shale, undermines it, causes it to split off and fall, thus beginning a canyon wall. So the irregular course of the river is due to understandable geological reasons. Yet as I watched these variations in the scene, so great a personality had the river acquired for me that I felt that mere whimsy on its part had turned it aside here where the mountains began, as if it had said, I will, I won't, I will and then no, I won't quite yet. Not for a bit anyway, and so it bent away to shape that U-curve that Powell aptly called Horseshoe Canyon.

As we came into it, I saw that the walls were formed by great blocks of stone such as a giant mason might have laid, one on top of the other, fitting them together till he tired of his task and carelessly finished by flinging on layers of porous, honeycombed rock. There was more buff color here, and on some of the flat surfaces there were dark stripes that looked like organ pipes, marks left by the mineral-laden streams of water that sometimes run down there. There were strange shapes too, carved by wind and water—blunted profiles, queer prehistoric animals we amused ourselves trying to give names to, and I remember one fat red chickabiddy sitting poised on a narrow ledge not half big enough for it.

The mouth of Horseshoe Canyon is but half a mile from its beginning, but we had the feeling that we had been a long way when we emerged into a brief valley, passed through a small rapid too negligible to make it necessary to detach the motor, and so came into Kingfisher Canyon. The river was wider here and the walls showed distorted rock, tilted in curving lines.

Charles shouted back to me that we were now on the hind side of that Sheep Creek Canyon through which we had driven in the jeep. I nodded to let him know I had heard his words above the chug of the motor, now growing louder as we entered deeper into Kingfisher Canyon. But actually I could not accept the fact. We had been so far since that sunny afternoon, we had traversed such variety of land and water, and now that we had entered these canyons, we seemed to be in yet another world. My sense of geography, weak at best, was outraged. Had I then been just going round and round, like the old horse at the end of the pole, turning the press that sent cane juice down into the boiling syrup vats of my childhood? Had I just been under the illusion that I had come a "far piece" as we say in that same country?

At this moment a jet plane streaked the sky with twin trails of white against the blue. How strange and incongruous that swift flight seemed, how unrelated to us! It was just as remote as the passage of a meteor across the night sky, and just as meaningless. It was traveling a far piece, but there are other ways— and in my mind I had come farther than any such plane, no matter if it put a girdle round about the earth in forty minutes.

We saw no kingfishers such as Powell had found in this canyon. But there were a few ducks. Now and then one or two, disturbed by the noise of our approach, flew up and crossed before us on busy wing. Surely no bird that flies makes such heavy work of it as the duck. Again a mother duck with a half-grown brood brazened out the danger, swimming along close to shore, hurrying her young ones toward a reedy stretch of safety.

But Kingfisher, like the other two, is not long, and there was still sunlight on the river when we entered Red Canyon. One side lay in shadow, maroon, while the cedars on its brim stood black against the bright sky. On our left the cliff rose blood red in the sun, all its cedars a brilliant green. Higher and higher the walls went up to a bluer and bluer sky, eight hundred, a thousand, twelve hundred feet and more. My neck ached from looking up to see them shoulder the sky. I leaned back and shifted some luggage to rest my head on, and now and then I closed my eyes against their very audacity. Don had cut off the motor and now the noise of the river was louder, the water moving more swiftly.

Before I knew what was happening we were in the midst of a rapid. B. W. had said, ages ago, back in Denver, "Don't fight it, go with it." I sat upright, pretending I was in the saddle, swaying to the motion as if I were a gyroscope that could not tip over. A wave splashed in my face, we ducked and rose—it was like jumping hurdles one after the other, white foaming barriers over which we poured, semi-liquid ourselves, sweeping on with the river. Now for the first time I began to see the difference between these waves and those of the ocean where one rises and falls with the swell and the sinking of a wave. Here one passed over it, and it seemed to remain behind, standing still.

We were not yet out of the turmoil of white water, indeed it seemed to me that we were still in the heart of it, when Les shouted, "Hold her, Bruce!" and, tucking his oar handles under his knees, he snatched out his camera and began shooting the rapids—while we were still shooting them. Bruce held her; he always did, as I discovered later when this same thing happened again and again.

So we came out of the swift water and very soon arrived at the place which Don had chosen for our camp. He knew this canyon well and had planned just right. It was around five o'clock when we drew in toward the left bank and tied up the boats at what surely must be one of the most beautiful campsites in the world, and deep, deep in the very heart of the world.

The sun, not yet quite cut off by the towering cliff opposite, was still shining down here. By a cleft in this wall and a wooded widening, a clear rushing stream dashed down over a tumble of rocks to join the river. Tall pines glinted silver and green, their straight trunks rosied by the sun. The ground sloped gently back to a more level spot under the trees where a rough table had been set, a board bench alongside it, for others had camped here. Carter's Creek. I shall never think of it but with a sense of completion, of fulfillment, as if here at last I had arrived at perfection.

Never before was duffel so quickly brought ashore, the platform table set up and the boxes of supplies ranged round it. Fisherman's zeal had infected everyone, for there were said to be rainbow trout in Carter's Creek. I found my duffel on the slope near the water, and without a word to anyone lay down, pillowing my head upon it and looking across the river at the changing colors on the opposite wall. The roar of the creek made such a din in my ears that the wind seemed to stir mysteriously silent in the pine needles overhead and the river, reflecting sun and shadow, rolled on without audible sound. This was for me a moment of utter peace and relaxation, one in which I was conscious of nothing but delight in my surroundings. I was tired, yes, but in a way that left me quite unconcerned about it. I knew that a few minutes here on the ground would rest me. No one stopped to say, "What, are you all in?" I suppose it was too evident that I was purely happy. Les grinned down at me as he limped by with the last load.

Don had a small ice-cream carton full of worms and he took off up the creek while the others were still getting their rods together. Tony, whose job was building the fire, rushed about getting wood and twigs to start it with. "My grandfather always said start your fires with tiny twigs," he said, breaking and rebreaking them with feverish haste. He had no fishing pole but Charles had an extra one for him. When the last of them had disappeared upstream, Fred looked after them rather wistfully. He would have liked to go along, I am sure, but the sense of duty is strong in the New Englander. He and I were responsible for dinner that night.

I was rested now and went over to join him. "What's on the menu?"

He was already reading Don's carefully prepared list. "Chicken and beans and cabbage-raisin salad."

"But the trout—"

Fred was a fisherman and he knew how tricky a business fishing was. "They may not get any. We'll wait and open the cans at the last minute."

"But we can't have chicken without rice." That was my Southern upbringing coming out. I used to think the rice must be some delicate anatomical part of the chicken that nobody ever spoke about. I said as much to Fred and his laughter rang out, wholehearted, spontaneous. I think we all loved Fred's laugh, and more than once when the sound of it came back to us from the small boat ahead where he and Bob and Don were, Charles and I exchanged a smile and wished we knew what they were talking about to call it forth. Many New Englanders I know laugh as if it were a confession of weakness or something pried out of them by an unwelcome pitchfork. Fred was not like that. Yet I suppose it was the strong New England conscience that made him add now that rice, after all, was not on Don's list.

"No matter. Who's cooking this dinner, Don or us?"

Fred just smiled and made no protest while I rummaged around till I found a box of rice and set it alongside the cans of chicken. He was already chopping the cabbage for salad. "You go about that like an old hand at such things," I said.

"I've camped out a lot."

"In Connecticut?"

"Maine. I'm a down-Easter."

Maybe that explained him, I thought as I spread the green-figured plastic cover on the table, set it neatly with knives and forks, salt and bread and butter, powdered milk and tin cups and cocoa mix. The tin plates I stood in a pile near the fire, ready for serving. There seemed to be nothing more that needed doing at the moment. But just as an extra flourish, and as consolation for the fishermen if they had no luck, I got Bob's one lone bottle of rye that was still holding out quite magically—none of us were real drinkers, in spite of my reputation. I set the bottle with cups and a canteen of water on the high board table. "The bar," I told Fred when he looked around inquiringly.

I hurried then to get my tent set up. I was getting to be more skillful at this all the time. Then I set out to walk up the sloping ledge that ran across the face of the cliff. It was leaf-covered, slippery with pine needles, and it rose steeper and steeper as I climbed. When I was altogether out of breath I stopped to look down to the river through sprawling green bushes. It was quiet here where a curve of the cliff shut away from me the roar of the creek. There were flowers blooming among the boulders. As I plucked a few small yellow blossoms and some blue starlike clusters, I wished we had a botanist along to tell me what they were. There were some lovely little white flowers in the shadow of a rock. I drew back my hand quickly, remembering Charles's warning that such places were rattlesnakey, but I got the flower. I have a friend who claims he does not want to know the names, common or Latin, of bird or flower. He says the knowledge distracts from the purity of one's enjoyment of them. But I do not agree. Maybe he has just had an overdose of those gardening ladies who go down the garden path murmuring Latin names in a kind of horticultural Gregorian chant. Or more likely he just wants an excuse for not having troubled to learn the names of anything. I know for a fact that he can scarcely tell a bird from a bee. But I would like to know, to give a thing a name. In the Egyptian Book of the Dead, there is a soul I have always felt sorry for. At the time of the final weighing, "Give, oh give me back my name," he cried. Whether one likes his name or not, having had no choice in the matter, it is inextricably involved with that precious thing identity, and to be deprived of one is to diminish or destroy the other.

I came down the cliff and put my flowers in a paper cup in the center of the table where they kept blowing over till I added some stones to weight them down. Tony came back about this time. "Any luck?" He shook his head rather sadly. "How about the others?" But that he could not tell so we were still uncertain whether to open the cans of chicken. Later we took our duties more nonchalantly, but this night being our first Fred and I were quite uneasy till Charles came strolling in with a very small trout and a grayling and a wild tale of how he had to climb a tree to get one of them. I said that indeed it had a light aerial look about it. But he explained that he had felt a bite and in an excess of enthusiasm had given the pole a jerk more suitable for a tarpon and had sent fish, hook and line flying into a treetop from which he had rescued them with difficulty.

Fred had already gone to work with the can opener, dumping the chicken into the big pot. I added the rice—a great mistake even though there was an abundance of juice. For the others still delayed their return. Darkness was filling up the canyon, there was only a sunset glow on the tops of the high pines when Charles, after shouting in vain, for his voice was lost in the noise of the creek, got out his rifle. I think he had been wanting an excuse to fire it. And what a roar it made! The sound echoed and re-echoed from the cliffs around us.

That brought them all stumbling back over the rough path along the creek bank. Bob, who did so love to fish, had none. Don had six. Not enough for a dinner for all of us, so we sat down to the meal Fred and I had ready, saving the fish for breakfast. They all admired and made much of the centerpiece of flowers. And I thought that, if all men realized the effect of a word of appreciation or praise, they might have women forever their slaves. Such a word is a shot in the arm, spurring one to greater endeavor. People wonder sometimes; they say, "How can that woman stand by such a worthless rascal of a man? He is hated by everyone, disgraced, a failure." I know. He is a man given to praise, to encouragement, to kindness in small matters. Or is it that I, having missed these things in certain vital relationships, give them undue importance?

The rice was rather mushy, the chicken was falling off its bones, but no one complained—owing perhaps to that good camping rule that whoever complains of a meal shall cook the next himself. Don lifted an eyebrow at sight of the rice which he had destined for some other meal, and for the first time I realized what a good disciplinarian he must be in his fourth-grade room in the public schools of Salt Lake City. He had crushed me with an eyebrow and I resolved to follow the menu henceforth at whatever sacrifice to my inherited traditions.

Bob washed the dishes. I have never seen a more efficient man at the dishpan. Sleeves rolled to the elbow, he scrubbed each tin plate as if he were sterilizing it, getting it ready for an operation. I offered to wipe but he said, "Only the silver. The wind will dry the rest." He looked askance at the only dishtowel I could find, so I took a paper one instead.

We sat long around the campfire that night. There was something about the place that made each one of us reluctant to end the evening and the experience of being amid such beauty, such grandeur. Even in the dark we could feel the presence of the towering walls of the canyon and always we heard the mad rush of waters. The yellow light of the fire played on the grasses and the low underbrush behind us, giving it an aspect of unreality, making it too yellow a green to belong anywhere but on the stage. It made me feel that not only was I there in the midst of everything, but I was also standing aside looking on, an audience. When a log blazed high, the upper reaches of the pines were pierced with swords of light. I tilted my head back to follow them upward. Not swords, I thought; they were rather like the notes of a violin playing without accompaniment, shafting its sound into deep silence.

At one moment when no one was speaking and Bob had finished rattling his tin cups in the dishpan, Tony, pad on knee, hunched over writing a letter to his girl, looked up and said to no one in particular, "Isn't it wonderful to know that thousands of miles away someone is thinking about you, wondering what you are doing, hoping you are all right, maybe wishing for you?"

In the next few seconds of silence, like sparks from some atom-powered Roman candle in the sky, our thoughts shot away across the miles so that each one of us was translated by that magic of the mind to other scenes. I knew these seven men better now—that Fred could be counted on to think first of others; that Don, in spite of his casual and often comical manner, was always alert to his responsibilities; that Les, a sort of modern Mike Fink for physical prowess, never worried, or hesitated before any danger; that Bob carried his laboratory efficiency into every phase of living, even to baiting a hook; that Charles, with his many endearing qualities, had the gift of understanding and probably knew us better than we knew ourselves; I had seen that Tony was quick to impetuosity in all his reactions, mental and physical; and I felt sure that Bruce, for all his youth, could, were we all incapacitated, take charge and bring us safely through. I knew too something of the homes they had left and to which their thoughts had sped now, set off by Tony's words about those who might at this moment be wondering how we fared.

And my own thoughts? They had gone shooting many ways—first to my four children, to wish them well in the full lives that left them little time to be worrying about me. I thought too of my own small house and the quiet life that goes with it, and only for one fleeting moment felt its emptiness of that sort of single-minded concern which Tony had meant. And in another lightning flash I thought too of four white sterile walls, of one sleep-drugged against hopeless pain, and wished that I could send a small dream of pines and campfire smoke and the echo of wild-running water into the bedimmed consciousness of one who had loved such things. Perhaps I did. Who knows? For the human mind is yet a mystery to science that has learned so much, and thought is more powerful than the atom.

chapter

6

The roar of Carter's Creek was in my ears all night but I did not really wake to it till daylight came and the sound of voices arguing.

"Roll them in cornmeal, I tell you." That was Don at his most positive.

"They'll be ruined," Charles was saying. "All you want with trout is butter."

"And plenty of it," Bob agreed.

"Cornmeal keeps the juices in."

"They're too delicate for cornmeal."

"But it brings out the flavor. Believe me, I know—"

"Well, a little flour, maybe. With salt and pepper," Charles said.

"We haven't any plain flour. Just Bisquick."

"Heaven knows what that'll do to them."

I got dressed, rolled up my tent and went to the scene of the argument. There was no cornmeal on the trout, but they were a beautiful sight on the long griddle, done to a turn, the delicious smell of them mingling with the scent of pine needles on the trampled ground, and the aroma of boiling coffee—for Tony had taken my suggestion that powdered coffee was improved by being brought to a quick short boil before serving. "This is the best breakfast I have ever had," I said, and I still can shut my eyes and taste that trout. The coffee and pancakes too were better than usual. Maybe the surroundings had something to do with it—the fresh, crisp coolness of the morning air, the clear water of the creek leaping down over boulders, bright foam rising to small points as if a thousand winged sprites of the stream tossed themselves in wild abandon as they dived down over the rocks. We were still in shadow here under the pines, the river dark and swift, cutting away at the opposite wall, which grew brighter and redder as the line of yellow sunlight widened downward, erasing the blue and purple shadows, changing the cedars to a brighter green.

I went up the creek on my morning stroll, beyond the pines into a scattering of small green trees and bushes that climbed up the wall of this side canyon. But I came back in a hurry, with scarcely enough breath for speech. "Charles, Charles—what does a—a rattlesnake sound like?"

"Where did you hear it?" He picked up a stout stick and followed me back along the path.

We walked gingerly, searching the slope on our right. "There—stop! Listen," I said. We stood still and I heard it again, not so much a rattle as a snap-snap, dry and crackly.

Charles relaxed. "Just a locust. A rattler doesn't sound like that. If you ever hear one, you'll know it."

I hoped I would never hear it. Of course I carried always with me the rattlesnake kit, a small package that fitted easily into my plastic bag. But I had no desire to have to use it.

When I got back to camp I found everything was packed and being carried down to the boats. This morning, however, there was a difference in the way things were stowed aboard. They were being fitted more carefully into place, ropes were passed through duffel-bag handles and tied securely. The life preservers were in a heap alongshore. "Pick out the kind you prefer," Don told me, "and keep it with you."

"Shall I put it on now?" I asked.

"Not yet. You'll have plenty of time." His voice sounded too calm, too deliberately nonchalant.

There were two types of preserver—one that had to be blown

up and looked complicated, with many straps. So I chose the other kind, more like a jacket, of kapok, and I tried it on to be sure I knew just how it should go. Then I went aboard. I did not look back when we pushed off a few minutes later. There was a new tension among the boatmen, an alertness that made me watchful, too, looking ahead and then down at the current which grew swifter as we rounded a curve between the high red walls.

It was my ears that first gave me warning. I heard a new sound, still faint and far off, but deep, unceasing. Les looked around at me and grinned. "Ashley Falls," he said.

I remembered then what I had read. Powell had stopped his boats well above the falls. There they had unloaded and made a difficult portage, lining the empty boats down with ropes, a back-breaking feat, and the men had grumbled, preferring to take a chance on running it. On one great rock that blocked their passage Powell had found the name Ashley and a date which he read as 1855, though later it was found that Ashley went through here with some hunters thirty years before that. Powell had heard that they lost a boat here and that some of the men were drowned, so he took every precaution.

I wondered how we were going to manage. Back in Green River, Wyoming, I had heard of Ashley Falls and how we might have to make a portage there. I had listened with some apprehension, wondering how I would make out, climbing up the cliff and scrambling over boulders. I looked up now at those we were passing. In some places there was a sort of shelf, a ledge. In others the canyon wall rose sheer from the water's edge. When we had talked about this place, back in Teton Café, I had said I wished they could line me down with ropes, the way Powell had managed his boats. Don said, "Yes, we'll put one life preserver on you, give you another to sit on and let you down in great style." Charles had added, "Or we can just give you an air mattress and you can float through." I knew that last was a joke, but Don had been so straight-faced when he made the life-preserver suggestion that I now wondered if he had actually meant that.

The roar grew louder and more threatening. The sound seemed to bounce from wall to wall, gathering volume, to beat down upon us, to assail us from all sides. The river moved more and more swiftly. We rounded a curve and ahead I saw the rocks that blocked our way—as if half a canyon wall had fallen down in midstream. Beyond the barrier, there was no more river in sight. It was as if it ended there. Yet the roar of falling waters did not cease.

Les and Bruce swung hard on their oars as Don turned shoreward some hundred yards above the falls. We followed close behind, crossing the river slantwise, and drew up in the shadow of boulders that rose steeply above a narrow ledge of crumbled shale. Don leaped ashore and went ahead to study the rocks we would have to avoid if we were to get safely past this hazard. He stood for a long time on a high boulder, a slender figure against immensity. There was no talking while we waited. Only Les and Bruce got out, secured the boats and went to meet Don as he came slowly back from his inspection. They stood together in a little huddle, out of earshot, talking earnestly. When they came down again to the water's edge, I still could not hear what they were saying, so loud was the roar of the falls. But I saw Bob and Fred scramble out of the small boat and up the steep side to stand there watching and waiting. I saw Don and Les get in their boat and start the motor. They moved slowly, fighting the current and with great difficulty, in spite of some help from Don's oars, they passed across stream to the other side.

When they seemed to be almost touching the canyon wall there, Les cut the motor and Don at the oars spun the boat around so it headed stern first downstream. Against the sheer red wall, it looked small and helpless, and there seemed scarcely room for it to pass between wall and rock. Don and Les had a queer humpbacked look in their life preservers. As they neared the fall and the perilous narrow passage, they moved with greater swiftness, caught, borne along relentlessly. Then for a long moment they seemed to hang suspended in time and space. To me, watching with held breath, that was a shocking pause that they made, more frightening than their swift movement had been. It was as if a mere thing, an inanimate boat hung back, afraid of the drop ahead.

The front of the boat plunged out of sight, Don's oars striking wild in mid-air. The rear kicked high, jerking sideways as it disappeared. We all stood motionless, our eyes now searching the distance beyond the great rock, searching for some sign. Where were they? Then between rocks lower down we saw the flash of a red oar. We let out a cheer and waved back. They had made it.

We waited for them to tie up the boat and come back alongshore and tell us what to do. Don had complete authority about such things. When it came to deciding where to camp or when we had better stop for the day, Charles had the final say. But he left responsibility for running the rapids entirely in Don's hands. Would Don tell me I had to walk? I had a feeling as I sat there in the bright morning sunlight that he would never in this world let me run Ashley Falls. I would have to scramble over those great boulders alongshore, climbing up the cliff to get round some of them, crawling halfway under others. I could do it, yes, but it would take me a long time and I would have to take off these canvas sneakers and put on my high leather boots as a protection against snakes. But which bag were they in and where were my duffel bags?

Don and Les came into sight now. They stopped to speak to Charles and Tony, who were perched high on a rock with their cameras, then came on down to the big boat. I waited while Don gave his orders, which I could not hear because of the roar of the falls. Then he came to me. "I've decided to let you run it."

"Wonderful!" I was terribly relieved. Anything would be better than walking. I had complete confidence in the two boatmen and in the boat itself. Sometimes in the midst of traffic I have felt fearfully conscious of being made of soft flesh and delicate artery and brittle bone, of being helpless among so many metal bodies. But now I felt as if I like the boats were made of rubber and could neither break nor drown, and as I tied on my life preserver, I was convinced that I was quite unsinkable.

"But you will have to lie down as flat as you can, here on the luggage," Don went on, his voice crisp and authoritative, "so you won't obstruct the boatmen's view."

"All right. Like this?" I threw myself down on my stomach embracing a duffel bag that was full of knobby hard objects—though I did not feel them at the moment.

"Fine." He gave the boat a shove and we were off, the red oars flashing as Bruce and Les pulled hard against the current. I could see that they were trying to get across to the other side, for there was certainly no passage here, where rocks rose like jagged teeth and the water boiled around and over them and shot in between as if bursting from a fire hose.

We did not make much headway upstream, yet we did hold our own across to the far side. There in the shadow of the wall that rose sheer from the water, Les shouted, "Swing her, Bruce!"

"Not yet!" Bruce cried.

Heavens, I thought, they'd better get together on this! But the river took us willy-nilly and Les's great thrust of the oar brought us around halfway, then, with Bruce's help, all the way, so we were headed stern first toward the falls. Now they could pull against the current, not really holding us back, yet partially guiding. And as they were facing forward, they could see what they were doing. I made myself as flat as possible with only my head lifted a little. The current had us now. The wall of rock shot past me, the roar of the falls grew deafening as our small channel narrowed. The great rock on our left loomed up as big as Gibraltar—and below it, blocking our slim passageway, was another, a low-lying rock over which water boiled in a fury.

We swung in toward it, were sucked in, drawn by the sweep of the water. Les jerked out his oar just in time to save it, flung himself across, arms outstretched to shove us away if we struck and I, bracing myself, turned on my side, stiffened my legs and prepared to give a push. We escaped by inches and then seemed to hang for a moment suspended, hesitating as the small boat had done. Only longer. Or was it that just now as I saw the drop ahead of us, the great pothole to the left with its backward-curving wave and on the other side the water tearing at the canyon wall, time stretched out to accommodate all I had to comprehend in that one swift glance?

The front of the boat plunged down at an angle, the rear kicked up, the center where I lay seemed to buck and then fall from under me all in the same instant. A wave washed over me. Two forces, one forward, one sideways, caught us, then on we went, leaping, plunging, the oars now deep in the water, now high in the air. It was like riding a bucking bronco as two currents fought with each other.

"Hard on the left!" Les shouted, his voice a roar of delight and defiance.

We cut through, waves splashed over us, up and down we went in undulations that became less and less violent. Then we were through, heading now for the left bank where the small boat was tied.

"We made it, we made it!" Bruce cried and, shipping his oars just in time, sprang out rope in hand and held us as we swung round in the current. With his feet planted far apart on the rocky shore he looked as sturdy and dependable as an oak tree.

Les gave me a triumphant grin. "Thought that rock had us for a minute there," he said. Then, shouting to each other above the roar of the river, he and Bruce reviewed each stroke of the oar, each swing of the boat, saying, "We hit it just right there— another inch and we'd have been done for—she took it like a live thing—" their voices high with excitement.

The others came in sight now, scrambling down over the rocks to join us. They were all envious of me. "The only woman ever to run Ashley Falls," Charles cried with a gay salute. I don't know that this was true, but it made me feel all the more set up at the moment. Indeed we were all exhilarated by the success we had had, and as we got under way again, without the motor, for the water was swift here, I felt that now for the first time in my life I had some understanding of the fascination of danger. I still felt little sympathy for those who sought it out unnecessarily, to no purpose—the daredevils, the big-game hunters, seeking a thrill. Yet once caught in a perilous situation, it now seemed to me that there was some compensatory element there of which I had not before been aware.

Moving on down the river, now and then running through a riffle of white water, nothing compared with Ashley, I wondered if this had not been my first real encounter with physical danger. Oh, I had had quick narrow shaves on the highway, I had clung to a runaway horse, I had had brief moments of peril such as anyone must occasionally meet with, but that was all. Or was it? After all I had five times gone through the dangers of childbirth, and it struck me now that there was a curious parallel between that and running the rapids. There was the same sense of being caught in a current, swept on, powerless to turn back. There was the same feeling of being stripped down to the last essential—the preservation of life—with all small extraneous things falling away. And both were singularly purifying experiences, followed in the end by the exhilaration of accomplishment and a new-made, bright and shining look to the world. I remembered that after Bobbie was born I stared up at that cross old night nurse standing by my bed and said, "How beautiful you are!" In the same way now all of us here in the boat were transfigured, aglow. The bright face of danger? No, it was we who had passed through it who had the bright faces. And I myself saw with clearer eyes the towering cliffs between which we were moving, I found the reds and greeens more brilliant, the sky a deeper blue, the air more pure and sweet to breathe.

I was recalled to the present by discovering that Charles had turned the camera on me. When he set it aside, he said, "Now I'd like to know what you've been sitting there grinning to yourself about."

"Would you, indeed?" I asked, stalling for time, trying to think how I could put it, and in the end only saying, "I was thinking what fun it is to be alive." And that perhaps summed it all up as well as I could have managed to do after hours of puzzling.

Then I thought, more seriously, yes, this is how it is when one comes safely through such an ordeal. But suppose one does not make it—what then? What then? Well, there might be, just briefly, this same sense of being stripped down to the final fundamentals, to the last flamelike essence of self. There might be a certain exaltation in the realization that here one was face to face with the last high hazard. And if this should be but prelude to dateless night? To the slow disintegration of the unconscious physical self? I looked up at a wisp of white cloud high overhead, floating serene across the face of the deep blue sky, I looked down at the fast-running water on which we moved, seeing the tiny particles of silt, glinting brown and gold in the sun, I looked at the broken shale along a ledge, at the accumulation of leaf and wind-blown earth that gave a cedar tree a place to sink its roots and grow against the blood-red cliff—and I thought that even such disintegration, such merging with the mute inanimate things of this world was a not ignoble end.

We stopped for lunch where the cliff drew back to leave room for a small growth of green cottonwood and elder, and close to the water a smooth flat surface of grayish sand and mud—though it did not look quite like either. Rope in hand, Bob sprang out of the small boat and tied us up to a silver log. He was only a moment fastening the knot for his fingers had the surgeon's dexterity, yet his feet began to sink down in that queer substance, and everywhere he had stepped was filling in slowly, covering up his footprints. "Quicksand," Les said when he saw me staring at it. "But it's all right if you don't stand in one place too long—and it's better farther back." No matter what we came upon, Les always spoke as if he had seen it before—as indeed he probably had.

While the men were unstrapping the luggage so as to get at the lunch box, I walked along the gunwale of the *Brontosaur*, stepped across to the small boat and then gingerly lowered one foot, then the other, down to that moist, slick-looking surface. It was a queer feeling, having it draw at my feet and try to suck me down. I did not linger to explore the sensation, remembering too well one of the characters in *Lorna Doone*, but took quick flying steps across to a more solid spot.

All the rest of the day we moved through swift water. Once the small boat with Bob, Don and Fred fell behind. They had stopped to have a look at a fresh-water creek. When we rounded one bend after another, looking back each time to see if they were yet in sight, I said they must have gone fishing. "They wouldn't do that," Charles said. Yet I thought he was a little uneasy and I began to feel the same in spite of Les's assurance that they were quite able to take care of themselves. It seemed to me we ought to keep together. We were too far from help, here at the bottom of the monstrous canyon world, with no human habitation near, not even a lonely ranch, just bare wastes of impassable rock and mountain extending for mile on mile beyond the rim of the gorge.

It was in the late afternoon that we began to hear again the unmistakable roar of rapids ahead. Perhaps because I felt some anxiety about the other boat, the sound fell on my ears with an even more ominous note than at Ashley Falls. Also, there was a curve ahead and we could see nothing. "We'd better pull over and wait," Charles said. So we swung across to the left bank. Tony sprang out and made the boat fast. I stood up to stretch—and saw the small boat coming toward us round the bend. To this day I do not know what had so delayed them. For at once now all hands were occupied with the problem of how best to run Red Creek Rapids. The river was wide here; it was difficult to get a good view of all the rocks that would have to be avoided. Don called Les over to the small boat and with the help of the motor they got across to the other side.

I climbed out with the others and up the rocky slope to look the situation over from this vantage point. Charles thought the only passage must be against the far wall of the canyon. Certainly there was little room elsewhere, for the river here poured itself over innumerable jagged rocks and there was at the same time quite a drop. Bruce said, "Old Don'll figure it out," gave me a quick reassuring smile, and went on over rocks and through bushes to get yet a better view from lower down. The others with their cameras passed me, Tony leaping from rock to rock, lithe and graceful. I trailed along in leisurely fashion, skirting the great red boulders where I could and climbing over when there was no other passageway.

It was here on the sloping side of the canyon wall that I came upon my first cactus in bloom. It was a low-growing variety, a bit stunted, perhaps by the scarcity of soil or sand. The strange, thick, prickly leaves were a pale gray-green. I knelt down to study them, to look in wonder at the satiny wide-open golden flowers. How could such a thing be? How could anything so delicate, so richly colored be created out of this meager scrap of sand between two great boulders?

The others were out of sight and hearing now. Across the wide river I could see Don and Les moving against the red wall of the canyon. They looked very small, disappearing now and then behind a boulder, emerging higher up and yet farther away, only to disappear again. I turned back to my cactus plant. It seemed to me that I had come upon a miracle, and kneeling there in the sand with the warm bright sun on my back I put out my hand with caution that was half reverence to touch the edge of the thick juicy-looking leaf. I brushed the sharp spines with my fingertips and took a petal between my fingers and felt its delicate texture. A plant physiologist could have explained to me perhaps how a stray seed had found a resting place, had swollen and sent out roots and a single shoot that spread and multiplied its form in wind and rain and sun. But who could tell me what secret knowing shaped it so, or what the initial impulse that impelled it to existence? As a living creature I felt akin to it in the mystery of our mutual being and left it with reluctance as if it were a part of myself.

The others came trooping down now from their inspection of the falls ahead. Across the river Don and Les were nearing the small boat. As we scrambled back to take our places we saw Les with his camera—he seldom let it out of his hands except when occupied at the oars. He was so intent on getting a shot of us that he did not notice he had reached the brink of the river, took one step too many and down he went into the water, camera and all. "There goes Les," Bruce shouted. Then his head appeared alongside the boat, Don gave him a hand and he climbed in. He was still laughing when they came across to join us. "Won't have to take a bath this Saturday," he said, as he jumped over to his place in the *Brontosaur* and sat down dripping. "We'll take it in the middle, between those two rocks," he told Bruce, and they manned the oars.

I lay down this time without being told, bracing my feet against the gunwale and finding the two ropes Bruce had arranged conveniently to hand. This time our boat was to go first. The roar of the water grew louder as we swept on toward the rocks. I lifted my head to see—it did not seem possible that there would be room for us to pass. I thought we would surely be carried straight down among those jagged rocks.

"Hard on the right," Les shouted. "Pull, Bruce, pull!"

They bent, grunting, to the oars, the heavy boat swung round, gaining all its length in the right direction, then stern first tore on through boiling water, passing with only a few feet to spare between the two great center rocks, dipping downward in one humping, almost human undulation, flapping and splashing through waves that drenched us. I thought we were through but Bruce's shout, "Hard on the left, Les, pull, pull!" made me see a new danger. A swift side current swooping in from the other wall was sending us straight for a rocky shoal. There was a scraping, grinding sound from the flat bottom of the boat. The oars struck bottom and could do no more. An instant later we were aground, white water foaming all around us, unable for all its velocity to budge us from this perilous resting place.

Don with Bob and Fred came flying through between the rocks, the small boat flipping sideways and up and down, lost to sight as the waves went over her, then emerging to shoot on downstream. But Don had seen our predicament and as quickly as he could came about while Fred sprang out, waist deep at the edge of the shoal and held the boat against the current. Don and Bob came wading through the raging torrent to our rescue. By now everyone but me was out of the *Brontosaur*, hauling and tugging—in vain, for the side current was holding us pinned there on the rocks. It took all of Bob and Don's added power to budge the heavy boat inch by inch off the sharp rocks. Then as it swung free, I thought for a moment that I would be left alone to float downstream. But they all managed to scramble aboard, drenched to the skin and breathless. Tony, the last to make it, got in just before we were swept out into deep water. Bob and Don were left standing there with the water rushing and foaming around their knees, and looking very much as if they had been made to walk the plank. As we tore on downstream I turned to watch them make their perilous way back to the small boat, Bob stumbling once and almost going down because the small, water-tumbled stones gave but precarious footing.

It was time now to stop for the night and dry out, especially as the wind had been rising and gray clouds were gathering. We had been all day in Red Canyon so we were not far from the end, and a short run brought us out into Little Brown's Hole, a good campsite. The duffel was carried far in, away from the river and, we hoped, out of the worst of the wind. But there was no escaping that. I chose a spot under a cottonwood that had as many dead as living branches, and after I had pitched my tent wondered if I had made a wise choice—I was afraid the wind would bring a branch crashing down on my head. But it was too difficult to shift. I'd take a chance. I stowed my luggage under army cot and tent flap, for there would surely be rain before long, then went to consult the menu and see what we were to have this night. Tony had a good campfire burning, for here there was plenty of dead wood scattered about on the sandy level ground under the trees. He had some trouble breaking up the wood and Les, on his way to the bushes to change to dry clothes, paused to help him. He took up a dead log that was twenty-five feet long at least, cried, "Look out," and swinging it as a boy might swing a baseball bat, he cracked it against a tree trunk, breaking off a piece of convenient size. He stepped a little closer and swung again. Another stick for the campfire, and another till the whole dead tree was broken in bits. Then he brushed his hands together and limped away without a word.

I searched through one box after the other till I found the

menu—beef stew was to be the *pièce de résistance*. I got out
the cans but the can opener was the kind that to me has always
been a Chinese puzzle. I turned it this way and that, presenting
first one side of it, then the other to the top of the can in the
hope that, if I kept on shifting, it would eventually assert some
sort of natural affinity for a particular spot. Fred took it from
me without a word and in short order had the six tall cans
open and ready to pour in the pot.

I sampled the mixture—"Tasteless," I said. "Haven't we any
onions?" We went through every one of the boxes before we
found them, in the very last. There were not many, Don could
not have meant them for a cooked vegetable, he must have
planned to use them in some salad. So I left enough for that, cut
up the rest very fine, browned them in butter over the fire and
added them to the stew. They made all the difference in its
flavor, and our dinner that night justly deserved the praise it
received. Canned food, like a ready-made dress, needs a little
personal touch to make it acceptable.

Charles had his radio out and was trying to get the Lowell
Thomas newscast, Fred and Tony were writing up their notes, as
was I, while Bob and Bruce did the dishes. The campfire,
whipped by the wind, blazed high and low and sent sparks
flying. I sat as close as I dared, for the wind grew colder all
the time. The sky was black with rain clouds and the pages
of my notebook kept blowing back in a noisy riffle every time I
lifted my pen. Don, with hands on his slim hips and shirt collar
blown up by the wind, was having some sort of argument with
the dishwashers and now and then they emphasized a point with
a bang of tin plates or cups. I paid no attention till Don moved
round to my side of the fire and I heard him saying, "But the
trouble with women is—"

As he spoke he sat down without looking to see what he sat
on. It was the collapsible canvas water bucket which Bruce had
refilled before supper. Amid our laughter, which he increased

by his comic air of outraged dignity, the argument was forgotten and now I suppose I shall never know what the trouble with women is.

Les, who had been back in the shadows searching through his duffel, had joined us while all this was going on and now he sat down on the other end of my log. He had a small book in his hand, and as he opened it a picture blew out and landed at my feet. "Look at it," he said when I picked it up.

"What a beauty! Glamorous and everything. Pin-up? Movie star?"

"My girl," he said with pride. "Next time I come down the river she'll be along. We're getting married in August. In the Temple."

Charles's radio was sputtering and groaning as he kept on trying to get Salt Lake City, which he thought to be the nearest big station. "Quiet!" he shouted now. "I'm trying to contact the outside world."

Bob, wiping his hands on a paper towel, said with a faintly surprised air, "Is there such a thing?" As if he had planned a real vacation and change but had not expected to forget his laboratory so completely.

I said, "Who cares whether there is such a thing or not?" And Bruce gave me a shy smile across the campfire that was lending his wide sun-bronzed face an even ruddier look. "I'm happy," he said.

Yes, I thought as I watched him lay another stick of wood carefully on the fire, you are just one of those lucky ones who are born happy. According to the psychologists he really should have been all warped and chuck-full of complexes, if not actually delinquent—his parents were divorced and both had married again. But with Bruce everything was just fine. He had told me how much he liked both his stepfather and his stepmother, and I was sure they could not help but love him. Maybe that was the real explanation of the way he had turned out.

It was a wild night. I woke more than once after the rain began, to wonder if the boats were tied securely, to cover my bed with a poncho, for there was a small mousehole in the top of my tent where water blew in. The wind roared through the treetops, flapped at the sides of my tent, and above my head the old branches of the cottonwood creaked and groaned.

chapter

7

Morning dawned gray and cold with a fine drizzle falling. I lay snug and warm till Les's "Roll out! Roll out!" let me know that it was time to be getting up. Pancakes in the drizzle, bacon sputtering on the griddle, eggs sizzling, all tasted extra good this morning. I ate some of everything—I, whose usual breakfast is no more than coffee and toast! Then I packed my duffel, for once glad of the exercise which kept me from feeling the cold too much. The boats were bailed out and inspected for leaks, for the rubber bottoms had taken quite a beating when we were stuck on that rocky shoal. But all was sound, so back went the duffel and platform. This morning nothing was tied down, so I knew we would have a quiet day.

We got off around nine-thirty, Don attaching the spare motor and towing the *Brontosaur*. On each side of us now there was gentle, hilly green country. Once we passed a ranch—a gray cabin amid a cluster of small outbuildings, with a wooden stockade, an old Ford car set up on blocks, and no sign of life anywhere. We shouted and got no response. Farther along we saw a small herd of cattle grazing close to the river. They looked up as we went by and stared at us, turning their heads to follow us with an air that was at once benign and superior, as if to say, "Well, all right, if that's what you want. As for us we prefer to give ourselves to quiet and contemplation."

There was more wild life here in this open area. Ducks and geese flew up from the river's edge and in one great dead tree we saw three gray cranes. Deer went bounding away through the underbrush. Our only canyon this day was low-walled with deep, still-running water. The sides were pale in color but made interesting by the great number of mud nests swallows had built there. There were thousands of them. It had been so when Powell came through and this short canyon was named in their honor—Swallow Canyon. There were far more nests than birds, and the effect was rather desolate. I have felt somewhat the same dreariness in winter when driving past closed cottages along the seashore.

By one o'clock when we stopped for lunch, the sun was out and only a few white clouds floated overhead. We were again in a tranquil open place, the Brown's Park area. It seemed strange to me that in the course of so short a time the whole aspect of the scene could have altered yet again. The river here was wide, with scarcely a ripple. Across on the other side were rolling green pasture land and trees. It was not unlike some of New York State's abandoned farm country. From the high bank where we sat eating lunch I watched three cows come down to drink and they lent a peaceful, pastoral note to the scene, standing there motionless as if in a painting. Behind them on the low hills across from us, cloud shadows passed, undulating as they followed the contour of the land. The sky was a clean blue with that rain-washed look that always gives it added depth and brilliance, and the sun felt delightfully warm as we sat there eating our sandwiches. Les, munching on a head of lettuce, for he seemed to prefer fruit and raw food, said, "Davy Crockett's fort used to be here somewhere."

I looked around eagerly. This would be something to tell my grandchildren about when I got home. So as soon as I had finished eating and while the others were mixing gas and working over the engine, I set out to explore the grove of cottonwoods behind us. If I could only come upon the remains of a brick or stone chimney somewhere here I could claim it as part of the fort and carry it home in my duffel. I walked back some distance to where the trees ended and the ground began to rise in a series of low hills similar to those on the opposite side of the river, but I found no trace of human habitation. There was not even a sign of a trail going out, though surely cowboys must come in here now and then to round up the cattle.

Many of the cottonwoods were old and gnarled, picturesquely twisted. As I came back along the river's edge I was interested in examining the younger tree trunks that had been gnawed by beavers. Some had been cut all the way through—without any apparent reason, for there was no sign of a dam anywhere. Maybe beavers eat the wood. The stumps, about a foot and a half from the ground, were pointed where they were cut off, and the point was right in the middle as if the beavers had not cared in which direction the tree would fall. Here and there a trunk had been circled and left to die. Those that had been a long time thus ringed around were already dead, standing there silver, bare and beautiful among the living.

As soon as we got on our way again, a strong wind came up, the brown river was flecked with whitecaps and the oars were needed even with both motors going full blast. It was a cold wind. Remembering the heat we had encountered earlier, I wondered that there could be such swift alterations in temperature when we had actually traveled so short a distance in miles, and most of it in a southerly direction. I hauled out my jacket and still I was cold. But at that I preferred it to roasting.

Each day the luggage was placed a little differently and after this noon stop I found my most comfortable position within conversational distance of Les as he pulled away at the oars with long steady strokes. I said these little wind waves made me feel as if I were riding a pacing horse and that got us started talking about horses. Les said he grew up with them on a Montana ranch, couldn't remember when he didn't know how to ride, and added, "I never lit hard off a bucking horse." As for boats, he had gotten used to them early too because all through childhood he had to row across a river to get to school.

Les was a good talker and I listened with interest, feeling I was getting the real flavor of the West in his manner of speech, and of the pioneer days as he spoke of his ancestors. They had come out from Pennsylvania by way of Kentucky and one of them was that John Smith who signed the Declaration of Independence. They had gone into ranching, raising sheep and cattle. "My great uncle," Les said, "got to be a real big rancher. Lost his nose in a saloon."

"Dear me! That was—unusual." I paused expectantly.

"Yes, it was," Les said and made no further explanation.

I suppose I shall always be wondering about this. For there is something unforgettable about an unfinished story; it teases the mind and will not let go. It may be that all scientific research is really the result of this common human tendency to be uncomfortable till one finds out, and probably the never-ending soap dramas on the radio run on the same principle. When I was eleven I read part of a book that was pronounced unsuitable for my tender years and removed from me before I could finish it. It was called the *Curse of the Cliftons* and I have been wondering all these years what the curse was. In the same way I shall now be forever haunted by Les's great uncle's nose.

We had struck a crosscurrent and were making little headway, for the wind had grown stronger and all the river was whipped to a milky white. Bruce gave a shout: "Hey, Les! Pull, pull!"

Les, who had shipped his oars while he was talking, took them up again. I waited till we were in easier waters before I asked about his limp. I had thought it might be from a war injury. But he had not been in the war, he said; he had gone into a Sabrejet factory while waiting to be called up and they had kept him there. Then he added, "My leg's just fine. I broke it last year but it's all right. I've just got a sore toe now; that's what makes me limp."

After a moment I asked, "How did you break your leg?"

Les grinned. "Got mad at a Cadillac car and kicked it."

It would be something like that, I thought. Before I could find out why he had lost his temper with the Cadillac car, a shout from the small boat ahead made me again conscious of my surroundings. Ahead, beyond a projecting peninsula which gave the river a sharp twist, I could see two great cliffs, one of them brilliant red in the afternoon sunlight. The Gates of Lodore, a beautiful name, and fitting. It was Powell who named this canyon. One of his men, Jack Sumner, had objected to what he called a far-fetched, flowery, foreign name. It ought to be more American, he said, and not one taken from an English poem. But Powell would not change; he liked too well Southey's lines about "how the water comes down at Lodore." Only these waters came down with far greater violence and fury, for here we would have to run Disaster Falls, Triplet and, worst of all, Hell's Half Mile.

But all that would come tomorrow. It was too late now to undertake such hazards, and besides, through the kindness of the Park Service, we had been offered the use of their cabin just a little way above the entrance to the canyon. It would be quite an experience, I thought, to sleep once more under a roof, and heavenly to have four walls against this cold wind which was literally freezing me.

We drew up under the bank, still at some distance from the entrance to the canyon. It was quite a walk back to the cabin, especially for those who had to carry our boxes and duffel. I went ahead with Charles, who knew where the key was hidden. And what a delightful spot it was! The log cabin, stoutly built, stood under one of the many gnarled old cotton-woods that formed a pleasant grove around it. In the level open space to the rear was a pump—that meant we would have good fresh water. And off to one side a little way was a small unmistakable structure—what a luxury that would be, after the bushes! Beside the entrance was a tall, feathery shrub covered with delicate pink and purplish blossoms. Bruce said it was a tamarisk.

Charles opened the door with a flourish and bowed me in. It was rather dark till he and Tony had pried the wooden shutters from two of the windows, but I could make out at the left a long table with benches, a sink on the right of the entrance, and a great black wood stove with a rocking chair beside it. I walked right over and sat down. What a delightful sensation it was, to have a willow seat for my rear, a back for my spine and a place where I could lean my head. One does not realize, till he has sat for days on anything that is available, what a remarkable thing a chair is.

Tony started a fire in the stove, and I have never met with more welcome heat. I sat between the stove and the partition which divided the six or eight bunks from this part of the cabin, and I did not move to lay out the dishes on the long table. I simply could not pry myself from the chimney corner or from that magnificent big old rocking chair. Don came in with a load of supplies. "I didn't realize your name was Uncle George," he said.

"What are you talking about?"

"Look behind you." I turned, and found there painted in large letters across the back of the chair—UNCLE GEORGE.

I shook my head. "I'm not Uncle George, but whoever he is, we are kindred spirits, and as long as he is not here to occupy this chair, I mean to do so."

Les and Bruce began bringing in the boxes of supplies. "There'll be no room for me to rock, if you bring all that in," I complained. So they decided it would be not too inconvenient to step outside for whatever was needed. Certainly there were already plenty of pots and pans on the shelves behind and beside me, even some supplies—sugar and coffee and cereals, as well.

The small cabin seemed crowded when we were all inside

there, everyone milling about except me. I stuck to my rocker and planned that I would move it later and set up my army cot here between the stove and the partition wall. Then I would be warm, and out of the way, all night. Les was too big for any one room; he kept bumping into things. Voices were magnified by the four walls, Tony's sounding high-pitched and at times irritating. Bob's laughter filled the room so there was no space left for breathing. It was a most puzzling effect that this confinement began to have upon me and indeed upon us all. We were enlarged, to our mutual discomfort. I thought that now I knew how men felt in submarines or enclosed in some small shack at the South Pole.

After a little Bob and Fred said they were going to set up their tent outside somewhere; Charles beckoned to Don and the two of them disappeared. Soon I heard the put-put of the motor and decided they had gone ahead to look over the rocks at the entrance to Lodore. Les went in and out, bearing great pails of water from the pump. These he set on the stove to heat. He was going to soak his sore toe, he said. Bruce brought in armloads of wood, Tony built up the fire till one stove lid glowed red hot.

Les poured hot water in a pan, shook in a handful of salt, and, sitting across the room from me, took off shoe and sock and gingerly lowered his foot down into the steaming water. I had a glimpse of his toe; it was truly in an alarming state, red, swollen, puffy-looking. "Any normal person would be in the hospital with a toe like that," I said. "You'd better get Bob to look at it when he comes back."

He shook his head. "A good soaking is all it needs. These doctors—" He spoke of them in the same tone he had used when, heaping that cheese mixture on the cabbage, he had said, "This plastic stuff—" He liked nothing artificial, I thought. He wanted to take life straight, on the rocks. With his rugged independence and his true appreciation of nature in her wilder aspects, he should have lived back in the real pioneer days. I was reminded of my own grandfather Burnley, setting out from Virginia on horseback with a wagon train of goods and chattels, traveling through woods, across rivers and down by the Natchez Trace to settle on a Mississippi plantation, his only doctor for any emergency among his family and a hundred slaves the leather-backed *Family Medicine* that still stands on my bookshelf. For external inflammation, soak in hot salt water, for internal, take slippery elm tea; for yellow fever, scald the patient's limbs with boiling water. Les would have fitted right into that era.

Tony, adding more wood to the already roaring fire in the stove, was speculating about Hell's Half Mile; Bruce was quietly opening the cans of meatballs and spaghetti, dumping them into a big pot on the back of the stove. All at once I felt too hot, too oppressed by these four walls, and could not stay in such confinement any longer. I went outside. The wind had died down, the air was cool and fresh-smelling, delicious, the sky rosy with sunset, as rosy as the tamarisk bush by the door. I realized all at once that I wasn't going to sleep in that hot stuffy cabin! Not with all this space out here where I could really breathe. I dragged my duffel away to where another great cottonwood spread its branches. There I set up my tent. There were anthills and millions of large ants disturbed by my activities. I considered setting the legs of my cot in tin cans of water so as to be sure they did not swarm up and eat me in the night. Then I decided it was too much bother and, besides, the ants seemed too busy with their own affairs to be interested in me. I walked across to the river's edge and waved to Don and Charles, who were chugging slowly back upstream from their brief excursion. I saw that Bob and Fred had set up their tent on a small knoll some distance away, and off in the open field that lay back of the cabin there were two sleeping bags in position for the night. So I was not the only one who had found the cabin oppressive.

Standing there on the bank of the river I suddenly remembered something Rilke said in one of his letters, and though he was speaking of marriage, which was certainly a closer and more permanent relationship than the brief crowding we were having at this moment in the cabin, there seemed to me to be a certain parallel. He said that living side by side required that each appoint the other as a guardian to his solitude, that the solitude of an individual was a sacred thing, not to be broken in upon and each should know and love and cherish the "distance between."

So in the cabin we had perhaps intruded upon each other's fundamental privacy, and we were too alien, too disparate a group for that. Outside, in the face of danger, under the wide sky, before the wonders we had looked upon, we were surrounded by space, both physical and psychological, and having such space between were able to move in harmony under the canopy of our common humanity.

We had a good supper, sitting at the table. I was over against the wall where I could lean back and take every advantage of our comforts. Now that I had set up my tent outside, I did not feel too confined in the cabin; only our voices still seemed too loud and numerous. In one brief moment of quiet I quoted a favorite line of my father's, from Dr. Holmes: "And silence, like a poultice, comes to heal the blows of sound."

This set Tony off, quoting poetry, and Charles too recited a few lines. I came in again with snatches from some of Keats's odes which I had once learned by heart. It is a pity, I think, that schools no longer require students to memorize. In my grandmother's day, it was quite the fashion—at least this was true in the old Morristown Academy in New Jersey where she was educated. And in her old age when her eyesight failed and she could no longer read, what a pleasure it was to her to sit by the fire repeating page after page from *Paradise Lost*, from Burns and Byron and even from the *Aeneid*, for she was quite a Latin scholar. Nowadays the old turn on television, and indeed it is a godsend to many. Yet there seems to me to be a richness lost, and I would not willingly give up the memory I have of my grandmother in her long gray calico skirts, a small white fluted cap on her smooth, reddish hair, repeating the lines she loved.

I remembered too, as we sat around the table in the cabin that night, how Powell had read aloud to his companions from Longfellow's "Hiawatha"; and not only around the campfire but during the quieter stretches when they were floating down the river he read "The Lady of the Lake." Those things were out of fashion too, nowadays. I wondered how some of our modern poetry would stand up against such a background, and did anyone memorize it? Yes, probably, but as for me I could think of none I had learned by heart lately except some of Robert Frost's and those four lines of Ezra Pound's that end, "But years and sterner grieving, It takes to fashion laughter." At any rate most of the things we quoted that night in the cabin at the Gates of Lodore were out of such old collections as Pancoast or *The Oxford Book of English Verse.*

After dinner Bob and Charles got out their cameras and began taking them to pieces in an effort to get rid of dampness as well as some grains of sand that had crept into vital places. The table was soon strewn with mysterious-looking inward parts. I was reminded of the way my boys loved to take an old alarm clock to pieces—and the trouble they sometimes had getting it back together again. I hoped Bob and Charles would have better luck with all these small bits and pieces—and stole away, out into the cool, soft, dark night to my tent under the cottonwood tree.

The next morning I found that only Don and
Charles had slept inside the cabin. So much for civilization's
comforts, I thought. And we were later than usual in getting
off. The cabin had to be swept, the pots and pans we had so
recklessly used scrubbed and replaced on the shelves, everything left in as good order as we had found it—and that was
very good indeed. Then the windows must be reshuttered, the
fire wholly extinguished, our scraps buried, the woodbox left as
full as we had found it. All this was far more trouble than
leaving an ordinary camp spot where tin cans were simply
tossed in the river and the wind quickly blew sand over all traces
of human occupancy. It thus became more than ever apparent to
me that the conveniences of modern life exact their toll in time
and effort.

Then too this morning all the duffel had to be tied down
securely in the boats. This was the day we were to run Hell's
Half Mile, and now that it was upon us we were all feeling a
sense of foreboding. Don was more serious than usual and his
mood affected us all. I dug down in my luggage and got out a
bright red scarf. This I tied round my cap. I thought that
if I went overboard maybe my head would bob up out of the
foaming waters and I wanted it to be visible.

While we were getting everything ready and the boats loaded,
clouds had again gathered in the south. Not gray, gentle-seeming
clouds, but dark blue and threatening. As we shoved off there
was a roll of distant thunder. It seemed fitting somehow, as

we headed toward the Gates of Lodore, that our entrance to so hazardous a passage, to a place of so poetic a name, should be heralded thus by warnings from the sky.

We rounded the point made by the peninsula of gray shale. It was dotted here and there with the green of cottonwoods, with clumps of sage and scattered grasses, and it lay like a bar to the Gates. The river moved with quiet sureness, bearing us swiftly along, curving back to enter the space between the orange-red cliffs that rose like a giant vise to clasp us. Clouds spread across the sun, colors changed to darker tones, shadows were purple and the same deep blue as the cloud that hung over one cliff. A long roll of thunder echoed down the canyon, a fork of lightning split the sky. I thought of Dante at the gates of hell. There was no "raging lion with hunger mad," and yet in that first moment of our entrance to the canyon of the beautiful name, the very air seemed terror-struck. No one spoke. It was as if the place had put a spell upon us.

Then suddenly the threat of storm had passed by, the sun broke through the clouds, colors brightened as the walls rose higher and higher, cameras were brought out to click and buzz all around me. I tried to make a quick sketch in my notebook and accomplished nothing but a hodgepodge of lines that kept running up and up above the top of the page so that my pencil hung in midair! How could one indicate those thousand-foot walls rising to the sky? Before I could note more than the angle at which they rose from the rushing water's edge, they had mounted yet higher, sloping back by irregular ledges that held long stretches of juniper and pine, as if giant green fingers had pushed back the stone and were keeping it there while we passed.

A great amphitheater appeared, set a thousand feet above us with the walls towering yet higher—stage for a performance by giant actors equipped with wings. Or perhaps there sat an invisible audience and we were the brief actors on a fluid stage.

The scene altered with every moment of our swift passage. A cloud went over the sun again and the red rock was blued to magenta; the sun came out once more and a stretch of sage on the shale took on a frosted look; and here ahead was a terraced, modern building with plain abrupt walls above and below, and decked with Christmas cedars.

In this canyon, I had been told that in a distance of twenty miles the level of the river descends over four hundred feet. For here it is cutting through the very heart of a mountain. So it was no wonder that, now we had really entered upon it, we found our boats caught in a swifter and swifter current, the water continuously white. Les saw me watching it. "This is nothing. We'll hit Disaster pretty soon, then you'll see something."

"Disaster? That's where Powell lost his boat, the *No-Name*, isn't it?"

Les nodded. "The Kolb brothers were three days getting through it."

He was continually surprising me by his knowledge of all the books that had been written about these canyons. I had not read Kolb's account but I remembered Powell's vivid story of how the two Howlands and Goodman went ahead in the *No-Name*, were caught by an irresistible current that bore them straight on between the rocks while the other boats were being drawn up alongshore for a study of the best course. Powell had run down afoot by the edge of the water and reached the first fall in time to see Goodman caught in a hole below the rock, the Howlands clinging to broken bits of the boat and with difficulty landing on a small rocky island amid-stream. They were rescued, but the boat was a total loss, its contents dumped to the bottom. As I was remembering all this, I began to hear a dull, threatening roar ahead. We were almost there. I was listening tensely when a shout and a gesture from Don motioned us to turn out of the current and go ashore. Tony sprang out into shallow water and, leaning back with heels digging into the sand, held the *Brontosaur*. The small boat came in, and Fred did the same for it.

Don and Charles were talking excitedly as they came toward us. "Old Fred was right on the job," Don said, admiration in his tone.

"Johnny on the spot, all right," Charles agreed.

"What happened?" Les demanded, for we had been ahead of the small boat and had seen nothing.

"Oar broke—heaven knows why—there was not a rock visible. Back in that last fast water. We slung around—it was a ticklish moment—but Fred had the spare oar in place in the nick of time. Nice work," Don said. Then he motioned to Les and Bruce to come with him. "We'd better go ahead and look Disaster over."

Charles jumped across and perched on the side of the *Brontosaur*. "You should have seen Fred. The rest of us just sat there sort of paralyzed, it was so unexpected. But he was quick as a flash."

I looked over at Fred, out of hearing, standing there hanging on to the rope, serving as anchor to the small boat, and, catching his eye, I clapped and nodded. He shrugged, grinned. He looked pleased, in his modest, quiet way. And I—I felt more than pleased, I was filled with delight that this gentle, thoughtful, bookish man, whom we had all come to love for those qualities and for his readiness to do his part and more, had won the admiration of these men of action. It was a vindication of some sort. Don's "Old Fred" had been spoken not disparagingly but with admiration and affection; his brief, "Nice work," was an accolade.

Curiously enough I now no longer felt any apprehension about Disaster Falls, Upper, Lower and Middle, and the roar of the water ahead was more of a challenge than a threat. So I was glad when Don and the other two came back with the news that we would run it. "It doesn't look too bad," Bruce said as he climbed back into his place, giving me a reassuring smile. "And we're going first this time."

"Good—and the badder the better," I said. "I'm ready for it."

There was a new spirit among us now. Gone were the small irritations of the four-walled cabin. Bob sat perched in the stern with his camera ready. I looked around and saw behind us the small boat, with Don rowing and Fred waving encouragement as the roar of Disaster grew louder. Charles and Tony had walked ahead with their cameras to get shots of us as we came through. When the foaming water came in sight, I lay down across the duffel and held fast. Down we went into the turmoil of waters. The *Brontosaur* shuddered, the stern was swung round to face forward, the bow flipped up. "Pull now," Les shouted. We dipped and plunged.

"She's all right," Bruce said with such confidence that I sat up, balancing myself easily, giving my body to the motion that took us dancing up and down and ever forward through one rapid after another. At last we came into smoother water.

"Swing round now," Les called. "We'll wait for Don." So we drew up in the quieter water alongshore and sat waiting for him.

The small boat was lighter; it flipped up and down far more than we had. One moment it was wholly doused in spray, then it rose again and came on, weaving among the rocks by the same course we had followed.

"We took them all at once—just wasn't any stopping in between," Les said.

"What do you mean?" I asked.

"That was Upper, Middle and Lower Disaster we just ran. Three sets of falls in Powell's day."

"They should be named Triplet," I said.

"We'll be to that bunch in a minute," Les said. Then, seeing

that the small boat was safely through, he and Bruce bent again
to the oars and we swept out into the main current.

The roar of Disaster had not really died away when the
sound of more falls began. Bruce stood up and studied the lay
of the rocks that obstructed our passage. "We'd better swing
right against the wall," he said. "Pull, Les, pull."

We shot across, passed a great boulder. Then a stronger
current caught us, bore us toward an overhanging wall, concave,
with dark waters sweeping far back under the rock.

"Pull, Bruce, pull!" Les cried, a desparate note in his voice.

I saw the danger and made myself as flat as I could—if
we went all the way under that overhanging wall, I would surely
be scraped off. But strong oars worked well in harmony and it
was only for one moment that I felt the rocky roof brushing at
my back. Then out and on we went.

The rest of Triplet Falls was pure delight, with enough
white water to be exciting, the waves not high enough for real
danger and the *Bronto* taking them with gay grace. If Hell's
Half Mile proved to be no worse than this, it would not be bad
at all. In any case, I was all keyed up to run it. Not so much
that I wanted to take wild chances as that I longed to be able
to tell about it afterward. Indeed I was already imagining my
grandchildren telling *their* grandchildren—and so on through
future generations, "My dears, you great great great—ran
Hell's Half Mile." Vanity, that was all. I've always been rather
intrigued by those odd bits and pieces of a life that are thus
preserved and handed down. For instance, I have one ancestor
quite unknown to me save by one deed—there was a certain
dining room chair he did not like. He said, "If this chair is
put at my place again, I shall throw it out the window." It was,
and he did. Of another I know only that Sir Walter Scott
wrote a poem to her—"Lines to Lady Mary G—". Was she really
a Lady? I don't know. By such small chance rememberings are
we immortalized, we who do no great deeds fit for the pages

of history. So, splashing down the Green River, I thought to have
my word-of-mouth epitaph made to order, not left to a more
unkind chance.

As we began to hear the roar of waters ahead, I asked Les,
"Do you think I can run Hell's Half?"

"Sure you can." Les never admitted that anything was impossible.

The sound was almost deafening, though we were still well
above the first fall. Don turned his boat shoreward. We
followed. Bruce sprang out and tied us to a little bush there.
The others started at once unloading the small boat. "What's
up, Les?" I asked, as he too began climbing out to help.

"Don wants us to line her down this first drop."

"And the *Brontosaur?*"

"Oh, we'll run her."

It took more than one trip, with all of them helping, to unload
here on this small level sandy spot and carry the luggage
down out of my sight. Then Don, hugging the shore, took the
small boat as far as he dared. Great rocks and the curve of the
river hid it from my sight now. I sat on, perched on the duffel
in the center of the big boat. I had a feeling that, if I stayed
right here, I would not be asked to get out and walk. The sun
shone down pleasantly warm on my back. I felt very much
alone as I sat there waiting. The roar of the rapids ahead seemed
to gather in volume. It was echoed and re-echoed like thunder
from the high red walls.

My eyes rested on the slender nylon rope that held the boat
against the current. What a small bush it was that the other end
was tied to! Suppose it gave way—already it was swaying as
the river tugged and wheedled at the side of the boat. If it
did, what should I do? There was deep water and swift current
between me and the shore. I could never swim against it.
Better to hang on to the boat and go down over the falls. I
imagined the shouts of consternation, the faces of dismay, as

the *Brontosaur* would loom into sight of the others, with me sitting here serenely, maybe even lifting a nonchalant hand to wave as we plunged down over a fearful drop. It was a delightful little scene I pictured in my mind's eye. I even went so far as to hope Charles would have the quick wit to keep his camera going.

But it was not to be. The rope held, the small bush was firmly rooted and, after a little, Bob came back and pulled the *Bronto* in so I could leap ashore. "You won't have to walk but just a little way, just below this first drop."

I followed him, rather sulkily, I am afraid, as he chose the easiest path, around rocks, over and above them, underneath branches that blocked the way. "Thank you for guiding me down," I said when we came in sight of the others. I don't think he heard me—he was hurrying on to help out with the lining. The others, ropes in hand, were stationed here and there along-shore as close as possible to the rushing water. Don and Les were perched on rocks that from my vantage point seemed to be in the very midst of the falls. I had arrived just in time to see the procedure which I had read about in Powell's account. I moved further down, and now the full height of this first drop of Hell's Half Mile was visible—and a fearful fall it seemed as I stood there, deafened by its roar. Water poured foaming down between two great rocks, fell some ten feet or more, swerving over hidden rocks to scoop two great potholes from which backward-sweeping waves would present yet another menace to any boat that ventured there.

I did not see how they would ever get the small boat through or hold it against the sweep of the water. And for a moment as it took the deep plunge, I thought they had lost it. All in an instant as it came down, a great log, left by higher water on top of the rock where Charles stood, was caught by the jerking rope, flung upward to come down square across the boat. A second later, Les was swept from his precarious footing, and down he went into the boiling waters. It was a long moment till his head appeared some twenty feet lower down the river and he caught on a rock and climbed out, to stand dripping while the others, running with the boat, held it, brought it into the quieter spot just below where I stood. Now I could see why Don did not want me to risk it in the *Brontosaur*. Indeed I felt uneasy as to how it would fare, heavily loaded as it was, and with Bruce and Les to weigh it down. They now set off upstream to bring it through.

Charles and Tony took their places high on the rocks to shoot the scene, Bob and Fred and Don had their cameras out too. I moved to a higher rock. We waited and waited. It was like arriving too early to see the Fourth of July parade in Duxbury. But the suspense was greater. At last above the rocks we saw the white cap Les wore and Bruce's bare head bobbing up and down. The great boat hung hesitant on the brink, then down she came. Les and Bruce seemed to sit for a second in mid-air, then they all came together in a welter of foam with the *Brontosaur* leaping and plunging. But right side up! I let out my breath—I did not know till then that I had been holding it all that time.

"All aboard," Don shouted, then as he passed me he added, "I'm going to let you run the rest of Hell's Half."

And with that I had to be content. The other falls in this half mile were not so bad as the first drop, yet we ran into one rapid aften another and the boatmen had to be constantly on the alert. As for me, I gave myself completely to the exhilaration of the moment so that it was a time of continual high excitement into which there penetrated no thought of the outside world or its difficulties. I was utterly absorbed in the moment, its event, until we tied up the boats for the night.

This camp spot was in a shallow space between river and canyon wall, a sandy, pleasant, wooded strip where a small stream of fresh clear water came down to join the river. Rippling Brook, it was called on the map. I set up my tent alongside a great silver trunk of driftwood and tied my rope to a tamarisk. As usual I chose a spot a little apart from the rest, the open flap of my tent on the river side. Behind me the cliff rose, dark with pines.

After such a day as we had had, everyone turned in early, but for a long time I could not sleep. The roar of the waters was too loud in my ears. In the dark, the river seemed all around me. I flung back the top of my tent and the black wall on the opposite side of the river loomed far higher and yet closer to me than it had by day. The rim seemed to be leaning over, tilted, trying in the night to reach the cliff that rose behind me. There was but a narrow strip of sky between, and it was soft as the inside of a jewel box, studded with stars that bombarded me with spears of light and yet remained undiminished in brightness. One cluster hung on the edge of the cliff. I thought it must be the constellation of the Harp and I remembered that somewhere not far from here Powell had seen it and had given a name to the cliff over which it hung—the Cliff of the Harp, he called it.

As I lay looking up, half awake, half dreaming, that group of stars became a real harp, strung with golden strings. The sound of the rushing water was a melody plucked by the ghostly hand of some harper of the canyon. The small stream pouring down over the rocks gave the higher notes of the tune, played a more delicate air. So surrounded by this harmony from the sky, I looked and listened in wonder and delight and at last fell asleep.

chapter

9

Our next morning's run was short, and magnificent as to scenery. The walls rose to yet greater height and, as we neared the end of Lodore, the reddish strata tilted downward at a spectacular angle and their place was taken by a sandstone formation of lighter color, with buffs that turned to gold where the sunlight struck. So before noon we came to where the left wall gaped wide to show the paler cliffs of Yampa Canyon, and the Yampa River moved in to join the Green. I was riding this morning in the small boat and it brought me into closer contact with what small rapids we passed over— I was well splashed. I felt almost a part of the river itself as we ran those last miles above Echo Park. In the quieter stretches Don had me hold the map and he tried to teach me how to read it. It was not his fault that I learned little—I was too busy looking at the scenery. But I realized what a good teacher he must be in his own classroom. He knew just how much to tell, how far to go with explanation, leaving something to be done by the student, giving one a sense of being challenged by the problem. Another few hours and I would really have mastered those complicated-looking lines that indicated height of cliff and depth of water as well as the meandering tortuous course of the river.

But now, passing the mouth of the Yampa, with its pale, square-cut flat-topped walls, I could see looming ahead on the right, thrust up to incredible height, the prow of Steamboat Rock. And as we came across to land on the left bank of the river, I saw how it rose sheer from the water's edge in a smooth clean-cut surface, as if sliced away by a giant knife. Monstrous in height, overpowering in length, the face of the rock was in the noonday light salmon-colored, pale purple, pink and buff. Powell had called it Echo Rock and the grove in which we came ashore is now known as Echo Park, being accessible by a road that comes in from U.S. Route 40. Here on this side where the canyon wall was set far back from the river, there were tables under the trees, fireplaces, "conveniences," and from lower downstream we heard voices—children shouting to Steamboat Rock to hear the echo thrown back, repeated again and again and dying away as if a single word were a whole conversation. It was at once evident that many people came here—picnickers, sightseers, overnight campers. There were several cars parked nearby with license plates from Connecticut, Wyoming, Oregon and other distant places.

Tony got out his horn and the notes were thrown back at us in a veritable avalanche of repetition. I shouted, "Hello! Hello there!" and my voice was tossed about, fainter and fainter with a dying-away sound that quite enchanted me. Self speaking to self, I thought, and remembered one time when I had been moving about too much to have news from home and I telephoned back to Duxbury trying to find out if my house had been rented. I had left it in the hands of a real-estate agent but had heard nothing. So, being economically-minded, I put in a person-to-person call—to myself at my own home, thinking if strangers answered they would say, "No, she is not here, we are just tenants," or if no one answered, I would have my information. When I heard the telephone ringing far away in my own house and knew the operator was prepared to ask for me if anyone answered, I thought, in quite unreasoning panic, "But if they get me, what shall I say?" The idea of being confronted by myself over the phone was a staggering one. I was quite relieved when it rang on and on with no answer at all.

So I felt the same way about the echo from Steamboat Rock. What was there, what great truth, what words of sufficient import in my vocabulary with which I might thus accost myself? I found none beyond a simple "Hello, hello there, you! Who are you? Who?" And the echo answered, "Hello-oo, hello-oo you-oo —who-oo-oo—you!"

While Bruce and Don were setting out lunch on one of the Park tables, I pitched my tent. I chose a spot close by the river's edge on the high mud bank just opposite Steamboat Rock, and anchored it securely to a box elder. Here I would be able to watch the rock change in color as the afternoon faded and at night I could hear the sound I had come to love, the sound of the river. As I untied my duffel and arranged my luggage I heard birds singing in the leafy rooms of the box elders above me, and the locusts that I now knew were not rattlesnakes went clack, clack with a dry persistent sound. Above Steamboat Rock the sky was a deep dark blue with a few clouds blowing. The air was deliciously cool.

By some miracle of prearrangement, Charles's jeep arrived just as we were sitting down at the table for lunch and the driver joined us, though at the far end of the table so I had no chance to talk with him. He had come to bring a two-way radio which the Park Service had asked Charles to try out at various places en route, and he was leaving the jeep so that we could all have a drive that afternoon to a place where there was said to be a magnificent view. I must see it, Charles said.

So immediately after lunch he and Tony with their photographic equipment, Bob, Fred and I got in the jeep and set out by a dirt road that ran behind the picnic grounds. We had gone but a short distance when clouds began to gather, the sky turned gray and the air colder, whipped by a high wind. The road, after a level stretch, wound upward, made its way on the ledge of a craggy, rock-strewn gorge, bringing us now and then out into a more open place where we could see barren bleak slopes.

I thought it was a brutal land, this country back from the river, harsh and without a redeeming feature unless one graded it on the quality of desolation. It would have a high mark for that.

The road wound as crazily as a bat flies and looking back we could see its zigzag line. Then all at once we were in the midst of a gentler scene, splashed with green-gray sage that turned to velvet in the distance. On the slopes where, in some wetter season, small streams must have run, there were green grassy rivulets that streaked the gray crumbling shale. Close by the roadside there were flowers—pink star grass, blue lupine, and when we stopped to examine one bright red clump, we found it was a low-growing cactus, as silky and soft and utterly amazing as the golden one I had come upon above Ashley Falls.

For the sake of Charles's pictures we kept hoping the sun would shine, but the sky was solidly gray when we came to our destination, the highest place for many miles around, Harper's Corner. From this point where Charles parked the jeep, they all walked down a precipitous winding path to reach an overlook where they would be able to take pictures showing the canyons of both the Yampa and the Green, and their junction. I stayed in the car, for they told me it would be nearly a mile straight down. I did not mind that—it was the mile straight up, coming back, that I did not care for.

Time passed slowly as I sat there on what seemed to be the very top of the world. A cold wind shook the jeep. Before me were wind-blown, wind-twisted cedars too old to care how they looked. To my right the earth dropped away to nothing, and beyond lay the bleak stretches of rocky land on the far side of the Green. Seen from this height, its canyon and the Yampa's were but tiny fissures in the surface of the world; they reminded me of the cracks in the old plastered ceiling I had looked up at so often from my bed in the "Yaller House." Only now I looked down upon them, like the blessed damosel leaning out from the golden bar of heaven. Behind me was the bleak country through which we had driven and away in the distance lay masses of soft blue mountains topped with snow which, against the gray of the sky, looked whiter than even snow should be.

Harper's Corner—it seemed to me it must be one of the four corners of the earth. And who was the Harper for whom it was named? I wondered. And it pleased me to fancy that he was my ghostly harper of the canyon who had played the harp of the heavens for me last night.

The others came back half frozen from their tramp, for it had been too warm for jackets when we left the park. Charles turned on the heater and we were soon driving along quite comfortably on our homeward journey. We saw several deer close by the roadside, and when one of them bounded off across the sage it seemed not so much that he was afraid of us as that he had suddenly remembered more important business elsewhere. We saw others, grazing contentedly amid the underbrush or springing lightly along a green slope. When we reached the bleak bare rocky stretch and followed the course of a dry wash down into its canyon, I noticed, as I had not on the journey going, how strangely the wind and rain had carved the rocky walls. I remember one stretch of cliff where wind-carved figures stood in frozen bas-relief, long-limbed, fantastically distorted, yet human—a woman with but a single breast, a man with hands, indeed with all his members pointing skyward. Other figures were turned away to face the stone. A little below this point we stopped to investigate what seemed to be a shallow cave in the canyon wall. Bending to make my way through the low opening, I did not see what a fearful place I was entering. But when I straightened up I saw the narrow black crevasse to right and left. And when I looked overhead and found a great rectangular rock of staggering dimensions hanging above me with no visible means of support, I turned and fled from the cave to wait by the jeep while the others took pictures.

When we came into camp we found that there had been a

veritable sandstorm—everything was covered. I had to shake out my sleeping bag, turn it wrong side out to get rid of the sand, and my tent had nearly been blown into the river; it hung by one rope to the box elder tree.

It seemed strange that evening to see the light of other campfires beyond us in the park, to hear voices. One solitary camper came and pitched his tent not far from us under the trees. He paid no attention to us but ate his supper at a table a little distance away and then by the light of an electric torch sat there reading.

The wind had died down to a pleasant, cool breeze and, as I lay on my cot bed with the tent flap open on the river side, I could hear the water again, above the faint rustle of leaves. The great bulk of Steamboat Rock loomed up, black and menacing. It seemed to lift the sky itself, to set the stars away at yet greater distance, pale and unconcerned. Just before I fell asleep, I felt a faint twinge of toothache. That tooth Dr. Ortolani, my dentist in Plymouth, had warned me about! "It is likely to give you trouble at some time when it will be very inconvenient for you," he had said. And I had argued, "But it is perfectly sound, isn't that true?" "Yes, but just the same—" And I had said, "I'll keep it and take a chance." The whole conversation came back to me vividly—my own obstinacy against his better judgment—and how much better, I was becoming more and more aware. It is bad enough to lose a tooth at any time. It makes one feel reduced, diminished, bereft. But if I had planned an inconvenient spot for having trouble, I could not have achieved a more difficult one than my present situation. I would just have to suffer in silence, I thought, as I fell asleep.

In the morning luckily the tooth was quiescent. I refused bacon, and took my pancakes with caution. We were to spend this day too and a second night here in Echo Park—but civilized as it seemed to be, compared to some of the remote places where we had been, there was no way of getting to a dentist unless I was willing to risk being left behind. Maybe after all it was just the cold wind at Harper's Corner that had given me a kind of neuralgia in that tooth. I would lie low and wait and see.

Charles was going to drive up the Yampa Canyon to take pictures this morning and he asked me to come with him and Bob, Don and Tony. But I said I had washing to do, as indeed I had, and made that an excuse not to go along.

So Fred—who wanted to rearrange his luggage and write up his notes—Bruce, Les and I remained in camp. We had visitors—a professor from some midwestern university who was sightseeing with his wife; two women in slacks with two children about ten years old who had been on a boat trip on the Yampa and were feeling very adventurous about it. They stared at me in amazement when they heard where I had been and where I was proposing to go. "All the way down the Green and Colorado?" they exclaimed. I enjoyed my little moment of superiority. "Pinky" Robinson came by to talk with us; I never discovered his real name, but he was the son of the Park Service couple who had been so kind and cordial the day Charles had taken me to Dinosaur National Monument on that first afternoon's drive from Vernal. He was serving as oarsman in one of the boats that had made the Yampa excursion. Another visitor was a tall, well-built young man named Rasmussen. It was a name I had encountered only once before—when I was a medical student, and I had, on first meeting, been quite terrified of its owner. I had entered school late that year, too late for a partner to be assigned to me in Anatomy. The dissecting room was divided into small cubicles, so that first day I was in one of them with my "stiff," partnerless. But a graduate student was dissecting over by the window. His name was Rasmussen and—someone had whispered to me as I went to do my first bit of dissecting—he was a Mormon! I had never before seen a Mormon—or a stiff. I was equally frightened by both. Now I tried to get news of him from this young man. He shook his head. They might be kin, he said, for there were many of that name in Utah, but he could tell me nothing of my old friend. So I left him and took my washing down to the river's edge.

While I was sousing things up and down in the water wondering if it really did them much good to wash them in such liquid mud, Bruce came down in his bathing trunks. He sat on the bank for a bit before diving in for a swim and watched me at my task. He was in favor of a bucket of hot water with soap flakes. That was the way he was going to do his washing, he said.

But I was already too involved with a cake of soap and the Green River. "At least I am exchanging dirts," I said. "No matter if I have to spend next winter trying to get these garments white again."

"Next winter?" He looked at me if it had not occurred to him that this summer would ever end. Then he said, "I'll be a freshman at Utah State—and on ski patrol weekends. I like the outdoor life. That's why I'm going in for engineering."

"You'll do all right, whatever you go in for," I said.

He stood up, gave me his quick shy grin and then dived in, his bronzed body cutting the water cleanly without a ripple.

I brought my washing back to where my tent was set up and strung it along a rope and hoped no sudden gust of wind would send it flying into the water.

At lunchtime the others had not yet returned from their excursion up the Yampa Canyon, so we sat round the table, the four of us, and had our sandwiches. On another picnic table Fred had spread out the contents of his duffel bags. He was arranging things, he said, and trying to decide what he did not really need, so he could mail it back home when we stopped within range of a post office. He had several books stacked up to send away. I looked them over when I had finished lunch. "You sending off this one?" I asked, holding up Stegner's *Beyond the Hundredth Meridian.*

"No, I want that—set it aside, will you?"

I opened it and was at once completely absorbed. Anywhere, it is interesting reading, but in this particular situation, I found it fascinating.

When Les had finished stowing away his lunch, he came over to my table with pencil and tablet.

"You writing up your notes?" I asked.

He shook his head. "Writing to my girl."

I held up the Stegner book and asked if he had ever read it.

"Oh yes, I know it well. It's a good one. Too bad he couldn't come with us." Then seeing my look of surprise, he added that Charles had asked him but he couldn't get away, had to stay on the West Coast—or was it New York?

There was something about the tone of Les's voice when he said New York that made me ask if he knew much about that place.

"Spent three, nearly four years there. The streets of New York! It's a dog's life you lead, there in the soot and the dust. But at that, it was the best years of my life. I was on a mission —that'll make a man of you if anything will." He laid aside his pencil, snapped the knife shut, leaned back with his long legs stretched out under the table and told me about it. He had worked in an office, bridge design, layouts, because the Mormon church expected him to support himself if he could. Evenings, Saturdays and Sundays his mission job was to visit people in their homes, talking to them, giving them pamphlets. He had had the district from Seventy-ninth Street to Ninety-sixth between Riverside and Central Park and had held meetings, too, down around Maiden Lane and Nassau. Sometimes there were only a few people in attendance; again there would be nearer a hundred, especially if there was singing.

I listened in wonder. In the city what a strange, incongruous figure he must have been, this great six-footer out of the West. But indomitable and powerful, I was sure, as he was in this more suitable setting. "But," I asked at last, "how did you know —how were you able to do such things? How did you learn to conduct a meeting and all that?"

"We're all taught that. From the time we are ten years old we are liable to be called on to take charge of a service. We all go on missions, you know. Most of us, anyway."

"Yes, yes, I had heard that." But how little I had known, really. I wanted to ask more. But he had gone back now to his letter writing, so I returned to my book and after a little went to my tent. It was not often that I had a chance to have an afternoon's rest and I thought I had better take advantage of this opportunity. I read and dozed and watched the changing colors on the great flat face of Steamboat Rock. It was different at every hour of the day. Almost colorless in full sunlight, now as the afternoon shadows came it took on richer shades. The purples deepened, the perpendicular stripes where water had left its mark darkened to black; there were salmon-colored areas that were reflected in the river, turning its muddy water to living gold. Yet still the Yampa's milky flow retained its identity, the two running side by side within their common banks as far as I could see downstream to the turn at the farther tip of Steamboat Rock. It was not really much like a steamboat, I thought. No ship, no Leviathan of the ocean displaced so mighty a weight of weightless air as this monstrous formation that now, with the declining sun, caught on its rim the slanting rays and seemed afire at the top.

When it was time to see about our supper, I went out and helped Fred search for the menu. Bruce built a fire and we got out the cans and Fred opened them. I wanted to make hot biscuits—the others, who had taken no lunch, would be starved and we would need something extra, I thought. But I could not find the Bisquick. There was a box of meal so I decided to make hoecake, Mississippi style. I mixed up the meal with salt and water and dropped it in small patties on the griddle. It did not taste the way it should, there was not that rich, nutty flavor I remembered so well. What was the trouble? The meal perhaps. This fine-ground meal was not at all like the coarse, home-ground corn that should be used for hoecake. But the cakes browned nicely, and looked all right. They just tasted awful. I felt quite ashamed.

When the others came, tired and hungry, it was almost dark. And having had no lunch, they made no complaint, but munched the hoecake with no more than an inquiring look in my direction They had had a wonderful day and had taken some magnificent views. "You should have come," Charles said to me.

I wished I had gone. And yet, if I had, I would never have gotten my washing done.

Next morning, June 18, we were off around nine o'clock after a good breakfast of the perpetual pancakes—I had worked up to three by now—fig jam, Spam, coffee and chocolate. A group of campers and sightseers came down to the bank to watch us push off; they evidently considered us a part of the sights they had come to see. So for once we had someone to wave to us as we headed downstream, crossing slantwise through the pale chalky water of the Yampa and into the muddy stream that came down from the Green, the great bulk of Steamboat Rock rising above us. We rounded its lower point in a hairpin curve and so came into Whirlpool Canyon.

Powell recorded one dangerous rapid here in this gorge, but time had altered it to a gentler state. Once, we were caught in a counter-current and sent spinning all the way around, full circle. But that was just fun and no trouble. The other small rapids were only big enough to splash us pleasantly—for the morning sun was warm. It was fast water but not perilous. Les read us Powell's account of his passage through here, of how his boats spun about, at first to their great alarm. But they soon found there was little danger in this whirling progress— "It is the merry mood of the river to dance through this deep, dark gorge, and right gaily do we join in the sport." Later, reading the Kolb account of passing here, I found that he too was exhilarated by these spinning waters, saying, "They put us in a joyful frame of mind." So little wonder that we were affected in much the same way. Small eddies dimpled the water's surface, the sun shone down upon these whirls and counter-currents so they glinted like spun silver. We had had two good night's rest at Echo Park—as had other voyagers before us—and today's run was to be a short one. We stopped before noon on the right bank just beyond the point where Jones Creek spreads itself and comes down to join the Green and give it for a little while, here close to the bank, a clear clean look.

We set up camp under a heavy canopy of box elders that shut out the sky. It was cool and shadowy there. There was a cabin, but no one even suggested that we use it. I think it was mostly for storage of supplies for short river excursions or for the horseback parties who could come by rough trail from Island Park, downstream. We had no sooner had our lunch than Bob, Don and Fred got out their poles and went fishing. Jones Creek was famous for its trout. I set up my tent below the campsite a little, close to the river where I could look out across a narrow stretch of wheat-white, tasseled reeds to the running water. There were thousands—or so it seemed to me, trying to avoid them—of tiny hard-shelled bugs or beetles here among the leaves. They were a beautiful, brilliant coral with black head and legs. They climbed over my duffel when I dumped everything out in an effort to get it arranged in a little more orderly fashion, they somehow got up on my army cot. I simply could not escape them. I do not think they made any sound. It was another, larger insect whose clack-clacking rose shrilly above the sound of the noisy water. "Lots of rattlesnakes here, too," Tony said as he got out *Moby Dick* and prepared to spend a safe morning stretched out on top of one of the picnic tables.

Charles did his washing, carrying pail after pail of clear water from Jones Creek and heating it over the campfire. I think he washed everything he owned, being finally reduced to bathing trunks for something to wear. "There's a wonderful spot back there for a swim in clear water," he told me. "Go through the woods past the little house and you will come to it."

I was warm from setting up my tent and rearranging all my luggage, so I took towel and soap and set out across an open reedy stretch. It was a pleasant shady little walk back through the grove to where I could see a right-angle bend in the creek. Here, running parallel to the river, it came down between pale yellow cliffs to sparkle in the sunlight. It poured over rocks and pebbles with a rushing sound. I remembered what Tony had said about snakes and looked around carefully before I stripped off my clothes to deposit them on the rocks at the edge of the water. I knelt first and bathed my face and arms—for the water was icy cold—then little by little I waded in. Here the stream was shallow and swift. I found a hollowed-out spot between two rocks and, stretching full length, let the water pour over me. It was a delightful sensation. How long had it been since I had lain thus in cold running water? It must have been in '39 when I was in the Vermont mountains and had come upon a small mountain stream far off the road. I shut my eyes now, and though I do not often think back, pretended I was there again. What had I been thinking that day as I lay on my back like this and let the water pour down? Oh yes—that man. I had really been fond of him. But how he would complicate my life! Too much, it wasn't worth it, I had decided, lying in the Vermont mountain brook. Well, I thought now—other days, other problems. I opened my eyes and saw how the sun, slanting downward was turning the cliff beyond me to salmon and rose, I looked up at the deepening blue sky, I let my arms rest on the water, hands turned palm upward, relaxed and easy, and I thought, well, the present isn't so bad. And tomorrow we should get to Jensen and I could go to a dentist. For once more I was beginning to feel that dull low ache.

That evening while Don and Bruce were getting our dinner ready, I sat on one of the low benches and watched the activity, glad for once that I had not been assigned to get the meal. Perhaps that tooth was sapping my energies. Bob came and sat beside me. I thought for a moment of asking him how he was at dentistry. There might be a pair of pliers somewhere in the luggage. No, I decided, I could wait till the next day. So I just told him how much we were going to miss him when he left us and couldn't he possibly take another week off from his work.

He shook his head regretfully. "I'd like nothing better but I'm already going to be two days later than I should."

Suddenly I remembered a doctor friend who had set out to be a dentist and switched over to medicine. Maybe Bob—"Where did you take your training?" I asked.

"Syracuse. I grew up near there." That set us off—with no mention of dental college—on the beauties of New York State. I had lived in Ithaca for fifteen years; we knew people in common. He had been a research fellow at Harvard, I discovered, had worked at the Rockefeller Institute, so we had yet more people to talk about, people whom we both knew.

He told me something of his work in the laboratory and I listened with a queer nostalgic feeling. So many years of my life—all my married life—I had spent listening to just such talk. How strange it was, to be sitting here on a rough bench, after so many years, by a campfire in the state of Utah, hearing the old familiar terms, letting my mind skim over the more technical details, which I less than ever comprehended, to grasp the essential idea back of them. This I had always been able to do, and I was pleased that I still could do so, in spite of the many advances in biological chemistry and my consequently greater-than-ever ignorance.

After a little Bob left me to finish his packing—for the next night we were due in Jensen and he had to be ready to take the plane for California. I moved over closer to the campfire, for I had gotten my hair wet when I lay down in Jones Creek and it now began to make me feel chilly. As always when the sun went down, the air was growing colder.

Don was disappointed not to have trout to cook for our dinner. "They're simply aren't any in Jones Creek," he said.

"There used to be—Powell tells how good they were. And

one of his men shot a deer somewhere around here," I reminded him.

"No deer now. And no trout. My Dad got fourteen last time he was here. There must have been a freshet lately that washed them all out—no other way to account for it."

"Are you as good a fisherman as he?"

"Well, I ought to be. He taught me." Don grinned at me as he turned another can of sweet potatoes out on the griddle. "Used to carry me fishing pickaback when I was too small to stand up against the current. That's when he showed me how to cast—and he was always more pleased when I landed one than if he had done it himself."

It was a pleasant little picture he called up with this memory and I was glad to add it to my impressions of him. In some ways I felt he was the most difficult member of our rather oddly assorted group to get to know more than superficially. I felt that his was really a complicated character in spite of his easy-going friendliness and that delightful comic gift of his that made it possible for him to set us all laughing with a gesture or a twist of a red bandanna round his head, making himself into a pirate. I still wondered what he was like underneath all that. I moved closer to the fire and turned my head to dry the back of my hair. As I watched, he flipped the sweet potatoes over with such skill that I asked, "What did you major in at the University of Utah? Cooking?"

He laughed. "This is just a side line. I majored in Sociology and Elementary Education."

"Then you always meant to teach."

"Right."

He had had the same quick decisiveness about this, I was sure, that he showed when he stood poised high on a boulder studying the lay of the rocks in the falls ahead, deciding where the safest passage was, then following it.

"Where is everybody?" He stood up straight and gave a shout: "Hey, dinner! Come and get it."

They came running out of the early dusk that had gathered under the trees, and lined up with tin plates to be served the sizzling ham and sweet potatoes—a good substitute for trout, we all agreed.

I slept soundly that night under the box elder—tree of doom, I have heard it called. But it laid no dark fate upon me. The coral and black beetles did not disturb me; my tooth was quiescent.

Next morning I noticed that our duffel was being tied down again—more rapids. There was no sign of them as we came out of Whirlpool. The river spread out wide and tranquil and here in Island Park there were green meadows beyond the fringe of trees along the river's edge. It was hot here under the sun and again I took to plunging my white veil in the water and draping it, dripping, over my cap, thus creating a little private air-conditioning system. The small boat was pulling us this morning and once I did my dipping at an unfortunate moment when the engine was spouting oil—and my veil was no longer white. But the cooling system still worked so I did not really mind.

One small coral bug had clung to my veil through all this dowsing and, spying it now, I thumped it off into the water, grieving a little that I thus made more brief his brief existence. Yet who could tell—there were perhaps compensations in that brevity—he knew no winter, knew neither age nor care. Nor toothache, I thought.

We were not moving fast enough to suit Les this morning. He got out his oars and began to row. "Got to help that little engine out," he said.

I watched for a while as he bent and hauled on the oars, the sweat running down his face. Then I protested, "It's too hot for you to be working like that, Les."

But he only grinned and shot the big boat ahead so that the tow rope sagged.

"You'll get a sunstroke or something." I really did not like to see him working so hard, when it was not necessary. Then I realized that the more I protested the more he was going to work. Well, I thought, now I know how to manage Les, if I ever have need for it. Order him not to do a thing and it is as good as done! "You're an obstinate man," I told him.

That made him laugh. But he did not stop rowing till he got good and ready—after I had turned away and ceased watching. Then he drew a small Testament from his pocket and stretching out in the sun read quietly for the next hour or so. That reminded me that this was Sunday and I would have suggested that he read aloud to us, only he seemed so absorbed that I did not like to interrupt. There was something simple and fine about the concentration, the complete attention with which he read.

Now in the distance we began to see the dramatic entrance to Split Mountain that rose high above the level plain through which we were moving. A long curve of the river took us first away and then back around toward it. The cliffs seemed to rise higher and higher as we approached; the great distorted uplift was gigantic, overpowering. The river entered quietly almost as if it shared our awe. This great curving swoop of rock is called Rainbow, and the other end of it is on the far side of the mountain. As we floated soundlessly by, save for the click of cameras, I remembered a water rainbow I saw once in the Hebrides, a complete arc from earth to sky to earth again. Delicate, diaphanous, transient, it was a brilliant unforgettable sight. But here was a rainbow of rock, the colors muted by the solidity of the stone. Only one segment of the arc was visible, yet it was no less imposing.

"White water!" Don shouted, and hastily cameras were stowed away, I tucked my notebook back into its Cellophane bag and reached for the ropes Bruce had left handy for me. For now we entered a series of violent rapids, one after the other without respite—Moonshine, S O B, Eagle's Beak, Schoolboy. Often there were few rocks visible, or they had all been pushed, as if by a giant hand, across to one side of the river. Again we swept close to a sheer dark overhanging wall, with waves rising five or six feet in height, splashing over us while the big boat plunged and bucked, danced and sidled, slipping in and out of a pothole and on, borne forward by the irresistible force of the river.

I had scarcely a chance to more than glance briefly at the walls—some three thousand feet at the higher points—of rosy sandstone, splashed with green, and, as we moved deeper into the canyon, hung with buttressed towers, and shapes like classic buildings. Tony pointed to one of these—"The Parthenon!" he shouted above the roar of wind and water.

Bruce glanced up. "H-mmm—not quite."

There was something about the way he said it that made me ask, when we came to a quieter stretch of water, "Do you know the Parthenon?" For he had spoken as one who knew more about it than a schoolboy who has happened to have a picture of it on his classroom wall.

He nodded. "I was over there for a year when I was fifteen."

"In Greece?" I asked, quite stupidly. Where else would he find the Parthenon? "How did you happen to go there?"

"My father took me—he was over in government service."

"You went to school there?"

"Yes, got so I could understand pretty well."

Then he told me he had sailed among the Greek islands, gone swimming in the Ionian Sea. All the classic names fell from his lips as easily as if no more alien to him than Billings, Montana, or Cody, Wyoming, or Salt Lake City. He had stopped in the Azores, he knew Portugal and Pompeii.

I was amazed. Maybe this would teach me not to jump to conclusions about people, I thought.

Around noon we came within sight of our stopping place—a stretch of sand, a concave cliff and the foot of the road that led down from the Dinosaur National Monument. There were tourists and sightseers roaming about there and they were all watching as Don brought the small boat to shore. We had drawn up on the far side because Charles said there was a cave over here on this cliff that he wanted to investigate.

"I don't see any cave," I said.

"It's hidden from the river. Come on and I'll show you," Charles said. He led the way across a level space, thick with tall grasses. Tony and I exchanged glances. Rattlesnakes? But we followed in Charles's footsteps. Almost immediately we came to a shallow stream. There was no way to get to the cliff without crossing it. Charles knelt down. "Climb aboard."

"I'm too heavy."

"Nonsense. No need of your getting your feet wet too."

So he took me pickaback. I would have felt safer afoot, for the stream was pebbly and deep in unexpected spots. But who was I to refuse a gallant gesture! Suppose the Queen had told Sir Walter no—it would have been a loss to history.

It was hot after we left the stream and approached the cliff. The sun beat down relentlessly as we passed through glaring sage-strewn sand, and there was no shade till we had mounted a slope, climbing over red rocks, scrambling around prickly bushes to come close to the overhanging cliff. Here all was yellow and gold except the narrow black line of shadow at the foot of the cliff. We climbed over a great rock and came abruptly upon the mouth of an enormous cave. At that moment there was a thunder, a rushing sound as if the whole thing were falling in—and three wild sheep dashed out, leaping over rocks to escape up the far side of the cliff. "Maybe they are not really wild—but they act like it," I said.

"We'll call them wild," Tony said.

A blast of cold air struck us as we came under the great arch of stone that covered nearly half the sky and deepened what was left of it to a dark sapphire. The high, vaulted ceiling was richly colored in yellow and gold with orange-washed stretches that darkened as it curved downward perhaps a hundred fifty feet from the entrance to end in a small black hole running in farther under the cliff. In the center was a heap of fine powder where the ceiling had sloughed off. I took some up in my hand and let it sift through my fingers. It was like talcum powder, light and soft, and it made me sneeze. "Better not breathe too much of that," Charles said.

Tony had been exploring in a far corner and he came out now with a hollowed-out small rectangle of stone."Indians have lived here," he said. "This was for grinding corn, wasn't it?"

We examined it and agreed. It was a good safe place for an Indian camp, so hidden that from the river one would never suspect that a cave existed, and big enough for a whole tribe. I tried to imagine them gathered round a campfire, warm in winter, cool in summer.

The sun was all the hotter as we came back across the open boulder-strewn field. We turned a little out of our way to pass by a small tumble-down cabin. The door was hanging on one hinge and we looked in but did not venture all the way inside, for Tony said, "Looks snakey to me." Indeed it did. There were two sagging bunks, the chimney had fallen in—a picture of desolation, dirt—and someone's despair. How different it was from the clean cool depths of the Indian cave! How transient this man-made abode compared to one of nature's building!

I waded the stream, coming back, and my shoes and pants and socks were almost dry again by the time we had crossed over the river to join the others in the shade of the opposite cliff. There we had lunch, and soon—again by some miracle of management by Charles—the Robinsons drove down to get us. Bob was anxious to see the exhibition of dinosaur bones at the diggings, so it was decided to let Bruce and Les take the boats on down river some ten miles to Jensen where we could join them later, while we went up to the headquarters.

It seemed strange to be returning to the place where Charles and I had driven that first afternoon, and again I had the odd feeling that we had been traveling in a circle—and in a way, we had. But by what a route! It was cool under the trees beside the Robinsons' house, but when we went up to the diggings, I thought I had never felt such heat. How those men could work on the rocky, chalky, white stone wall digging out bones, I could not understand. I took one look and came inside the corrugated tin building which is a temporary shelter for the exhibition of skeletons. There it was at least shady, and after moving about trying different spots, I finally seated myself, wilting, in the doorway where a breath of fresh air came in to restore me. There were a number of visitors that day; I just moved my feet rather ungraciously, and let them by the narrow door. I was too hot to get up and be polite for them. I felt almost overcome, as if I might get a sunstroke or something, I felt sticky and disheveled and altogether a disgrace to the human race. For that morning, thinking to be cooler, I had put on instead of jodhpurs a new pair of blue jeans—surely the most graceless garment ever invented by man. It must have been man—no woman would have dreamed up such a thing. Mine were stiff in all the wrong places, and since I had gotten wet as I came back across that stream, they had a rough-dried bulging look around the knees. I had abandoned my nylon shirt that morning in favor of one of those Ed gave me, of cotton, all nicely starched and ironed when I put it on. Now, looking down, I found that it had begun to disintegrate at the armhole and here I was with one shoulder bare. I was a most disreputable sight. Well, no matter, I thought. I was too hot to care.

One of the visitors, coming back from a trip up the path to see the men at work, digging away at those great bones, stopped and spoke to me. "Are you the lady who is traveling down the river with this Expedition?"

I said, "Yes, I am," thinking I looked it, too. But I stood up. She had such a lovely gentle face I could not but respond.

She held out her hand. "Good luck to you," she said, and added, "I didn't know you would be so beautiful."

Beautiful! I was simply overwhelmed. Maybe her eyesight was bad. In any case I was grateful to her for that kind of word; it bucked me up at a low moment. I don't know who she was—she came from California, she said. But I shall always remember her. I might even recognize her if I met her "in the middle of the big road," as we say in Mississippi, or strolling down the golden streets.

When we got back to headquarters, Bus Hatch, Don's father, had come for us in a big bus driven by the same young Rasmussen whom we had left two days before in Echo Park. How he got there will forever remain a mystery to me. Someone had sent Charles a copy of *The New Yorker* with a write-up of the Expedition and he read it aloud to us as we sat there in that hot bus waiting for Bob to get through taking what he called a quick look at the museum. I imagined my children at home reading it, and wished I had some way of letting them know that I was surviving what in cold print seemed to be an exceedingly hazardous enterprise. I think few things are as bad in their performance as they sound when written about. The imagination of the reader—or the writer—can sometimes leap to greater and more horrifying detail than reality is capable of achieving.

"But they don't mention you," Tony said.

"N-no," I said. "But don't you see, if they had said that a fragile, elderly, gray-haired woman who couldn't lift a duffel bag was going along, it would have quite invalidated all this idea of the dangers of the Expedition."

Everybody laughed. "They don't know you," Fred said.

So by bus we came back into the town of Vernal where I had first arrived to meet Charles. I felt a little surprised that it was still there, all unchanged, just as I had left it. We stopped at the Hatches' home. I did not go inside but sat down in the shade on the green close-clipped lawn. It was the most comfortable

spot I had come upon in some time. The grass felt cool and
dampish, delightful; I had not realized that I had grown so
accustomed to walking on crisp, dry ground, or heavy, hot sand.
People came and went—a Sierra Club group was arriving for
a trip in one of the canyons the next day. Charles seemed to
know everyone; people joined us till the circle in which we sat,
there on the lawn, was enlarged almost to the street. Among
those who arrived was a young English doctor who had gotten
in touch with Charles by the two-way radio. He wanted to come
along as cook, and it seemed like a good idea. I studied him
with interest. He looked husky, tall and heavy-built. With Bob
leaving, we would need some more good muscle—as well as
scientific procedure in the way of dishwashing. Also, it would be
reassuring to have a doctor along for the rest of the way. This
young man's name was Leslie, but to avoid confusion, we
quickly decided to call him Doc. He said his name was not pronounced quite like Les's—the s was like a z. But that seemed
too fine a distinction to make clear in an emergency.

Bob and Fred had disappeared to telephone home. Now Bob
came back smiling. He had talked with his wife, everything was
fine, he had his reservation and he would be home before morning. Already in his mind he seemed to have left us, he was
back in his life, and glad enough to be there. He had had his
vacation, a good time, now he was ready to return to the real
business of living and working. Fred came out of the house in
a few minutes looking troubled. He sat down on the grass beside me.

"Couldn't you get your call through?" I asked.

"I got it through."

"Is anything wrong?"

"No, no—only I don't know that they would have told me if
it was. Esther and the children want me to go on for the rest
of the trip, but I don't know that I really should. The bookshops—"

"Forget them," I said. "Besides, how could I ever get along without you?"

He gave me a rather weak smile. He too was surrounded by his life now, drawn back into it, concerned about how things were going in his absence. I said it would be a pity to give up now, when he had for so many years dreamed of just such an expedition as this, but I might as well have been talking to the wind. He was not listening, and he remained thoughtful the rest of the afternoon.

Don's father moved about among us as if we were all his invited and very special guests. Genial, hospitable, ruddy-faced, heavy-set yet stepping as lightly and quickly as Don, he was in and out of the house, meeting people, telling stories, greeting everyone like an old friend, arranging details of the boat trips he was organizing for the next week as well as the morrow. Someone had told me that he had run Cataract Canyon—the worst of those that were ahead of us. I knew that Don and Charles were looking forward to it with some uneasiness—there had been so many disasters there; twenty-nine of the fifty people who had tried it over the years had perished. So I was concerned lest I be told that I could not take that part of the trip. I watched my chance, and caught Bus Hatch as he was crossing the lawn, for once not surrounded by people.

"Just a minute, Bus," I said. "I want to ask you something."

"Yes, ma'm."

"Is it true that you have been down Cataract?"

"Yes, ma'm."

"Then tell me, honestly. Do you think I could make it?"

"Of course you can."

"Thank you, thank you—just what I wanted to hear," I said and let him go. But I should have gotten him to repeat this in Don's presence.

Charles suggested that we all go to the Vernal Hotel for a good dinner before going to find the boats and camp. It would be a sort of farewell party for Bob, who would get his plane soon after. A real dinner with chairs to sit on! With waiters to wait on us! It sounded delightful. Only—I looked down at my disreputable state. Well, there was nothing I could do about that, I thought. Maybe no one would notice me. They would have Don's wife to look at. For Charles had invited her to come with us—and she did look lovely, so fair and young and blonde in her fresh summer dress with bare arms and shoulders.

Just as I had come to this conclusion, a woman whom I had noticed because everyone seemed to know her, to be glad to see her, came across the lawn to me. "If you are going to the hotel to dinner, why not come over with me now? I have a nice room and bath—you can have a good hot shower before the rest of this gang gets there."

"It sounds like heaven to me," I said and went with her most gratefully.

As we walked the three blocks down the street to the hotel, I discovered that she was Charlotte Mauk, secretary of the Sierra Club, that she was going on their trip and that she was the one responsible for making out the menus for the expedition, doing the marketing, as well as attending to all the preliminary correspondence.

In her room, I lost no time in stripping off my outer garments and diving right into the bathroom. I closed the door and looked around. How beautiful it was! Every fixture seemed a work of art. Never again, I thought, would I take for granted such luxuries as these.

When I emerged, clean and refreshed, I found her sitting cross-legged on the bed putting the last stitches in my torn shirt. I almost burst into tears! How very kind and thoughtful! No wonder all those people back on Bus Hatch's lawn had seemed to be so glad to see her! So it was that I was at least decently cleaned and mended when I went down with her to meet the rest of the party for dinner. It was a gay meal, and a delicious one. I had an enormous steak and everything else in proportion.

Fred was late getting there, but he came in beaming and took his place beside me. "I just talked with them all at home," he said.

"But—you called from Bus's house—" I began.

"I know." He gave me a little embarrassed smile. "But I couldn't say anything I wanted to say with all those people milling around and listening to every word."

How very New England, I thought, and how utterly delightful, too. "Then everything is all right?"

He nodded. "They're making out fine—I talked to the children, too. They said they would never forgive me if I didn't go on. And Esther is taking care of everything at the bookshops." He was as lighthearted as a boy. Everyone was happy that he would be with us; he had somehow managed to make a very special place for himself in the group.

Dinner over, I found a moment to speak to Don's wife as we went through the lobby. There was something I had to do the next day—which, it had been decided, we would spend here getting in fresh supplies. "Could you tell me the name of a good dentist?"

"I know one, Dr. Shimmin—" She looked across toward Don, hesitantly.

"He'll be all right," I said quickly, making mental note of the name. For I didn't want anyone to know about my difficulties. "It is just—well, I think I may have lost a filling and I thought tomorrow I could have somebody take a look—it's not really important." A filling? Well, maybe I had lost one, but the way that tooth was feeling at the moment, it would be a miracle if I did not lose it too.

We said good-by to Bob, gathered up our new cook's luggage and the doctor himself and set out in the jeep to find the boats at Jensen. Don was spending the night in town and would see us the next day. "You'll find them below the bridge," he called after us. Below the bridge was rather indefinite, we thought, when we had come to what Charles said must be Jensen. It seemed at this hour of the night to be a wholly imaginary town —there were only a few buildings, dark and low-lying on the far side of the bridge, a silver span in our headlights over a black void that must be the river. We drove up and down the road, looking for a campfire, for some light to guide us. At last Charles turned off by a bumpy trail and drove as close as he could to the river. Then he got out of the jeep and shouted, again and again. Tony shouted, too.

At last a faint answer echoed back out of the darkness and after a moment we saw a light beckoning us on. There was a field across which we could drive and we were soon down by the boats where Les and Bruce had camped and had gone early to bed. I had to set up my tent in the dark with only a scraggly bush to tie my ropes to. Mosquitoes buzzed round me as I worked. But luckily the air was cooler now and when I crawled into my tent I was able to be comfortable inside my sleeping bag with the indispensable Egyptian veil hung over my face.

chapter

11

We had had no mail in a long time, so by nine
o'clock next morning we were at the small post office on the other
side of the bridge. Mine—the first I had received—reassured me
that if all was not wholly well in my world, at least nothing
was very different from the way I had left it. Tony and Les
had letters from their girls and seemed quite cheered by what
they read. We left Tony to stand guard over the boats. He said
he would be able to entertain himself, rereading his letters and
reading *Moby Dick*.

The Vernal in which this day was spent seemed like a
different town from the one to which I had first come. I did not
return to the wide street where I had spent the night at a motel,
but was all day in the business section—about three blocks of
stores. We scattered, Don and Les to get supplies at the one
large grocery store there, and I went off in search of the dentist.
It was cool and pleasant in his office. Yes, an emergency, he
agreed, and he'd fit me in.

"There's no doubt about it," he said after one look. "This
tooth is abscessed and must come out."

With what I considered admirable decisiveness, not to say
fortitude, I said, "Go ahead." If 'twere done, 'twere well,
'twere done quickly.

He was skillful and quick. I took one look at myself in the
little mirror over his chest of shallow drawers full of instru-
ments, saw the great gaping space my tongue had explored
and found even bigger, and said, "Now can you fill in that place
with a false one?"

135

"Of course. If you are going to be here for a few days."

"Just today."

He shook his head. "Impossible. These things take time."

So I had to decide. If I stayed over, I did not know when I could rejoin the Expedition, for our next weeks would be in even more remote regions than any we had yet traveled through. Should I miss everything for the sake of vanity? No. I would just control my smile. I stood up. "Will you take my personal check, doctor?"

"Be glad to," he said, and added, "Three dollars."

I felt silly making a check for so little. I had thought it would be fifteen or twenty at least. Maybe I should return to Vernal for any future dental work, I thought as I thanked him and went down again into the street.

It was hot outside, glaring—if I only had an umbrella! People here did not seem to mind the sun, they went about bareheaded, apparently without a qualm. I wandered in and out of stores asking for an umbrella. The salespeople looked as if they had heard of such a thing, but had never really met up with one. "What do you do when it rains?" I asked.

"It doesn't rain much here." At last in the drygoods department of the big grocery where I could see Les and Don surrounded by cans of food, checking their list to see what else was needed, I found a small parasol. It was the sort of thing one might have carried back in the nineties to a garden party. It was the silliest little thing I have ever looked at—plaid with lots of red and green and yellow. I bought it. It would distract attention from my missing tooth—and indeed it did. I saw people turn to stare. But I found it shaded my head and shoulders very neatly even if it was not the big black umbrella of my dreams.

I turned in at a drugstore for a milk shake or something for now I was feeling rather shaky and found Fred perched on a stool at the counter having an ice-cream soda. So he treated me to the same. I was really quite dizzy by this time so I told him I'd had a tooth out and please don't mention it to anyone else. I just wanted someone to know, so that if I should swoon on the sidewalks of Vernal they would know what was the matter with me, and not cart me off to a hospital.

This was a long day for me. I sat for a while in the bus that was already half filled with supplies. But it was too hot there. So when I noticed a small shoe-repair shop I went in and asked the proprietor if I could sit on the bench close by the window. "Help yourself, lady," he said and went on working, resoling a shoe. The place smelt of leather and shoe polish— not unpleasant smells really. I watched people passing on the street. An Indian stopped and looked in the window as if he were trying to find someone. I was disappointed in his appearance. He was not young and he was very fat. He wore no coat and he bulged above the belt that held up his trousers, and hung down over it. He had jowls. He was not the Indian of either TV or the movies, or of Fenimore Cooper. Later someone told me that the Indians in this country are rich, from oil on their lands, that the government is now paying them fabulous sums for oil illegally taken over a long period of years, so they are getting a great deal all at once. I do not know if this is true. Across the street I saw an Indian woman wearing a long full skirt and a shawl, both beautiful in color—brick-red and brown with bits of yellow. It was as if she had taken the colors from the canyons and woven them into her garments. But she was fat, too.

A dark young woman came into the shoe shop. She wore a blue cotton print dress and holding tight to her skirt, following close beside her, was a lovely little girl about six years old. The child had rich bronze skin, large soft dark eyes set wide apart, high cheekbones. She smiled at me, then shyly hid her face against her mother. Only then did I notice the mother was carrying in her arms not just a bundle, as I had supposed, but a blanket-wrapped baby. As they stood there, apparently waiting for someone, I beckoned them to come sit beside me, and then I asked if I could see the baby.

The young mother smiled and turned back the corner of the blanket so I could see the little thing. It was incredibly small, fawn-colored, pale compared to the mother, with perfect little features. "How old?"

"Five days."

"And you—you have come into town so soon?" I know the fashion is nowadays to get young mothers up and around very quickly—and heaven knows I had read stories of how Indian women merely retired to the bushes for a bit, then overtook and rejoined a tribe on the march, babe in hand, or rather slung across the back.

"No," she said, "I've just come from the hospital and I am waiting for my husband to come and take me home." She spoke very good English. "Oh—there he is now—"

I turned the corner of the blanket back over the tiny baby's face and said good-by. Then I looked out the window to see her husband, who was already climbing into a large modern truck parked across the street. It was the same fat old Indian I had noticed earlier. I felt shocked, outraged, somehow. Something was wrong—the great shiny truck, the heavy, slow-moving man, the lovely, gentle little wife and children—it was as if something had gone wrong over the years since all this country had been theirs.

It was late afternoon before the whole group was gathered round the bus that was now loaded with provisions and ready at last to set out for camp. I felt I had had enough of Vernal, for the moment anyway. I was glad when we got out to the campsite just an hour before sunset. The air was fresh there, the mosquitoes ravenous. I think Doc Lez, our new passenger-cook, was a bit dismayed by them.

"Are they always like this? Everywhere?" And he seemed

relieved to hear that these were the first we had encountered.

"But they may get worse as we go farther south," I said. At the moment I was looking on the dark side of everything.

I took a walk along the banks of the river and wished that we could move on. This was quite a dreadful, low spot, too close to the road, with the sound of cars and trucks rattling over the bridge. The river here was wide and tranquil. A dull scene, I thought. I studied the clouds as I walked and tried to forget both tooth and earthly surroundings. The clouds were unlike any I had ever seen. They floated across the sky like jellyfish, like the Portuguese men-of-war, bell-shaped, with streamers hanging down.

When I came back to camp I was delighted to find that dinner was ready—and that Charles had decided we would load the boats and float on downstream till dark to find a new camp spot. So, thanks to everyone's pitching in and helping, before sunset we were floating down the river, feeling the cool evening air rise, refreshing and restoring, from the surface of the water. Les—always adventurous—was all for keeping on till bedtime. But I was glad to have the last remnants of daylight to set up my tent by, in a tangle of bushes close to the water. The others scattered about, Don and Tony carrying their sleeping bags high onto a shelf of the long low cliff. Les slept in the boat that night and next morning complained that the beavers had kept him awake, flopping in and out of the water. I had heard them too, for it was a wakeful night for me, and I had thought it was Les diving in for a swim at odd hours, and belly-flopping every time.

The next day was one of almost unendurable heat. The river was wide and calm, flowing lazily between banks bordered with stunted willows and tamarisks, pink with bloom. Set well back from the river were low, flat-topped mesas, dull gray-brown in color. There were geese flying overhead now and then, ducks along the marshy spots and cows standing idle as if too hot to graze. The motor droned steadily in my ears. Even it sounded hot. I kept dipping my veil in the water and draping it round my head. This made me sufficiently comfortable to take some note of my companions, and now I saw that Doc too was feeling the heat. He probably was even less accustomed to it that I, I realized, and I began to be rather concerned about him. He looked white around the mouth; he seemed to be having trouble breathing.

Charles, who had been studying a map, shouted to Don to head shoreward. "There's an old gold mine along here somewhere and we ought to have a look at it."

No mine paved with gold could have induced me to any extra exertion. Doc seemed to feel the same way so we two were left alone in the big boat. He took off his shoes and dangled his feet in the water. "If you can cool off the arteries in the ankle, it is a help," he said.

"So is my wet veil." Then rather hesitantly I offered to dig something out of my duffel that he could wet and put on his head. I was really afraid he was going to have a sunstroke.

"That would be most kind of you," he said.

I had brought along a piece of an old skirt, thinking it might come in handy for something. It was the remains of a dress I had made during the war when materials were scarce and I had cut it out of linen dishtoweling. It had been great fun to wear because people would look at it, puzzled, and I could almost hear them thinking, "Now where have I seen that before?" For nearly everyone has at some time had a dish-towel of natural-color linen with a red stripe for border. So it rather amused me as I dug down into my duffel bag, feeling for it, to think that its final end would be saving an Englishman from sunstroke. Provided, of course, that he would not be too proud to wear it. I still remembered a remark I overheard many years ago when I was watching a tennis match at the Club Leopold in Brussels. One of the players had put on a headband so sweat would not run down and fog his glasses and a woman behind me asked, "Is he English?" and another replied indignantly, "Of course not. No Englishman would wear that thing around his head!"

But this Englishman received my offering gratefully, dipped it in the river and wore it the rest of the morning, looking rather like a stray Arab chieftain. After lunch, Les, not being needed with the motor going, got out a big sheet of canvas cloth and with spare oars constructed a sort of tent for me in the stern of the boat. And when he saw my lips were cracked from heat and wind he gave me his tube of Camphor Ice. "I have another," he said. But I don't think he really did. So canopied with canvas and cushioned on duffel I floated like Cleopatra down the Nile. Doc joined me for most of the afternoon. He did not seem to feel like talking at first, so for a while I amused him and myself by reading aloud from my tiny copy of *Twelfth Night*.

Later we talked. He said it was not so much the heat—though that was bad enough—as it was that he was subject to asthma and the first sleeping bag he had bought (he had gotten another our second day in Vernal) was padded with something to which he was allergic and which had brought on an attack. He would be over it soon, but in the meanwhile he was afraid he would not be able to do his proper share of hauling duffel and doing other chores. This greatly troubled him, and that was why, he said, he had been so dull and unresponsive all day. He did not seem so to me, and I soon found myself telling him more about my own life and various reasons I had had for taking this trip than I had confided to anyone else.

It is a curious thing, this business of talking with strangers. There are times when one can say almost anything, feeling safe, I suppose, in knowing one will never meet this transient traveling companion again. I have heard all sorts of odd bits from seatmates in bus or train. On shipboard, there is always the next morning to consider. That is inhibiting. The briefer journey is better for confidences and a night trip is better than day. Once on a coach in Texas just before daylight a man told me he was a murderer, and how it weighed on his mind sometimes. And on a night bus from New York to Boston, I heard the most lurid details of a love affair that was not going too well at the moment.

But now it was I who talked. And Doc in his turn told me something about himself—Oxford, interning in a Hamburg hospital, travels on the continent, his ambition before he settled down to medical practice to explore the great rivers of the world.

"How did you hear about this one?"

"I was driving out to Salt Lake City from New York, taking a truck out there—it was one way to get to see the country—and I heard one of the radio announcers describing this Expedition. Then when I was visiting the Dinosaur National Monument on my way back the Park Service people there told me more about it—and so here I am."

I thought it most enterprising and adventurous of him to seize such an opportunity. And to be willing to take on a job as cook in order to see the Green and Colorado rivers. "How are you at cooking?" I asked.

"Not too good," he admitted.

"It is mostly a matter of opening cans. And washing dishes."

"That's what I thought," he said.

Now and then as we talked, I lifted the side flap of our tent and took a look at the scenery lest I miss something. Tamarisk still edged the river, pink and green, and a slim cottonwood was reflected in a zigzag pattern in the moving water. As the long, hot afternoon passed, the mesas drew in closer. We began to see a formation that becomes more common lower down, on the Colorado. In these places the mesa wall has apparently disintegrated into broken small bits that have slid down, fanning out like wide skirts from a small waist. Here they looked to me like kneeling girls in gray dirndls who had bowed their heads and been covered over by the upper layers of stone, leaving visible only these outspread skirts.

As usual the air grew cooler in the late afternoon, and by the time we reached our camping spot it was quite comfortable. I wondered what these rapid changes of temperature would do to the human body—mine especially. But by this time I felt no pain in my jaw and indeed was feeling more energetic, when not prostrated by heat, than I had in some time. I decided that tooth had been poisoning me, and was content to be rid of it. Also by now, having no mirror save one that was only about two inches square, I forgot my gaping void and was no longer self-conscious about smiling.

We passed under a slender bridge where the Utah State Route 88 crosses the Green, and tied up for the night close to a pleasant grove of cottonwoods. Ouray was the name of the place. There was a house or two in the distance and a small store and post office and that was all we could see. Ouray is an Indian reservation, named for a chief of the Uncompahgre Utes who was always friendly to the whites and for his services was granted a yearly pension of a thousand dollars. He had spent part of his boyhood, back in the 1830's, attached to a white family who called him Willie, and the Ouray, according to Powell, was the result of the Ute attempt to pronounce that name. Other authorities say it means Arrow. In any case, the name is preserved here where several hundred Indians live, along with perhaps half a dozen white people.

We were just about to sit down to our dinner when one of them, the postmaster, came down and joined us, so he was invited to share our meal. He was a thin, wiry man with that still, listening look one often finds on the faces of those who live in lonely places. What is it they listen for, I wonder? The sound of another human voice? Or for something more deep and significant than may be heard in the roar of cities?

I kept hoping that some Indians would come down and look us over, thus giving us a chance to do the same for them. But no one came. A truck full of people went by on the road, a child waved. That was all. I went early to bed and dropped off to sleep while I was still hearing Charles's voice in the distance reading aloud to the others the directions for proper procedure in case of rattlesnake bites. I was more than ever glad that I had my army cot, which lifted me above the normal path of any stray rattlers.

The next morning we were off to a good start before nine o'clock. We passed the mouth of the Duchesne River without knowing it. This was a time of low water, so we mistook it for one of the small creek beds that came in now and then. Les read aloud to us Major Powell's account of how he and his men, somewhere near here, came upon an abandoned garden with potatoes growing. One of the men had said that potato tops made good greens and that as they had had no fresh vegetable for some time it might be a good idea to gather some and cook up a mess for their evening meal. Evidently these potatoes had been planted in the wrong time of the moon—as we say in Mississippi when a plant is all tops and no potatoes—so there was an abundance for all to eat heartily. And they were violently sick afterward.

Doc was still not feeling well, though the heat was less oppressive than it had been the day before because now we had a wind in our faces. I could not hold my little plaid parasol upright against it. Canyons seem to act like funnels to the wind, drawing it in, always upstream, and making of it yet another obstacle to fight. Our little motor chugged away valiantly, yet we made but slow progress till Les and Bruce helped out with the oars.

Gradually the surrounding territory changed in character. The gray, gently rolling slopes of the Utah badlands, which we had been passing all morning, drew in closer, gathered height, and now ahead we could see where they almost met— the beginning of the canyon Powell named Desolation. It measures almost a hundred river miles in length. To the east lies the Tavaputs Plateau and on the map one finds nothing but blank space and a winding small road that travels to a place called Dragon, and stops there. The Uinta Mountains had been left behind. The gorge we were entering had a solemn, solitary aspect, more strange and desolate than any we had yet seen. Tony got out his horn and played for a while—no gay tunes, but a sort of improvised imitation Gregorian chant which served to increase the somberness of the atmosphere.

I was reminded of other bleak bare places I had seen—the Coolins of Skye, the cliffs of Rhum. They were all akin—and curiously akin to something deep within my own spirit, so that I was not depressed by them. At first, the gray walls had a faintly purplish tinge, then they took on a more drab pale khaki color. As we moved on downstream strange shapes jutted out from the walls between which we passed. Some were pyramidal in design with a curiously Egyptian effect. Others had an unearthly look so that we said it must be like this on some other planet. I remembered the small town on the map, the one named Dragon. In such a place as this all myths and monstrous tales might come true, dragons might well be bred. For surely only monsters could inhabit these weird structures formed by wind and blowing sand and the water that had cut such a cleft in the earth.

There was little or no vegetation here. The walls on each side of us cut a straight bare line across the sky, sharp, uncompromising. As we moved yet deeper into Desolation, however, I began to feel a quite unexpected sense of satisfaction, as if I had reached the limit of barren bleakness. There is always a satisfaction—I can think of no better word for it—in reaching the limit. Even in pain. When the walls of pain close in so hard and fast, so glaring and pitiless that there is no escape, the human spirit must take heart, knowing things can be no worse than this, knowing that now the body can endure no more and the senses must withdraw into unconsciousness. This is equally true of mental anguish, I think. One reaches bedrock there too, and strangely enough one finds something firm and unyielding on which one may stand defiant, akin to the spirit of Lear crying, "Blow, winds, and crack your cheeks! rage! blow." Or as Hopeful said to the sinking Christian, "Be of good cheer, my brother. I feel the bottom and it is good."

The canyon walls widened out toward afternoon, the river swept round in the great curve Powell named in honor of Jack Sumner—Sumner's Amphitheater. It was a place of astounding sweep and grandeur, the high walls set back in curving tiers that did indeed suggest a vast amphitheater. Only what play, what tragedy could be played against such a backdrop? King Lear, perhaps? Or were we, weak humans here below, in our fragile small boats, with our lives wrapped round us like varied costumes, the players in a drama whose end we did not know?

I think most of us were affected by the scenes through which we passed that day and when toward evening we came upon a place where the right wall moved back, leaving a bush-grown, weedy space at its foot and a few trees, and a strip of sand at the river's edge, we were glad to stop for the night. Doc still was not feeling well, and Les and Bruce, observing this, though they said nothing, helped him with the preparation of dinner.

As we sat round the table we began to speak of how we would get out of this canyon if it was necessary. This subject of escape had not come up before, and it seemed to me that it occurred to us now because Desolation Canyon was so utterly remote, so complete in its bleakness.

Tony said, "It would be easy. See that cliff back there?"

We all turned and looked. We studied the slope set back from the level ground—a ridge, a crack, a foothold here and there, then a blank sheer rise and another ledge. Charles shook his head. "You know those angles flatten out, seen from here. But if you were there on the side of the cliff, you would find them very different, and much more difficult than they seem from here."

Tony sprang up. It was almost as if, oppressed by the day's journey through Desolation, he had to find some exit, as if he were driven by necessity to prove it was possible to get out. "I'll show you. I'll do it!"

"Oh no you won't," Charles said quietly.

I tried to think of something to say, to lighten what all at once had become an intolerable situation. But I could think of nothing, and there was real danger. Tony could slip, fall to severe injury if not worse—and what could we do, so far from any help? It seemed to me that I sensed in him the same sort of desperate oppression I had once felt when I was younger than he, in New York City for my first year there and for the first time experiencing the press of throngs that filled streets and sidewalks to watch the Hudson-Fulton celebration. I had felt that I must strike out and thrust these pressing bodies from me, make my escape somehow. On the other hand, I reasoned now, looking at Tony standing there, eager and excited, perhaps he had just made an idle boast and, being young, felt he must make it good.

Charles said, "How about trying it up to that first ledge?" and then turned away to pour himself another cup of coffee as if he had no great interest in the matter.

Tony set off at once at high speed, around boulders, then across the level stretch where reeds and grasses grew high. Did he stop to think of snakes? I wondered. We lost sight of him for a little while—I had not realized the distance across the open space was that great. My eyes had become so accustomed to looking at large distances, such as Sumner's Amphitheater, which was miles across, at great heights—thousand-foot wall and more—that my sense of measurement was all askew.

Tony's red sweater appeared at last at the foot of the slope; we could see the flash of color bobbing around boulders, quickly mounting higher till he came out on the long upward-stretching sweep of shale. There against that gray background, he seemed infinitely small, and he moved more and more slowly. "It gets steeper there," Charles said. We were all watching now with increasing uneasiness.

Don said, "It's all right if he doesn't try to get beyond that ledge."

But would he stop there? we all wondered, watching his slender figure as he mounted higher and higher, tried one side of a great boulder, then another, disappeared, then was visible on top of it. "The young idiot," Charles said, and yet with a trace of admiration in his tone.

The next step up was twice his height. "Let's give him a cheer, and maybe he'll stop there," someone said. So we all shouted and waved and clapped hands as if we thought he had attained his goal. He looked up at the cliff above him, waved to us—and started downward.

I was quite exhausted from the strain of watching, and as soon as I saw him nearing camp I slipped away to my tent, which as usual was pitched close down by the river. There were mosquitoes there. I got out my bottle of insect repellent, but they did not know it was a repellent. They seemed to enjoy its smell, and along with some larger insects came in droves to savor it—and me. Luckily the air was cooler now and I could cover myself completely without roasting.

chapter

12

Next morning when I told the others at breakfast that I had entertained gallinippers all night, they looked at me as if I had said dinosaurs, or some other prehistoric animal. "Didn't you ever hear of a gallinipper?" Not one of them had ever heard of such a thing—common enough in Mississippi.

"What is it?"

"An oversize mosquito, of course. Though how it got that name I cannot tell you."

"Maybe because it nips the gals," Don suggested. So we left it at that.

The baggage was well lashed this morning. There would be rapids ahead. And I think we were all delighted at the prospect. As we moved on down the river that morning of June 23, the scenery became more and more spectacular. Gray rock changed to browner, richer tones, to buff and yellow. The cliffs rose higher and higher to jagged tops, toothlike and strange. Wind or water had washed holes up there so that we looked as through windows and saw bits of sky set like jewels high toward the crest of the wall.

White water appeared ahead; we danced over the waves. I was in the small boat most of this day, and as always when I rode in it, I felt more a part of the river. I rather wondered why Doc and I had been asked to shift. I had a feeling that Charles was much concerned about the latter, because it was evident to us all that he was far from well, and while making a gallant effort to do his share, he simply was unable to take hold as had

149

been expected. Now I imagined that Charles had taken this
opportunity to talk things over with Les and Bruce or perhaps
with Fred, whose advice he often sought.

In any case, here we were in the small boat, the waves
kicking us high, the wind blowing a gale in our faces. The
backs of my hands had begun to blister and this morning I had
gotten out of my luggage some white gardening gloves. So there
I sat, veiled, white-gloved and holding, when I could manage it
against the wind, that silly little plaid parasol over my head.

There was all at once a shout from the big boat—Charles's
hat had blown away. It sank before we could turn and head back
for it. Next, a map went overboard and Tony plunged in after
it, watch, hunting knife, notebook and all. He retrieved the
map but lost his knife. Charles rather scolded him for diving
in head first, not knowing how deep the water was. I suppose
it might have been dangerous. Yet when one acts quickly, one
does not stop to think of such things. I had a good illustration of
that a few minutes later. We had just come through a lively
stretch of rapids and rounded a curve when the wind hit us full
blast, caught up Don's lavender shirt he had stripped off for
coolness, and away it went over the side. Without a thought, I
like Tony bent to the rescue.

Not that I dived in—I simply leaned over the side and
reached for it, missed, and was reaching again, when Doc caught
me by the ankle and hauled me back. "But I'd have had it in
another second," I complained.

"And we would have lost you," Doc said.

"Oh—I hadn't thought of that. Well, anyway, thanks for
saving my life."

"It wasn't so much that," he said with a dry, comical glance.
"I just didn't want to have to dive in after you."

So we laughed and no one said anything more about it. But
I knew just how Tony felt. Rather foolish.

We had fruit juice to drink at lunch, for our supply of fresh water, laid in at Jensen, was all gone and we had been unable to get water at Ouray. I was back in the big boat now and I asked Bruce what people did when they had no fresh water. He pointed to the river. "I've been drinking it for days," he said. So I thought, well, why not? We were miles from civilization and any possible contamination, and I remembered how, when I was a child, everyone drank water from the muddy Mississippi or the Pearl, that misnamed river near us that was almost as full of silt as the Colorado. So I scooped up a cupful and drank it down. "The mud—or something—gives it a delicious flavor," I said. And really, it did, and allayed my thirst till we stopped in the early afternoon at Rock Creek.

This was a superb camping spot, the best we had found since Carter's Creek. It lay above a bend of the river on the right bank, where a grove of cottonwood trees stood, gnarled and wind-swept. I pitched my tent under one of the biggest, so great in diameter that my rope barely went round it. Downstream little Rock Creek came dancing over small stones to join the river. Its valley—no doubt filled with water in the spring freshet times—lay behind our camp spot, wooded but sparsely, so I could look beyond the branches of my cottonwood and see far off a green-splashed height, a blue mountain topped with snow. It might have been one of the peaks of the West Tavaputs Plateau. In any case it was a beautiful view I had, framed by the gray willow branches.

Everyone disappeared with fishing poles. I found soap and towel and, after quite a search, a tube of Prell for my hair, which was by this time, thanks to my pouring river water over my head, caked with mud. I crossed the rocky stretch of dry creek bed and came to the stream itself, and it was a welcome sight under trees that shaded me from the western sun. No privacy, alas, for I could hear voices just a little way higher upstream. So I just took off my shoes, waded into the creek with all my clothes on. Water could not hurt my blue jeans or nylon shirt, I thought.

I'd wash them on me this time. So there I sat in the clear, cool water, stopping for a sip now and then, soaping my clothes and letting the current rinse me, lathering my head and then lying down to wash the Prell away.

In the distance upstream I could hear shouts—"Catch him! There he goes! Here's one, get him!"

Not trout, surely, I thought. And when Les appeared briefly on the bank I called to him. "What are you chasing? Rattlesnakes?"

He laughed. "Grasshoppers."

"What on earth for?"

"Bait," he said and dived into the grass. "Got him," he shouted and disappeared again.

I finished rinsing my hair and the garments I wore, then I made my way back over the stony ground to our campsite. Others had camped here—I saw a heap of tin cans that had been covered over and then washed half free of sand. And some enterprising camper had constructed from driftwood a little straight chair. I set it up, shaky as it was, and set myself down upon it. It was better than the ground or a log. The sun came through the gap of the valley Rock Creek had made and shone warm on my back and my hair. The wind helped dry it, too.

Before me, the river swept in a great curve to rapids below the mouth of the creek just out of my sight. The roar of water over rocks came pleasantly to me with its promise of excitement tomorrow. Across the river the other wall of the canyon still caught the sun and the lower rocks were rosy with its rays. Higher up they were turned to buff and gold. At the very top, pointed pines were a brilliant green. The sky was pale and cloudless. I sat there alone with all this splendor and wondered that I was here, that I could be here. What had I ever done to deserve the sight of so much magnificence?

I had just finished putting up my hair when the fishermen returned triumphant—Don had twelve beauties, Charles had eight and Fred almost as many.

What a feast we had! There is surely nothing more delicious than fresh trout cooked as Don cooked them that night over the open fire. Did he use cornmeal? I cannot remember! But I do remember how the stars came out in the clear cool sky, and that as I went to my tent I looked over my shoulder to the west and saw a slim new moon hanging on the edge of a far-off peak. I thought of how when I was on the Isle of South Uist in the Hebrides I had looked out my window one evening and had seen three young girls standing on a wet rock at the water's edge. As I watched, they faced the new moon and bowed low before it. Nine times they bowed in unison. So now I did the same, and made a wish—though I did not know for sure whether the ceremony included wish-making in its good-luck charm.

Next morning as the boats were being loaded, I noticed that Les was not taking his usual part in carrying the heavy boxes down from around the campfire. Then I realized that he had been already in his place in the boat when I came out of my tent, that he had not come to breakfast. Well, I thought, maybe he just did not feel very well this morning, maybe that was why he did not go ahead with Don and Bruce to look over the rapids we had heard all night beyond the curve of the river below us.

And when Bruce came back to report that he had seen fresh tracks of a mountain lion, I was too excited over that to notice that Les was unusually quiet. Suppose that lion had come creeping through the bushes as I sat all alone in camp at sunset! Or suppose in the night—but I had little time to tremble over that. "Life preservers, everybody," Don shouted as we pushed off in the face of a high head wind. No sooner were we out in midstream than Charles noticed that Doc had no life preserver—his had gotten in the small boat by mistake. Someone tossed it back to him, for we were still close together. But the wind caught it, sent it far out of reach. Bruce jumped overboard, swam after it—and lost his hat. No chance to go back for it, as we were now at the beginning of the rough water and Bruce himself had just time to scramble back into the boat and snatch up his oars. "We'll take it to the right, Les," he shouted. "Pull now," and Les pulled.

We grazed the one bad rock, swept on, dipping and plunging through the waves. It was a long rapid, though not a specially dangerous one, and beyond it we had swift water for the rest of the morning. As we neared the end of Desolation the character of the canyon changed. The walls grew even higher and were topped by reddish formations which resembled apartment buildings with elevator shafts projecting against the sky. So we moved as between the silhouettes of towns and cities, all empty, deserted—"and not a soul to tell Why thou art desolate," I thought.

The plan today was to stop early at Florence Creek, another good fishing place. But the water was so swift that we overshot our mark and had gone almost half a mile beyond it before Don, consulting his map, called back to say we had gone too far. We drew up alongside a bank of tamarisk and shrublike willow that left no landing place, and after some consultation it was decided that we would try to make our way back upstream. Both motors were attached and all oars were manned. We got across the river to where it was shallower and looked to be less swift —and there we stayed, just holding our own, no matter how hard Bruce and Les, and Don in the small boat, pulled on the oars. Thus for the first time I truly comprehended how strong the current was even when there were no rapids and the fall of the river bottom was imperceptible.

"We'll have to get out and pull," Charles said and jumped into the water. The others followed him, all but Don, who kept the motors going, and Les, who stayed by his oars. Wading knee to waist deep, they put all their strength to it and slowly we began to make some progress. I watched a bush on the shore— that was the only way I could tell that we were making any headway. It really did not seem to me that a good campsite, especially so early in the day, was worth such a struggle. But having had a taste of good fishing, I suppose they just had to have more.

We were almost opposite the sandy stretch of wooded shore that we were trying to reach when the big boat ran aground. There was a scraping dull sound as the bottom raked against stones, and then with all hands grunting and hauling, swung free. At that instant, there was an explosion from somewhere underneath. I nearly jumped overboard—just as the others swung up and crawled in. "Only a bottle of fruit juice," Les said. "Probably got too hot, blew up. Happens sometimes."

We crossed the river diagonally and I saw that we would be able to draw up within a few feet of our planned campsite. Doc was beside me. He was shivering; he was having trouble with his breathing. "You should not have gotten out into the water," I said.

He shrugged. "They needed me." He was game all right.

Why hadn't Les jumped in to do his share? I felt quite cross with him, though it was the first time he had not been in the midst of everything, doing his part. He could not be sick—he was pulling away at the oars with all his great strength, bringing the big boat round and close in shore.

"We'll have to unload," Charles said. "Those pieces of glass are too dangerous. May have cut a hole in the bottom already."

It was quite a job, taking everything out of the big boat. I went ashore and walked back to the protection of a cottonwood. The wind was stronger than ever now and it blew the fine white sand in a cutting storm. I sat down on a log and wrapped my nylon veil closer, turning my face away from the wind. The sand blew into my sleeves at the wrist, it sifted down my neck and into my shoes. This seemed a dreadful spot to spend the rest of the afternoon, fish or no fish—and I could see no sign of any stream. Our luggage was by now strewn helter-skelter on shore;

Don was down in the bottom of the boat, recovering bits of the broken bottle. Les sat on the gunwales doing nothing.

Tony came up with the cameras and a canvas to cover them with, against the sand. "What's the matter with Les?" I asked.

Tony hesitated. "He doesn't want anybody to know—but it's bound to come out. He broke his leg back there at Rock Creek—the bone that was broken last summer and hadn't healed completely, maybe."

I mentally begged his pardon for having found him slow to help today. "But how can he—"

Tony grinned. "That's Les for you—says he can row as well as ever so why make a fuss about the leg. It'll be all right, he says."

"But he must have attention right away. Doc and Bruce—they could at least put a splint on it, do something till we can get him to a hospital."

"Les doesn't take much stock in such things, though he likes Doc all right. I don't know—Charles has found out about it now. He'll see to it."

"But how on earth did Les think he could get away with this —not telling anybody and going on as if nothing had happened?"

Tony started gathering sticks for a fire. "Beats me," he said. "But that's Les."

Yes, it was just like him. And—of such stuff myths are made. I thought of Paul Bunyan, even of King Arthur. My sympathy at the moment went to Charles too. Out of the seven of us Doc, Les and I were unable to help, either in the regular chores of the day or, worst of all, in any emergency. Of course I had always been something of a liability. But Les—how could we manage without him?

"We'll be at Greenriver, Utah, tomorrow," I overheard Charles saying to Don as they folded up their maps and set out on an exploring walk. "Then we can see about it."

When they had all scattered, I went down to the boat and

talked with Les. He had been so kind to me, making that canopy against the sun for me, I hoped I could do something for him. But he said he was fine. "It's nothing—doesn't even hurt so long as I am still."

"But shouldn't you get Doc to put on a splint?"

He shook his head. "It will heal just as it is."

I gave up and came back to the shade of the cottonwood. Fred had come back for his fishing pole so I asked him to lend me his Stegner, and then I settled down in the shade, protecting myself from the blowing sand as much as I could and resigned to spend a long afternoon. Luckily the book was interesting enough to make me forget wind and sun and sand, and so it seemed no time at all before Tony and Bruce came back with news of a deserted ranch they had come upon. "You ought to see it," Tony said.

"How far?"

"Not far at all—straight back from here."

I was about to go alone when Charles and Fred came along. They had seen the ranch only from a distance and decided to go with me. We set out then, scrambling up the sandy bank that had cut me off from all view of our surroundings except for the cliff across the river. Now I saw how this canyon wall was set far back to ascend in a series of ledges. Atop one was a formation that might have been a Spanish walled city, and now in the slanting sunlight it was blood red, and where the shadows fell it seemed to be veiled in diaphanous green. We walked toward it over an open field which had that regular irregularity which remains long years after the last plow has turned rows for planting. We crossed a reedy, marshy stretch and mounted a bright green slope where water trickled down and the ground was soft. It had a queer feel underfoot, after all the crisp dry ground I had walked over.

At the top of the slope, amid a tangle of small trees, was the spring, running clear and cool from the base of the cliff.

Watercress—planted who could tell how many years ago—grew in a green mass that spread part way down the slope, following the outspreading flow of the spring. There was an old pipe there and Charles said, "They must have taken water from here down to the ranch." The pipe was broken, the people gone, but still the spring came from under the rock.

From this vantage point we could see where the ranch lay and now we set off across another field and through a neglected, half-dead apple orchard. Someone had set out these trees in hope and courage—and now look at them! "It is a sad place," I said.

We climbed over the remains of a fence—the gate was the only part of it that remained intact, less passable now than the fence itself, and so came upon several small buildings. In one we found bits of harness hanging on nails, a forge in one corner with blacksmith's tools all ready for use. "It's like the *Marie Celeste*," Fred said.

Charles who had gone ahead, called to us as we came out. "The house burned, that's why they left." And there stood the walls and chimney with all the rooms of the house open to the sky. "I wonder who they were," he said and stepped inside.

I went up to the side wall of the house and examined it. "He was a Scot, I know that," I said. For the walls were made of carefully cut blocks of red sandstone from the canyon, and each block had been struck a hundred or more blows with a hammer, chipping small pieces out to leave an irregular surface that would not weather or crack. "It is exactly the same construction as Ardross Castle in Ross-shire. Whoever he was, he came from the north of Scotland, the man who built this."

Inside there was nothing, no trace of its former occupants, only a cellar gaping wide, making it too dangerous for walking. But we explored another small one-room building and with a stick I poked about in a heap of rags and rain-browned papers. "There were children," I said, prying out the remains of a small toy bear, a broken doll, and a little girl's faded print dress with puff sleeves. "They left around 1910," I said. "This is just about the right style for that year."

"Come on, Sherlock," Fred called, and I followed him out to the corral. There I could see how a thirty-foot ledge of the cliff came around like a man-made wall to form one side of the corral, indeed it curved around the whole southern side of the ranch. Here against it there remained the stoutly-built feed shed, and on the other side, what must have been a hen house. It was dark inside but we could make out a long row of empty nests which had been cut with an axe from a great log, scooped out, each one a separate hollow.

Outside the corral there was still a trace of the road that came in from the valley, and here at the entrance the remains of a gateway. "I wish I'd brought my camera," Charles said. "But the light is bad now."

Halfway across the field, I stopped and looked back. The sun had sunk behind the western cliff, darkness was already filling up the valley here. And as I stood there looking, the whole place seemed to come alive again for me. A wagon with a team of horses was rattling down the road, a cowboy was opening the gate. The house was roofed over once more, smoke rose from the chimney. From the glowing forge came the ring of hammer on anvil, from the corral the sound of horses' trampling feet, from the valley the lowing of cattle. The green apple trees were laden with fruit, and little girls in print dresses with puff sleeves were playing there with a doll and a woolly bear.

"Gives you a queer feeling, doesn't it?" Fred said as we started back toward the river, facing a rosy sunset sky.

I said, "The loneliest spot on earth isn't an unexplored peak of the Himalayas or a blank waste of the ocean. It's a place like this. Or anywhere someone has lived, and now lives no longer." And I thought of that Biblical line, "and the place thereof shall know it no more." It seemed to me the saddest line I knew.

So we made our way back to camp. We had no fish that night

for dinner, but the Salisbury steak was good and hot and we all had appetites for it, even Les, who still could eat, even if he could not walk. I dreamed of the deserted ranch as I slept in my tent by the river, but when I woke could remember no more than that my sleep had been haunted. Later, after I was home again, Cecil Atwater, one of my Duxbury neighbors, loaned me a book by one of the Kolb brothers who had come down the river in 1911. They had stopped here at the McPherson ranch. The house had burned some time before that and the family had moved to Greenriver, Utah, but Mr. McPherson and two cowboys were there at work in the blacksmith shop. He owned quite a heard of thoroughbred cattle and they had just been driven down from the mountains to winter in the canyon. Mr. McPherson had recently lost a fine bull, he told the Kolbs, killed by a brown grizzly bear, and he had spent several days and night tracking him down. The cinnamon-colored pelt was hanging on a tree. He did not like the river, he said. His father and two men had been drowned in it and, though he often swam his cattle across to pasture on the far side, he never went in a boat without a life preserver. He did not think too much of the idea of traveling the river for pleasure, but he made the Kolb brothers at home and put them up for the night in one of the tents in which he and his men were living. So the picture I had seen in my mind's eye of the ranch alive again was rather accurate after all.

The next day was a muggy, hazy one and most of it was spent in Gray Canyon—named Coal Canyon by Powell because of the streaks of lignite along its cliffs. I found the walls more brown than gray. They were gray only in feeling, being bleak and for the most part bare of vegetation. We took the rapids in tow to the small boat. Some were rather rough and I was surprised that Don risked smashing the engine. Then I remembered— he was probably doing this to spare Les from rowing. In any case we passed through even the roughest stretch without mishap, though once I thought Doc was going to be knocked overboard.

Most of the afternoon he had been stretched out across the bow of the *Brontosaur,* making up for some of the sleep he had lost the night before. He looked quite limp and helpless lying there, the brim of his hat drooping dispiritedly over his face, one arm hanging across the gunwale. It was Les's great shout that roused him just in time to get out of the way. Our big boat, running through one of the swiftest rapids faster than the small boat that was towing us, came within an ace of crashing into it. The motor projecting from its stern was of course the danger to Doc, but he roused up and rolled away, escaping the blow. Then he dozed again. I thought he could not be having a very happy time, wondered if he regretted coming.

Les, who had been amusing himself working over his maps and notebook, now announced that we had come 387 miles since we left Green River, Wyoming, and that in that distance we had dropped a little over four thousand feet. A staggering descent. But when I thought of all the falls, big and little, it seemed credible.

Toward the end of a gray afternoon, we came out of this canyon through an open, desertlike stretch. Then of a sudden, rounding a curve, we saw the great bulk of Gunnison's Butte. High above drifts of broken rock and shale rose the battlements of a wind-and-weather-made fortress of tremendous proportions. I thought it looked like the walled city of Jericho, and the drifts of disintegrating rock were like the tents of the children of Israel encamped around about it, and that if Tony blew his horn the walls might come tumbling down. It was perhaps no more than seven hundred feet above us, yet rising from river level with no higher canyon walls near to dwarf it, it seemed an imposing monument to mark what is known as Gunnison's Trail. There is neither highway nor railroad here, though it was to mark out a path for the Pacific railroad that Gunnison came through, surveying in 1853, and with seven of his men was murdered a few miles to the west by the Pahvant Utes.

We were still some seven miles above Greenriver, Utah, when we came upon a spillway where the water poured evenly all its width down to a lower level, quite unlike the irregular rock-made falls and potholes through which we had come. On the left bank there was a motionless waterwheel and a wooden trough into which the buckets of the wheel, turned by the river's current, could dump water that was then carried away through other troughs to irrigate a field. The wheel stood some twenty feet high and seemed as sound as ever, indeed had been used very recently, Charles said. On the opposite side of the river toward which Don was steering us in order to take the spillway slantwise, some six or eight people suddenly appeared out of nowhere and stood watching as we sidled and slid down the spillway and out into the pleasantly-ruffled water below. They cheered and waved as if we had just accomplished a remarkable feat.

From here on down to Greenriver, the river was wide and open. In the distance we could see the snow-topped blue mountains of the Uncompahgre range. Off to the right against the sky there stood a long-stretched-out formation that from here looked like a cut-out of a Grecian city set at different levels and topped by a columned temple. Ahead, there appeared now the bridge by which Highway 50 crosses the Green. But where was the town? Tony and Don landed high on the left bank and made their way up a steep slope that was so thickly covered with small trees and underbrush that they were instantly lost from sight, indeed could only keep track of each other by shouting back and forth. And after investigating the lay of the land and discovering by inquiry at a small café that the town lay on the other side of the river, nearly a mile from the bridge, they made their way back to us, well scratched by the bushes they had had to pass through.

There was a steep bank on the other side too, but not so heavily overgrown, and we now made for that at a point just above the bridge. Cars went shooting across the bridge at what seemed to be a terrific speed. "How silly they look!" I thought. "Like mad things." And then I realized that I had not looked at traffic for so long I was seeing it now as if with eighteenth-century eyes. Great trucks rumbled across, red tanks labeled GASOLINE in large letters. Others were marked DANGER—EXPLOSIVES—ACID—most ominous of all. They seemed quite horrible to me, menacing, wicked.

And when I had sprung out and mounted the bank to what was to be our camping place, I felt that we had landed in the midst of a yet more unpleasant danger—other humans had camped here, too many of them, and left their spoor. I went past these bushes and small trees and there was only a reedy, open space without a trace of shade. On the left was the highway with a bare embankment that formed the approach to the bridge. On the right was a barbed-wire fence beyond which lay a field with a sparse scattering of alfalfa. It seemed to me that I had never seen a less inviting campsite. There was no privacy and the rumble of traffic was fearful to ears which had grown unaccustomed to it.

If I had known then that we were to stay in this god-awful spot for four long days and four hot nights, I think I would have rebelled. Before I realized how the time was going to stretch out, I had become too involved to be willing to leave. Perhaps too, the knowledge that I could walk a mile down the road and find reasonably decent quarters at a motel made it possible for me to endure the discomforts of this place. If I should find it at any time unendurable, I could leave, I kept telling myself.

First of the delays was the problem of a new boatman to take Les's place. Don set off at once to telephone around to see whom he could find. I imagine that Les had to be argued with—I am sure he felt that there was no reason why he could not continue, since he could row as well as ever. I felt sad about his not

being able to continue with us. He had been so kind and thoughtful all the way and he had had his heart set on making the
journey all the way through. Also, I knew he had been alone in
a canoe through Cataract; he knew every inch of that fearful
canyon. None of the others had been through it. So when they
were all occupied setting up camp, phoning Les's mother to
ask when she could come and get him, I went down to the boat
where he sat and commiserated with him.

"I'm afraid they will never let me run Cataract without you
along, Les. What do you think? Could I make it?"

"Sure you can, with or without me—and I do wish it was
going to be *with*." He gave me a rueful smile.

I felt so sorry for him that I wrote: "Lines on the Departure
of Les"—

> Oh how I wish that Leslie Jones
> Had been more careful of his bones.
> It grieves me sore to have him go
> From where the river rapids flow.
> He built a tent when I was baking,
> Cheered me up when I was aching.
> He plied a mighty, skillful oar
> And filled my head with river lore.
> The woods will echo with my moans
> When I must part from Leslie Jones.

This I copied off neatly and presented to him the next morning, knowing he had to go that afternoon. He seemed pleased
and spent several hours composing a long reply in which he
mentioned each one of the party and gave us all some excellent
advice.

chapter

13

Breakfast among the weeds, cars slowing up on the highway to stare down at us and move on, the radio bringing us the Salt Lake City Tabernacle organ playing Bach, the sun striking my back, lying across it like a hot old-man-of-the-sea— those things I remember.

It was still early that morning when three men in a Mercury car drove in from the highway. The driver—Jim Nixon was his name—talked with Charles for a while, asking about the expedition, then said, "You need a car—to pick up supplies, do errands. How about taking mine while you are here? I won't be needing it."

What incredible generosity, I thought. This was the West at its best. People were used to helping each other. Charles at once invited him and his two friends to come for dinner. They accepted in the same spirit in which the car had been offered and accepted. It seemed a pleasant way to live, without suspicion, ready to give a stranger a chance.

Other cars stopped from time to time—a woman from the Grand Junction paper, to interview us. Where had we come from? Where were we going? What was the idea? She lined us up and took our pictures. The sun grew hotter. A reporter and two photographers from the Greenriver *Journal* came. Questions again—and we all went down and got in the boats with Les, so pictures could be made. In the intervals between such comings and goings, I crawled in among some bushes where there was a little thin shade and worked on a Double-Crostic I had tucked in my notebook when I left home and had had no time for till now.

Doc, looking very dejected, joined me in the late afternoon, "They tell me I can't go on."

I sympathized with him, told him I was just waiting to be thrown out myself. "It's Cataract they are all worried about. Evidently it is a bad canyon, and everybody has to be able to take care of himself."

"I'd be over this asthma attack before then," Doc said. "I know I would."

"Well," I said, "I suppose we have to do as we are told—after all, Charles and Don feel the responsibility. What will you do now?"

"Go on back to New York tomorrow, take the first boat home."

"It's a shame!" I said. "But you have gotten something out of it, haven't you?"

He nodded and left me then and went down to talk with Les in the boat. At any rate, I thought, he had met Les—and I was sure there was nobody like him in all the United Kingdom. But I felt as if the whole party were breaking up—Les and Doc going tomorrow. And maybe I, too—only why couldn't they just tell me it was too dangerous farther along down the river, at least let me know? Or was it still being considered?

I was not long finding out. Don and Charles came back from town and as we sat around waiting for our guests to arrive they began to say nice things about me. "You know," said Charles, "this trip has done wonders for you. Fourteen days and you have lost fourteen years."

"Oh yes?" I said, understanding at once what this was leading up to. "And if we kept on another few weeks I'd be back in a prenatal state, no doubt. Listen, why not just come right out and tell me the truth? I know you had to argue with Les, persuading him he could not possibly go on. And"—I nodded in the direction of Doc who was turning the chicken on the griddle—

"I know it was hard having to tell him he'd have to leave. But you don't need to smooth it over for me. Just come right out with it."

Don, who was standing behind me, put his two hands on my shoulders. "You're too precious to risk, that's all there is to it."

I looked round at him and laughed. "You diplomat! sugar-coating it like this!"

"But we have it all arranged," Charles said. "We've just been talking with the pilot who will fly in supplies to Hite. You can go on with us from here as far as Anderson's Bottom." Anderson's Bottom? It sounded like the tail end of civilization.

"Yes, and he will stop there and pick you up, fly you on down to Hite, where you can wait for us with the supplies while we run Cataract."

"What kind of plane?" I asked.

"It's a cub, very good and safe, all they ever use around here," Don said.

"And Jim Nixon says the pilot is one of the best."

Actually I was terrified at the thought. All I said was, "I'd be less scared in the boat, running Cataract."

Just then our guests arrived. It was a gay meal—chicken and sweet potatoes browned on the griddle, salad and for a special treat ice cream that Charles had brought back from town along with several bottles of fresh milk—the first we had had. The sun had gone down, but the clouds were still pink when I heard the sound of a plane and looked up.

"There goes your pilot now," Jim Nixon said. "Good little plane he's got."

That tiny little thing? The last rays of the sun struck it as it went by, high overhead. The wings glinted like tinsel as it wobbled across the sky. It looked like a toy, tiny and tinny, and the engine was too noisy, altogether too sputtery.

"Um-mm," I said. "It seems to be moving." That was the best I could say about it.

After dinner we all got into the two cars and drove back to the town—little more than a crossroads, it seemed by the light of sparse street lamps—and went to Jim Nixon's hotel room to see some pictures he had of the country. He and his friends were here because they owned a number of uranium claims and these pictures were some taken during their trips to remote regions. They were very interesting, the colored slides he threw on a screen for us. But I found myself nodding from time to time in the darkened room. I was not used to being up so late, and the air inside these four walls made me yawn and yawn. I think Bruce even dozed off, for when the light came on, he gave a great start and blinked as if he did not know where he was.

Back at camp, it was cool—a good night for sleeping. But all night there was a rumble of trucks on the road—trucks marked ACID, DYNAMITE, URANIUM, GAS. Obscene and horrible, they were. Well, I thought, between waking and sleeping, this will be my last night of listening to such things. But it wasn't. Next day Charles discovered something wrong with one of his cameras. He worked at it himself all the morning, looking more and more worried. He was afraid he would have to take it somewhere for expert repairs. I began to feel that we were destined to stay forever in this ungodly spot. But there were visitors. Uranium hunters—loneliest of lone men. They just wanted someone to talk to, I discovered. One of them sat on his heels in the broiling sun and talked to me for an hour or so, his truck, piled with equipment, parked on the level ground below the embankment that led to the bridge. He asked the usual questions about our Expedition and I gave him an account of it. Then I said, "And you—are you out for uranium?"

"Giving up," he said, pushing back his hat and mopping his round sun-blistered face with a blue bandana handkerchief.

"No luck?"

"Too many others before me. I'm sick of it. Off alone in this dry, rocky country, day after day—hot as—excuse me, ma'm, but that's what it is."

"What will you do now?"

"Go back to fishing."

"Fishing?"

"Salt-water man, that's me. I had me a boat on the West Coast, went all along the California shore and down into Mexican waters. Fishing. It was a good life. But what did I do? Give it all up for uranium. Uranium!" he snorted. "No, I'm going to sell my stuff I've got here and go on up to Alaska, get me a boat and go after salmon. They tell me the salmon fishing up that way is fine."

"It will be different from this anyway."

"You bet it will."

So I wished him luck and he went on his way.

I had just dragged my army cot back into the best bit of shade I could find when Doc came by. He had finished the breakfast dishes long ago, but with Bruce's help had rearranged all the contents of our supply boxes. He had listed what was in each and Bruce was now painting signs so there would not be such frantic searchings before every meal. "I think I'll go across the bridge to that little café and have some coffee. Want to come along? They say it's air-conditioned."

I looked at the long hot bridge, open to the broiling sun. "I'll just stick it out here, thank you. Mind you don't get a sunstroke on the way."

"I'll take it slowly."

"When will you be leaving us?"

"This afternoon, when Les goes. He'll take me to where I can get a bus. Around four I'll be leaving." He started away, then turned back. "I feel as if I hadn't been too good a companion on this trip. But—well, you know how it's been with me. I'm not always this way—I was a commando in the war—I just haven't felt up to the extra exertion of—"

"I know. It's too bad it worked out like this," I said, "so we didn't really get to know you at all. But we all liked you." I wanted him to know that.

I watched him climb the bank to the road and move, as slowly as an old man, across the bridge under the hot sun. It is like this so often, I thought. We meet people and never go beyond the first step, the opportunity passes without our ever reaching each other. Adrift, alone, we move on. It seemed a pity.

Well, what would I do now? I had finished my puzzle. Everyone was gone but Les, down in the boat, and Bruce, painting red letters on the boxes of supplies. I could write up my notes, maybe. Only they would be mostly expletives, I thought, watching another truck roll by. Yet why should I revile these trucks and wish to escape them? I had come out to see the world hadn't I? And they, with their ACID, URANIUM, GAS, EXPLOSIVES, DANGER, were certainly a part of the world I was living in. So why shrink from the sight of them? They were facts to be faced.

A car drove in under the embankment. A man and a girl got out and walked to the bank of the river just under the bridge. They stood there, in profile to me, looking at each other, talking, looking at the river as if they did not see it. Her blond hair hung down on her shoulders, metallic in the sunlight. She had rather large bold features and her figure in a sun-back print was what used to be called overblown. The man, tall and faintly disheveled, had the pallor of one not often in the sun. They were utterly absorbed in each other. But they were not having much fun, I thought, as they turned and went back to the car, enclosed in their own minds and bodies, wrapped in a palpable madness, seeing neither our camp nor the boats nor Les sitting there waiting, seeing nothing in this world but themselves.

Tony came back and he and Bruce and I had sandwiches with fresh tomatoes—a real treat. Bruce took lunch to Les in the boat. By now the sun was everywhere, there was not a bush that gave me any shade. Tony saw my struggle to find a cooler spot and rigged up a blanket on two boards and an oar, and that gave me some protection from the sun, though it cut out what breeze there was.

In mid-afternoon a car drove in, a woman and a girl got out.
I knew them at once—that beautiful girl Les was engaged to.
"Where's Les?" she cried and dashed down the bank to the boat.
The older woman was his mother, I was sure, so I went to speak
to her, and invite her into the shade of my blanket.

"I won't go down the bank," she said. "And I'll just sit
if you don't mind—I have a wooden leg."

So we sat and talked while Bruce and Tony gathered together
Les's baggage and Doc's and put it in the car, then went down to
help Les up the bank. I reassured her as much as I could about
Les's injury, though she seemed to have taken it without anxiety.
All he needed was to rest and give it a chance to heal, I said.
"Doc has put an emergency cast on but it ought to be X-rayed.
Les doesn't want to go to a hospital. He ought to, and I hope
you will make him." She seemed so gentle and quiet that I
wondered whether she would have much influence with Les, who
when he made up his mind was hard to budge. "He is obstinate
as all get-out," I said. "You probably know."

She smiled. "I know how obstinate he is. But he will go
for his X-rays, don't worry." She sounded as if she was quite
accustomed to managing whatever she needed to take charge of;
she sounded as if she could meet any disaster undismayed. And
she was really a beautiful woman, I thought, as we sat there
talking about our journey, about the girl Les was to marry so
soon. She had lovely, regular features, dark curling hair without a trace of gray, and above all an air of grace and serenity.
No matter what had been the tragedies of her life, she had
transcended them all. What was it that had made her like this?
Was she just born so? Was it the Mormon religion? What was
it? I wanted to ask her. But how could I so intimately question
a stranger? I did say, "Now I've met you I can understand
how it was that Les, who looks so big and tough and rough—"
I floundered, thinking I had said too much.

She nodded. "I know. Those river clothes of his—"

So I went on, "I see now how it was that he was so kind and

thoughtful of me in every way. He could not have done more for me if I had been—you."

"That's nice to hear," she said.

They came up the bank now, Les with Tony on one side, Bruce on the other. He hopped along, his girl following with an armful of extra jackets, his canteen and other small belongings. "Hello, Ma," he said. Then looking around, "Where's Doc?"

"You'll find him at that little café down the road," I said, "trying to survive the heat."

So we said good-by. They got in the car and drove away to look for Doc. And now Doc was gone too, something of a mystery to us all, and we perhaps the losers by it, I thought.

So the afternoon passed—and ended with bad news. Charles had been unable to get his camera mended. He would have to take it to Salt Lake City. Fred was going with him, to keep him company, he said. "How about coming along too?"

I considered it. "I might. I have friends—" But my address book was in my civilization suitcase waiting for me in California and I had forgotten, or at least at the moment could not think of, the names of those delightful people I had met at Fontaine-bleau—all from Utah—who had invited me to stay with them if I ever went West. "Or I could stop in Provo—that is on the way, isn't it? I have friends there—at the University. The Bailifs and—" But they'd probably be away. "No, I'll stay here." It seemed simpler. Besides it had come to be a little private endurance test. I was going to stick it out.

Fred said, "Well, sleep in my tent. It will be better than this—" he waved a hand at my disheveled-looking arrangements. "You will like my air mattress—the air usually stays in it till you get to sleep and then it doesn't matter."

"Maybe I'll try it," I said and laughed and waved them good-by.

I did look at it. It was a beautiful tent, but the air mattress was right on the ground, I would have to leave the flap open for air—and I kept thinking it would be like an invitation to rattle-snakes to come right in and make themselves at home. So I went back to my own quarters.

It was just a little later that another car came. The new boatman had arrived, a young man with a week-old beard; he had just come in from another boat trip, he said. His wife, Virginia, was with him, had driven him down from Provo. She would spend the night and go back the next day. She was slim and tall and quick-spoken and wearing the smock which is nowadays the equivalent of an announcement. He was not so big a man as Les, but he looked husky and well able to swing an oar. And that was what we needed. I was at once interested in his name, Alden Galloway, and as soon as he had unloaded the car and come over to join his wife and me, I asked him where his family had come from, and were they related to the Mississippi Galloways. I suppose it is my Southern upbringing that makes me sniff like a bloodhound on the trail at the sound of a familiar name. I have noticed the same thing, however, in other places—New England, for instance, and Scotland.

"No," Al said, "I don't know of any Southern kin. My folks were Scotch, way back."

"Well," I said, now I had had a good look at him, "if you ever want to see your portrait, especially if you let that beard of yours grow a little longer, just drop in at the chapel at Millsaps College in Jackson, Mississippi." The resemblance was truly striking—the same high cheekbones, wide forehead, the very set of the eyes, the same rather deliberate movement, yet with a suggestion of power behind it. For I had known Bishop Galloway from my childhood, he was one of my father's best friends, and I remembered not only his looks but his manner. "You'll see yourself hanging on the wall there," I added.

"Well, I always thought I might hang—but I didn't expect to see myself at it," Al said.

The next day was a long one. Virginia got off early. Bruce,

Tony, Al and I amused ourselves playing games—one of Tony's
—"My grandmother told me to go up to the attic and fetch her
a—" Then each one added another item, repeating all that had
gone before. Bruce was very good at it, also at a game I remembered called teakettle, where two talked, substituting *teakettle* for as many homonyms as we could think up for one word,
the others guessing. Then they all went off to have a cool drink in
the town and I held down the camp. A good moment to have a
fine cool bath in the river, I thought.

It was shady down the bank, but there was the little problem
of the traffic on the bridge. I felt rather like someone taking
a bubble bath on the stage—the Green River mud substituting
for bubbles. The boats were some protection and I managed to
have a most refreshing scrub without too many cars slowing up
as they went over the bridge. I was dressed none too soon. As I
climbed back up the bank a car arrived and a young man got
out and came over to me. He asked all the usual questions, went
down and looked at the boats and came back again.

"I've just come off the river—up about Echo Park," he said.
"I wanted to keep on, come down this way too. But the friend I
was with said it was too tough. And here you are, going all the
way to Lake Mead."

"Yes." I did not consider it necessary to explain that I was
not being allowed to run Cataract; I thought the plane ride
a far more perilous undertaking.

"Well, I wonder—would you let me snap a picture of you to
take home with me and show him?"

"And tell him a gray-haired woman is doing what he was
scared to do?" I laughed. "All right, go ahead." So I stood there
beside a tamarisk bush and he took my picture and went off
happily to shame his friend with it.

There were others who came. Three men in khaki who just
wanted to talk. "Uranium?" I asked.

"Oil," they told me. "Only it was a dry hole," another added.

"Too bad," I said. "I've got land down in Mississippi. There's a big oil field there and it stopped right where my fence begins. So I know how you feel."

"Oh, we don't care."

"No?" What superhumans were these, I wondered, who were beyond having any use for an oil well? I wasn't that far gone myself, and they were forty years my juniors.

"Well, it's this way," one of them said. "We just dig. So it makes no difference to us. We're setting out tomorrow for another location forty miles south of here."

So there were the gamblers and the diggers, and the diggers were the richer by not caring.

When they had gone I went back down to the edge of the river to enjoy the shade and the breath of coolness that came over the water. I sat in the hollow of a step we had worn in the bank with our passing up and down, my hands clasped around my knees. The river made a pleasant small rippling sound as it struck against the pillars of the bridge. The tamarisk petals from the bushes on the bank drifted past me like pink snow and I felt all at once quite happy, to be alone, to be here. It had not been so bad, this awful spot with the trucks and the heat and probable typhoid germs. I had gotten more of the flavor of the country from just staying here and having people stop by to pass the time of day than if I had traveled all the way to Salt Lake City with Charles and Fred.

In spite of the addition of Al Galloway, it seemed a diminished group that gathered round the table that night. Don had done his marketing, and as usual just before leaving civilization we had steaks for dinner, each one about the size I would serve to three people at home. And there were extras, as Don had thought Charles and Fred might be back in time to eat with us. But all the steaks disappeared without too great difficulty. I went early to bed and before I slept heard Charles and Fred arriving. Good, I thought; we would be off tomorrow right after breakfast.

14

At breakfast Charles reported that everyone he had talked with said it was a shame for us to go through Cataract, that remote and unexplored canyon, without a Geiger counter. There was a good chance of uranium through there. Why not form a company, buy a Geiger counter and stake some claims? So we sat long, talking about that—what should we call the company? The Hit-or-Miss Company, someone suggested. Then there was the question of legal agreement. If we should really find a claim worth millions, then we ought to have everything all settled so there could be no disputes about who owned what. It seemed to me this was going to take forever. At last I said, "See here, are we not all honorable men? Can't we just agree among ourselves to share equally and go on?"

So it was settled, and Charles went off to buy the Geiger counter. I got my duffel packed, Bruce and Al began loading the boats and we swapped ideas on what we would do with our uranium money if and when we got it. Then the Howland brothers arrived with the pretty young wife of one of them. They were farmers, sons of Wild Bill Howland, they said. "But that's a lot of newspaper nonsense," one of them told me. "He went in and got a desperado who had fled into the canyons and the sheriff had not been able to find him. So the papers made a big to-do about it."

"There were two Howland brothers in the Powell expedition," I said.

Yes, they told us, kin. Same family. They were interested in

176

my living in New England. Their folks had come west long ago, had come from Plymouth originally. So I told them about the old Howland house which is still preserved there.

After the Howlands had gone, another car drove in. I really felt we should have had refreshments to serve—we had so many visitors during our stay here. These were of a different sort. Easterners—and even after so brief a stay in the West I knew them at once for that. Just as abroad we are always spotted immediately as Americans. This was a couple from Philadelphia, the Merckes, with their children, "doing the West," as they said, and evidently having a good time. They were interested in everything, looked at the boats, asked where we had come from and where we were going. Mrs. Mercke said, "It seems to me I read in some magazine about an expedition like this—surely there could not be more than one—"

"This is it," I told her.

So off they went, feeling that meeting us had been a real event. The next people who drove in were not visitors. Theirs was a shabby car with a trailer, and looking across I saw that it had been halted for repairs. Two men and a young woman were at work taking off a wheel, hammering on a piece of metal. A small boy had jumped out and gone to the river's edge, where he was throwing stones into the water. Two little girls were walking around investigating their surroundings, and an old woman sat in the car. I went over to her. "I see you are from Oklahoma," I said, when I had read the license plate and had come to the door of the car. And, I thought, you are straight out of *The Grapes of Wrath*.

"Yes, ma'm, that's where we come from. Won't you get in out of the sun and set a while?"

"Thank you. It is hot." I climbed in on the front seat and sat turned around so I could see her. She was a broad-faced, shapeless old woman solidly, stolidly planted on the back seat, and she fanned herself with a comic magazine. Her gray-streaked hair was drawn back tightly to a small knot at the nape of her neck. The two little girls came and sat beside her, their wide-apart brown eyes fastened on me. They had very pale brown hair and the most level straight dark brows I have ever seen. This gave them an air of great earnestness and intensity.

"My oldest daughter, she's helping with the trailer. Broke an axle or something back yonder a ways. That's her little boy. These here are my two youngest."

Heavens, I'd taken her for the grandmother. She must be years younger than I—unless she was another Biblical Sarah. "Where are you bound for?"

"Oregon."

"That's a long way." I looked through the back window at the trailer, heaped high with household goods. "You going to settle out there?"

"Well, we might, then again we might not. Just depends on how things look."

"Goodness, you've got courage—leaving your home and setting out—"

"Well, things weren't so good back there, so we just picked up and left. We got kin in Oregon."

"Oh. That's good. They can help you get settled."

"Yessum, that's how we figgered."

"Did you hate to leave home? I mean, it will be quite a change, moving so far—"

"Well, no, ma'm. We're used to moving. Lived all over Oklahoma."

"We've been through seven states, so far," one of the little girls said.

"And we'll be in twelve before we get there, and—"

"Or fourteen, depending on how we go," the first one broke in. They had soft, low voices and spoke quickly without taking their eyes from my face, without change of expression.

"That's a pleasant way to learn geography, isn't it?"

"Yes, ma'm," they said together.

"Those your folks over yonder?" The old woman gestured with a thumb in the direction of our camp.

My folks? In a way they were. I nodded. "We've come from upriver and we're going downriver." I felt as if only the fundamentals would be a proper answer. Anything more would be nonsense.

"Well, I declare." But she said it without amazement; she said it as if nothing in this world would surprise her.

"In the boats?" one of the girls asked.

"In the boats," I said. Somehow, the whole Expedition had taken on an aspect of unreality, of remoteness from real life.

"Just out for pleasure?" the woman asked.

"Well—yes, in a way. One of us is making a picture of the canyons, a movie."

"Oh," she said. All three continued to regard me, their faces calm and earnest, unchanging.

I pushed the car door open, looked back at the little girls. "You have beautiful eyes."

"Thank you, ma'm," they said and almost, for a moment, I thought they were going to smile.

"Well," I said, rather awkwardly, "I'd better be getting back." I climbed down from the high front seat of the old Ford. "I wish you luck on your journey."

"The same to you, ma'm," they said in unison, and with singular dignity.

I went slowly back to camp. Tony, carrying a box on his shoulders, said, "Been talking to the Okies?"

"Don't call them that!" I cried so fiercely that Tony looked at me in some surprise. "That's the trouble in all the world today—turmoil, revolution—don't you see? We who have more—or think we have—we must grant them their dignity. That's all they're really asking."

Tony was thoughtful for a moment, then he gave me his charming smile. "Okay, no Okie," he said.

We were about ready to take off. But Charles had gone to return the car to Jim Nixon. While we waited—for it was a mile and a half to town—other visitors stopped by, a tall man in dark-rimmed glasses with his teen-age daughter and a young son of about seven who tore right on down to the river's edge to look at the boats which they had spied from the bridge. The father introduced himself; Worth Offet was his name, and he was here looking after some uranium claims. He had over one hundred here and there. He knew the country rather well, and when we told him where we were going, he said he had seen some of that section, it was hard going and lonely. He got around fairly well in a jeep in spite of there being no roads. He said there were some low cables across the river not far below here and we had better look out for them. He told how he got stranded once in one of the canyons, ran out of gas and had to climb out and walk miles to get some. He had to lower it down into the canyon from the top of a three-hundred-foot wall. A lonely country, he said.

"Did you ever hear of Anderson's Bottom?" I asked.

"Oh yes. In fact I expect to be there myself June 30."

This was a great comfort to me. I had pictured the place as the end of nowhere, just from the sound of the name. Now I had a vision of a delightful small village, a veritable oasis in the blank, bleak empty spaces of the map. And of course it would have to be a fairly big place, to have a landing field. I should have thought of that before. Now I felt reassured. For I had resolved that I would not let the expedition be delayed there on my account. If Jim Hurst was not there with the plane when we arrived, I could find a nice hotel and be comfortable and get a good little rest while waiting for him. Charles had said that when we left Greenriver we would be completely out of touch with the world. But he perhaps did not know about Anderson's Bottom. In my imagination it grew into quite a little metropolis.

It was after eleven when we finally pushed off, Jim Nixon
and a friend—they had very kindly driven Charles back to
camp—standing on the bank to wave us off. We passed under
the bridge and looked back at it with what I am sure were
mingled feelings. I was delighted to be leaving it, escaping the
cars, the great rumbling trucks with their terrifying EXPLOSIVES,
ACID, URANIUM signs.

Charles, cranking his camera, said, "Take a good look. We'll
see nothing like it for the next three hundred miles."

That was a sobering thought. We were off again, on our own.
And no doctor. But we had the medicine chest—and Bruce, who
knew how to bind up broken bones. I opened my red plaid
parasol and faced forward. "How far to the geyser?" I asked
Charles. For we had heard there was one within a short distance
of the river, not far away, a natural wonder we should not miss.

"Not more than six miles," he said. "On the left. We'll have
to watch for it. A road comes in to it, off the main highway."

It was lunchtime when we saw two cars parked, as if waiting
for something to happen. This must be where the geyser shot up
every hour or so. And it must be nearly time. So we landed and
taking lunch and cameras mounted the bank and walked across
a hot open rocky space to where there were indications that
water had spouted up and run down over the slope to the river.

"Now," said Charles when he had set up his cameras and we
were all gathered around the lunchbox making sandwiches,
"when the thing goes into action, I want you all to dash across
and stand there looking at it while I get the picture."

We agreed, and were just well launched on our sandwiches
when there was a rumbling sound and a white column of water
shot up. We all sprang up—some to their cameras, the rest of
us rushing forward as Charles had directed. It was a beautiful
sight in the sunlight, this white plume of water at least 150 feet
tall and bending, swaying in the wind. It was supposed to continue for half an hour. But as soon as it had reached its height

and before the cameras could possibly get to work, it began to die down, and was gone in no more than a minute.

My dash had carried me quite close to it, sandwich in hand, and so I went on to scoop up some of the water that was running down over the rocky uneven surface. It felt warm to my fingers and had a queer, chemical smell. In one place the recurrent fall of water had dug out of the rock a small bathtub-shaped depression, open at the lower end. The action of the water and its chemicals on the hollowed-out rock had flaked its lining and colored it so it looked like curly fish scales that were yellow, orange, chartreuse and brown, and that glistened now, wet with the geyser water and illuminated by the sun.

Coming back to join the others I felt all of a sudden that a breeze was blowing where a breeze had no business to be. I stopped short; one hand went to the seat of my pants.

"What's the matter?" Don asked. For all his air of easy nonchalance, he never missed anything.

"I've got a—hole—a rent—as big as a house." Well, it felt that big—a three-cornered tear I could not cover with my hand. "Why didn't somebody tell me?"

"We didn't see it." Tony laughed.

They all laughed then, and I said, "I'll go down to the boats and change—give me three minutes."

Luckily I had another pair of blue jeans in my duffel. And perhaps when I got to Hite I could mend these. I was allowed more than three minutes, but at last they came over the rocks and down through the tamarisks to join me, and we set out again.

This was a stretch of dead land we passed through, with low walls, with a wind that blew without ceasing, and sand, sand everywhere pouring down over the cliffs in little rivulets. The engine droned steadily in our ears, and the heat of the sun was a weight across my back. I lay down on my stomach across the gunwale and asked Tony to scoop up a bucket of water and pour it over my head and shoulders. This was a great help. The others tried it; they called it the "treatment" and said it was a great invention.

Everyone was for the first time a little bored, this day. Al had brought a stack of murders with him and he lost himself in one with a busty belle on the back. You would think that the general public ought to be fed up with the female bosom by now. What with the ads and the paperbacks. But they seem insatiable.

Tony in the small boat ahead found a jar of salted peanuts and pelted Al with them. He just turned his head and caught them in his mouth. Bruce and Fred fenced with oars—and nearly fell overboard. For a while I amused myself studying Don's back. He sat in the small boat, looking ahead, bare to the waist. There was not an ounce of spare fat on his back; each muscle was plainly visible. I tried to name them—once I could have done it—trapezius, latissimus dorsi,—I used to know them all. I could get no further than that. Was I losing my memory?

"What are you sitting there looking so solemn about?" Charles demanded.

"Oh yes, I remember now, it is the spini erecti."

Charles looked at me in some alarm, as if he thought the heat had at last got me.

"It's Don's back; it's so beautifully clear, the muscles, I mean. I'm dissecting them—in my mind. Trying to name them."

Charles shook his head. "With Al reading a murder and you carving up Don, this trip is getting really dangerous."

At this moment a piece of paper blew past me and Al let out a yell. "What on earth—" I began.

Al looked back at the paper, floating for a moment, then caught and drawn under the surface of the water. "It's the last page of my murder. Now I'll never know—"

We all laughed at his expression of despair. So with such small amusements the day passed slowly. We came to the mouth of the San Rafael and moved on. Fred, who had been reading Powell, said it was here that Powell's party stopped for a bit of exploring and found many Indian relics, arrowheads and flint chips. Tony was all for going ashore and finding a few to take home. Charles vetoed that. "We've got to get on down river." He looked worried as he got out his map.

I must have shown my surprise—this was so in contrast to his usual leisurely way of taking things. "Are you thinking about getting me to Anderson's Bottom to meet the plane?"

"It's partly that. But mostly because of the river. They told us at Greenriver that it is falling fast. If we want to get through, we have to hurry on."

For the first time then I began to notice the watermarks along the banks. It was evident that the level was far below high water. That was a hazard that had not occurred to me. Suppose the river ran dry? Did it ever? It should be getting bigger and deeper as more streams came in. But the San Rafael had been a mere trickle. "Maybe it will be better when the Colorado joins us," I said.

"Maybe," Charles said.

Now in the late afternoon we began to enter another canyon. This was Labyrinth and well named, for the river took a tortuous course through it. The walls mounted higher, and from over the rims of scalloped red and yellow sandstone, orange-colored sand poured down in small waterfalls. What a desert there must be out there on each side of us, I thought. The walls were at first for the most part homogeneous, then odd shapes and various-colored layers began to be visible. There was one bulging formation jutting out from the cliff wall like a roundhouse built of fluted horizontal ribbons, mud-colored and orange and a queer pale green we had not seen before.

It was difficult to find a camping spot. We tried several places, drawing up under the bank where the walls had withdrawn to leave a space thickly overgrown with stunted willows and tamarisks. But either the bank was too steep or too quicksandy or had too thick a tangle of growth for landing. In one such spot,

Fred leaped out with rope in hand, only to have the bank cave away underfoot so that one moment he was balanced precariously there, the next he was in the water up to his chin, looking altogether surprised and very solemn with mud covering his glasses so he could see nothing. But still holding the rope.

A little later we came on a beautiful campsite where the high east wall curved back in a great concave, shelved sweep, and beyond a growth of stunted low trees there was an open level space with a rock floor. Charles found enough small stones to build an excellent fireplace; Tony hustled about gathering wood and soon had a good fire going so Fred could get dry. He was shivering from his plunge in the river. I pitched my tent a little apart, among the bushes on the river's bank. And Don and Bruce had dinner ready by the time I had finished. We had a delicious beef stew. It is remarkable what comes out of cans nowadays, especially when taken with good appetite. And there was a superb salad of fresh lettuce, carrots, green peppers and cucumbers especially mixed by Fred. As we ate the canyon began to fill with darkness but the sky was a dusty yellow and rose and the top of the cliff behind us caught the last rays of the sun and turned to brilliant gold.

That night I lay awake for a long time on my army cot with the tent sides flung back. Don and Bruce and Al had taken their sleeping bags to an upper ledge of the cliff and I saw their flashlights moving about there, then darkness. The young moon went down and the stars grew brighter. The Great Dipper lay on top of the cliff and slowly dropped behind it.

Next morning for the first time I overslept. Everyone had finished breakfast by the time I was dressed and packed. The coffee had boiled away so I had only half a cup, but strong. There was no wind this morning; the river ran calm and unruffled save by small rosettes where a counter-current formed a whirlpool. We got off early—or so it seemed to me, having wakened so late. It was a relief to have no wind. I could keep my plaid parasol open now. The scenery grew in magnificence as the morning passed. The red sandstone was streaked with purple and black streamers; there were caves in the wall of the cliffs that now held not even a small sprig of sage. Now and then we ran into swifter water.

Suddenly on our left, high on a sheer red wall, we saw carvings and stopped to investigate and take pictures. I sat in the boat while the others went up over the crumbly talus and the boulders to set our sign there with the others. Charles made an outline drawing, Bruce and Al with our prospector's pick chipped away at the rock till they shaped an oval camera lens with an arrow going through it and 1955 below. It was hard, hot work and took them nearly an hour. I copied down the other signs— "Neville's Expedition, 1938" and insignia of the U.S. Engineers with the date 1900. There was a reclining, cupidlike figure, the significance of which I could not imagine and something else that looked like a buffalo head. All rather recent, unlike the Indian petroglyphs we had been told we would find further down the canyons. There were several names too—Clyde Eddy, Bert Loper and USGS, 1915.

The walls rose higher as we went on that afternoon, a thousand feet or more of Navajo, Chinle and Moenkopi sandstone. Every now and then we came on white painted marks or a heap of stones with a stick propped upright, showing that a uranium claim had been made. This rather discouraged us as to our own prospects, but here the river was still easily navigable from Greenriver and it was perhaps but to be expected that claims would be staked out. Further down, in Cataract and below, we all thought it would be unlikely that prospectors had ventured.

The river doubled back on itself more than once, so that after an hour or more we were directly behind the spot where we had lunched on a narrow sand spit. Now and then we heard the dull boom of dynamite, and once where the left wall had moved back to leave a long slope and an open space we saw three men digging. Then the cliffs closed in again, sheer walls reaching up to the sky with fingerlike formations, pointing into the cloudless blue. We passed from Labyrinth to Stillwater Canyon in the course of the afternoon and here too there were manmade, but deserted holes dug out on the slopes, and everywhere uranium claims. In one place we saw what seemed to be a working mine with tents for the miners and a rough road that came curving in from the outside world.

It was late in the afternoon and we had seen no sign of life for some time when, as we passed close to the right bank, a solitary man emerged from the bushes. He shouted and beckoned and above the drone of the motor I heard his call—"Hello, hello—coffee! . . . Come in, come in." Don shouted something back, I did not hear what, and we chugged on downstream. The man stood there looking after us, a lost, lonely figure that haunts me to this day. He has somehow come to mean to me all the lonely people in the world, crying out to the rest of us, saying wait, wait, listen, there is something I need to tell, and you to hear—like the Ancient Mariner—wait, wait—but we passed by on the other side.

The scene around us took on more color as the sun dropped lower in the sky. With the red, which was now so familiar to us, there appeared chocolate streaks, lines of powder blue, aqua and bright yellow. Ahead, the cliffs loomed yet higher, hiding the sun so an early twilight came upon us, and far in the distance the Butte of the Cross seemed to block the passage of the river, saying, "Go no further." Don studied his map in the dusk, bent over, intent. Where was Anderson's Bottom? Wherever there were a level space and trees we looked, in vain.

Then on the left bank Bruce discovered some signs of life and we moved over in that direction, too late for anything but shouts, for the current carried us below the figures there. Don cupped his hands to his mouth. "Anderson's Bottom?"

A man holding up a small child and a woman with another child clinging to her skirts and a third apart a little stood there shaking their heads, their words lost to us.

Don cut off the motor. "The landing field, where is it?"

The man pointed behind him. ". . . one here. Not Anderson's."

"Where's Anderson's?"

He shook his head. We drifted on, the motor began again its noisy chugging. I kept looking back, and as long as light held I could see that small lonely family standing there watching us. Dusk began to fill up the canyon; a young moon came over the edge of a high black cliff. We had never before been on the river so late.

Don headed in toward a bank where there was a tangled growth, dark and mysterious. "It's got to be here," he called back to us. Here? There was nothing here but a thicket and the dark beyond. Fred jumped out of the small boat. His feet sank deep in the boggy sand while he was tying us up. Don plunged into the thick bushes, Charles and Al at his heels. We sat waiting till a shout told us this was the right place. Bruce at once got out the axe and began hacking at bushes, throwing them down on the shelf of sand to make a passageway possible. The river, shrinking to a lower level, had left this damp soft shelf. Al came back for the axe. "We have to cut our path through," he said.

I sat silent, watching all this activity with a sinking feeling in the pit of my stomach. So this was Anderson's Bottom, this bog, this thicket with no passage through till it was hacked out—and what was beyond? I made my way along the *Brontosaur* to the small boat, jumped off and, pushing brush aside, mounted the bank and with difficulty passed through the thicket toward the sound of an axe. Al was hauling a dead tree trunk out of the way, Don was chopping branches. They paused to let me pass. I ducked under a limb and came out into an open space, a rough field bound on three sides by the black bulk of rock rising to jag the moon-bright sky. There was not a light—unless that was one on the far side, dimly shining through the trees. Of all the desolate Godforsaken spots! And it was here that the plane was to land tomorrow morning and take off with me.

Tony, who had followed me through the jungle, got to work building a fire on the edge of the field and by its light I set up my tent not far away. Fred began opening cans of spaghetti and meat balls for our dinner and some cans of pineapple and apricots for dessert. It was rather a silent meal that night. We had had our longest day on the river and everyone was subdued. What talk there was was all of Cataract, which they would enter tomorrow. I was wishing I would be with them. Maybe—"Can a plane land on this small a space?" I asked, thinking that if it couldn't, there would be nothing for me but to go on with the others through Cataract.

"Oh sure," Don said. "Those small planes don't need much room."

"Suppose Jim Hurst doesn't come."

"We'll wait till he does," Charles said.

"No, you must get off early tomorrow. You can just leave me—with some cans of food. If you wait here, the river may be too low for you to get through at all."

"We're not going to leave you."

"Well, we'll see about that tomorrow," I said. But the prospect was not a pleasant one. I looked across the field to where I thought I had seen a light earlier. There was no light there now.

In my tent I could not get to sleep; I turned and tossed on my army cot, which had never before seemed so hard and narrow. I heard the others moving about, then quiet. For the first night of the whole journey I could not hear the sound of the river. It gave me a queer blank feeling. I remembered all at once how it was one night in the middle of an ocean crossing when the engines broke down and stillness awoke me in sharp alarm. It was as if a clock had stopped in a silent room, as if someone had stopped breathing. I flung back the flap of my tent. A bright, cold moon shone down on the rough, dry grass of the field. Its light fell on the great cliff on the other side and seemed to bring it close, so there was little room left, not nearly enough for a plane to land.

Then when the moon was high in the sky, the birds began to sing. The thicket behind me was alive with their voices, as varied and persistent as the mockingbird's, with answering small trills and calls from far away up and down the river bank. I could not sleep for their din and for thinking, thinking, about tomorrow. The birds sang on for hours while the moon crossed the open sky, hung for a little on the edge of the black wall of a cliff and then dropped at last behind it. Why was it that on other nights there had been no birds? Why had they all gathered here tonight? As if to answer me there came from above and very near a repetitive cry—"Tee-deet-tee do, tee-deet-tee-do." To pick your bones, to pick your bones, it seemed to say.

All right, all right, I answered. Go ahead and welcome—if

you get a chance. They'll be no further use to me. But pick them clean, pick them clean. And after that I fell into an uneasy sleep, broken by the first light of dawn. I dressed quickly and packed my bags, moving quietly about my task. There was no stirring from Fred's tent or Charles's. Beyond the dead campfire the others lay like mummies in their sleeping bags. I left my tent without rolling it up—lest I wake them—and set out across the field toward the far corner where I thought I had seen a light the night before. If only there was one human being here then maybe I would be allowed to wait, and not delay the others. The dry grass crackled under my feet; I stumbled over rough places. It was chilly this early morning, the field still in shadow of a towering rock that rose, triangular as a gigantic bulky flatiron, from what seemed to be the middle of the river. There were a few trees at the far side of the field. I passed under them, looked back to get my direction right and went on beyond several great boulders that had fallen from the purply-red rocky wall that bound the field on the far side. There was no sign of human habitation here, only the rocks, a few bushes and what might have once been a narrow trail. Then the red wall closed in again. That light must have been nothing more than the moon shining down on the dew-wet surface of a rock.

The first rays of the sun struck the top of the cliff above me as I turned to come back to camp. I would just stay here alone, I thought, for courage had come with the sun. After all, what was there to harm me? And hadn't that man—the one with the pretty young daughter—Worth Offet—hadn't he said he would be at Anderson's Bottom on the 30th of June? I could wait for him if Jim Hurst had cracked up, forgotten, or maybe never really planned to come at all. With the river falling every day, the rocks of Cataract would leave no room for the boats to get through. They must go on at once. I did not want their blood on my head. But Charles had said in that quiet tone of authority which he so seldom used, "We'll wait." Yes, they would wait, no doubt about it. So now I began to wish with all my heart for Jim Hurst and the plane.

Suddenly there was a whirr, a buzz, a roar over my head. From the edge of the red cliff the redder plane was coming down, down to touch and bounce and run on to the far end of the field and turn to taxi back. Thank heaven, I thought, thank heaven for all people in this world who do what they say they will do, who arrive on time.

Before I could get back to camp, it had come to life, everyone crawling out of tent and sleeping bag. The plane had come to a halt nearby, Jim Hurst had sprung out and now, going round to the back of it, he picked it up by the tail and turned it round for the take-off. It was that little and light!

"But you'll stay for breakfast," Don was saying, and Tony was already gathering sticks to start the fire.

Jim looked around and up at the sky. He was a sunburned young man with wide-set eyes, grave lips and an air of matter-of-fact confidence. "The wind is coming up," he said, as if that were an answer. "Are you my passenger?"

"Yes, and I'm packed—all but my tent, and maybe I'll leave that to come in the boat."

"Good idea. I'm already pretty heavily loaded."

"Then maybe I'd better leave my duffel too—I can manage." I had a swift vision of the plane trying to get up and failing to rise above the level of the cliffs.

"No, no, I reckon that'll be all right."

He reckoned, did he? Just reckoned it would be all right! "I'll roll up my tent, then I'll be all ready."

Charles started off through the thicket, calling back, "Just let me get my camera. I want a shot of this."

I wanted him to get it—it might be the last ever seen of me, who could tell? Also I was desparate for my coffee. Surely nobody could ask me to mount this perilous little mosquito on an empty stomach. I looked around and saw that Tony was just filling the coffeepot from the canteen. The fire he had started looked weak and pale. Maybe by the time I got my tent rolled up—

Fred said, "Never mind your tent. I'll attend to that for you."

And Jim Hurst said, "We'd better not wait. The wind is rising fast—in a few minutes I won't be able to take off."

Bruce threw my duffel bags in on top of the boxes of supplies that filled the plane to the brim. Jim went round and climbed into his place. I looked at the others standing about, a quick glance that passed from one face to the other. Then I said, "I wish I had had some coffee—is there anything left in that can?"

Tony ran and got it. "Half an apricot," he said.

I reached down in the can and took it out in my fingers and choked it down. "Good-by," I said rather breathlessly. "Good luck on Cataract. I'll be waiting for you at Hite. Say good-by to Charles"—for he had not yet come with the cameras. Then I bent myself around to fit, and Fred helped me up and into the small front seat beside Jim Hurst. I suppose they all said good-by—I could hear nothing. All my attention was fixed on looking nonchalant. Then the roar of the engine drowned out everything and we started bouncing down the field. Jim reached across me. "That door—it doesn't fasten very well," he said. He opened it and slammed it shut, shook it—and let it go. Maybe it was tight and maybe it wasn't. I looked around for something to hang on to—nothing but the worn, slippery leather seat.

At the end of the field we turned and came to a halt while the engine roared louder and louder, shaking the plane till all the landscape round about us seemed to quiver and quake. Or was it just me? Both, no doubt. Then we were off, bouncing and wobbling over the rough field. I don't know when we left the ground, but I suddenly knew we were no longer bouncing, just wobbling. We were up, circling—and I saw the campsite, the plume of smoke from the fire and small figures waving, Charles pointing his camera up toward us. I tried to wave and my arm would not move. I must relax, I thought, and shut my eyes and made each small muscle go limp. Now to be light as a feather, to be lighter than air. I opened my eyes as we cleared the cliff and mounted higher. Keep on turning, engine, I kept saying in my mind. Turn on, roar and spit but turn on, gas keep flowing, and all you little metal parts, hang together now.

Jim Hurst was shouting in my ear, pointing downward. "The canyon . . . Colorado . . ." He tilted one wing down and I had to look lest he tilt still further. There below us shadowy still was the gorge of the Green and another canyon coming in, brown water joining brown water. He straightened the plane and we went on, yet so vast was the expanse of bleak, bare, rocky land below us now orange and rosy in the sunlight that we seemed not to be moving at all, but hanging balanced on uneven keel in the midst of space. The Butte of the Cross was only a small hump, disappearing behind us.

I gathered my voice into sound. "No rapids," I shouted.

". . . wait . . . show you . . ."

Conversation was impossible. Again I spoke to my muscles, saying, relax, relax, the rock down there will be hard whether you hit it tied in a knot or limp. I crossed my knees and leaned back and took long deep breaths. Again I wished I might have had some coffee. Surely that was why my stomach felt so queer. The slow moments passed, the engine roared on, the plane shook its way through the sky. Then Jim was saying something, he was tipping the wing. I looked down. We were skimming the brink of the canyon, weaving in and out, following its winding course. Sheer walls fell away below us a thousand, two thousand feet or more to where a narrow white thread of water made its way. And yet from here it seemed motionless, without a ripple.

"Rapids," Jim Hurst shouted.

I nodded. He straightened the plane and on we went, leaving the canyon and the Colorado and taking a beeline for Hite. We had been up less than an hour when he said, "There—Hite."

I looked down—and saw nothing.

"We'll wake them up." He banked and turned and all at once we were skimming low.

I saw a few shacks, some tents, a gully with a sparse sprinkling of green along its banks, the river, broad and brown, then we headed away from all of that. I caught a few words of what Jim was saying: ". . . mile out . . . landing field." Then that was Hite back there! Where on earth could I stay in such a place? I should have brought my tent. And how would I get back there if the landing field was so far away? Meanwhile—to land, that was the immediate problem. We circled round between the river and a brown level butte. There was even less room here than there had been at Anderson's Bottom. I held my breath till bump, jolt, we hit the ground, taxied to a quick stop.

Another small plane was parked here; a truck was just turning around to leave. Jim sprang out and shouted, "Hey, wait a minute, will you?"

The truck came to a stop and the driver jumped down, came toward us. I climbed out stiffly and felt the good solid ground once more underfoot. Jim said, "Can you take my passenger to town?"

"Sure thing. Get right in, ma'm." He helped me up into the high seat of the truck.

"Good-by, Jim, and thanks a lot," I called.

"Okay, ma'm." It was all in the day's work, meant nothing to him, just a job done. Maybe he had not realized how scared I had been. For now he had turned away; he was asking the truck driver if he would mind carting the boxes of supplies along, too. The truck driver did not mind. Nobody in this beautiful, terrible country seemed to mind doing anything for anybody else.

Jim waved good-by and shouted, "Ask for Eloise; she'll look after you."

As we drove away, I heard the little plane's engine roar and I looked back till I saw it safely off the ground and heading away into the sunny sky. "Do you know Eloise?" I asked.

"Sure, everybody knows Eloise. Sorry—this road is rather bumpy."

That was putting it mildly. I had some difficulty staying on the seat and my words seemed to be shaken out of me rather than spoken, as I made some brief explanation of my coming here to wait while the others of my party ran Cataract.

"Yes, that's a toughie, Cataract." Then, pointing to a small shack by the road, he said, "The man who lives there has taken five million out of his mine, and more coming in every day."

As we passed, I looked in through the open door and saw a white iron bed with tumbled covers. "Heavens, think of that! Uranium, I suppose?"

"Yes, ma'm."

"Well, how about you—have you got mines too?"

"I just drive this truck, ma'm. Oh, I've got a few claims here and there—there's always a chance—"

We had come into the town now—if one could call it by such a name. On the left was a sandy open space and then a brown, low, rocky ridge. On the right were two small shabby buildings over one of which was a sign, CAFE. We passed several trailers set up on blocks, a cabin or two and stopped before a combination store and two-room house. Over the door of the store was a sign, WHITE CANYON P.O. It did go through my mind that it was rather odd, since this was Hite, that the post office should be called by some other name, but I did not give it much thought for I was at once involved in the problem of what to do with these great boxes of supplies that filled the back of the truck.

The driver said, "I'll set them over in the shade for you—sorry I can't wait, but I'm running late this morning." He began carrying the boxes around to where a small, crooked, young willow tree shaded the entrance to the post office—store.

The last two of the cartons broke as he lifted them out; cans went scattering everywhere in the dust. "Don't bother. I can pick them up. You've already been too kind." I wished I could give him something—what would I have done if he had not been at the air field? Just sat there in the broiling sun for a week? But he did not look like a man one would tip, so I just thanked him and read the sign on the side of the truck and thought, "Well, bless you, Kerncopter Co., whoever you are, for having such a kind truck driver."

Then as he backed out and disappeared with a wave of his hand, I began picking up cans from the dust and carrying them a few at a time across to the big pile by the door. I felt like the old crow in the endless repetitive tale—"And then the old crow came back and got another grain of corn, the old crow came back and got another grain of corn" and so on ad infinitum.

All this time there was no sign of life about the place. I had about finished my task when the store door opened and a tall, slow-moving man came sauntering out. "Good morning, ma'm," he said, and without another word began helping me.

When everything was stacked up in a great heap by the door, I thanked him and said, "Can you tell me where I'll find Eloise?"

He jerked a thumb in the direction of the other half of the building—"That door."

So I went and knocked on it. I was feeling rather empty and all-gone by this time, uneasy, too, about where I could stay. The door was opened by a tall, handsome young woman in a sun-back blue cotton dress that matched her blue eyes. Her bare arms and shoulders were beautifully shaped. "Are you Eloise? I'm sorry—I was just told to ask for Eloise."

"Come in."

I stepped inside and she closed the door. "Air-conditioned!" I gasped as I felt the heavenly coolness surround me.

"Yes," she said. "And the only bathroom within a hundred miles." She gestured toward a chair and introduced as her sister the young woman who was sitting on the sofa with a cup of coffee in her hand. "I'll get you some coffee," she added and crossed the living room to an open alcove where I saw a spotless, modern kitchen.

All this before I had explained myself at all. I accepted it gratefully, then sitting there in the soft, luxurious comfort of a real chair, sipping hot coffee, I told her how I had come and why and asked if I could have some place to stay for maybe as long as a week, depending on how the rest of my party got through Cataract. Yes, she reassured me at once, she had a place for me, and I could get a good breakfast just down the road a piece at the café.

"Finish your coffee and I'll show you."

The place she took me to, across the bare dusty yard, was a long blue trailer under a spindly willow tree. There was one narrow room with chair and sofa and table, a sink with running water and a stove. Through a door I could see a tiny room with a bed that almost filled it. At the moment it looked quite luxurious to me—but hot, hot as any tin box would be in the broiling sun. She opened some windows and a faint breath of hotter air came in. "How much will it be? And if you have a weekly rate—"

"Fourteen dollars," she said.

A day or a week, I wondered, and did not ask. I had to have it, at no matter what cost. "And my baggage, and all those boxes—the supplies—"

"I'll get my husband, Mr. Free, to bring them down for you after a while. The toilet's out back, down by the wash. You'll see the path," she added as she left.

Well, one could not expect everything, I thought, and washed my face and hands at the sink and set out for the café. It was a one-room affair with the kitchen visible through an open doorway. Two men were finishing breakfast, studying a road map and talking in low tones. I was served by a man and a woman—

pancakes, bacon, coffee that was weak but hot. The two other customers left. No one else came in. "You don't have many here, do you?" I said to the man as he poured me a second cup of coffee.

He laughed. "We've fed fifty-two since five this morning."

When I got back to my trailer, I found my baggage and boxes inside the door. Now I had nothing to do but wait, so I lay down on the bed and slept till noon.

The next four days I lived in solitude, eating from the supplies—after all, why go to a café when I had everything right here practically underfoot? That first day I had canned chicken, bread and peanut butter and many cans of V-8 juice. I read the old magazines, I bathed, I washed my hair, wrote letters, wrote up my notes, I slept and for the first time in a mirror saw how I had burned and tanned, even right through my nylon shirt. At the end of the third day I went out for a walk in the cool of the evening. A little way off to the right I came upon another small cluster of trailers and shacks, with children playing. Two young couples were pitching horseshoes. I stopped to watch them for a minute.

"You like to pitch?" one of the men called to me.

"I used to—but you finish your game. I'm out for a walk— I'll stop coming back." I went on down the road, crossed a small bridge over the wash that was almost empty of water, and followed a winding dirt road. On my left there was a ridge that rose to a peak, topped with the remains of what looked to be an old fort. It was crumbling to pieces, just walls and fallen stone. On my right was the brown Colorado with a crude pulley ferry anchored on the far side. There were trees over there, and beyond, the familiar red-brown wall of rock. I turned and walked back.

The game of horseshoes was over. One couple was waiting for me, standing in the middle of the road, two small children playing in the ditch beside them. They wanted to know what I was doing here, and I told them. "Are you out for uranium too, like everybody else?" I asked.

The man shook his head. "I make my money the hard way. I'm a driller." He and his wife had lived all over this part of the country; they had pictures of Indians remains, if I was interested. They lived in that blue trailer over there and wouldn't I like to come in some evening and see the pictures? I said I would.

That night thunder woke me. I thought of Cataract Canyon and wondered how thunder sounded there—or could it be heard above the roar of water? I lay awake for a long time, hoping all was going well. It is so much easier to be in the midst of danger than to be safe and think of others there. All the next day I felt uneasy, and when I heard the sound of blasting in the distance, I thought of those great cliffs where masses of rock hung poised and ready to fall down, needing only a jar, a slight vibration to stir them.

chapter

16

Late on the afternoon of the Fourth I heard voices shouting—somebody celebrating, I thought, and went on working at my notes. Then there came the sound of a horn—"Look away, look away, Dixie land, I wish I was in Dixie—" Before the second *look away* I was out of my trailer, running to the riverbank. Where were they? Not upriver. I looked downstream. They had gone past. And there was only one boat! How many were in it? I counted—six. All safe. But they must have lost the *Brontosaur!* The cameras, the luggage, that $300 box of medical supplies—all gone! I waved and shouted and they ran ashore, tied up the boat and made their way toward me through the tangle of bushes along the bank. I began to shout questions at them long before they came within hearing. But "You made it, you made it!" was all I could say when they reached me at last. I gave each one of them a hug and a kiss—even Al with his great black beard. "But where's the big boat? Did you lose it?"

"It's at Hite," Charles said.

"Hite? What do you mean, Hite? This is Hite."

They all laughed. "This is White Canyon," Fred said.

"There's nothing at Hite but the other end of the ferry," Don said.

"Then I didn't miss anything by not going there."

"You missed us," Tony said. "But I knew Dixie would raise you out of somewhere if you were dead and buried."

"I'd rattle my bones like castanets to that tune. Come on,

I think there's a place here where I can treat you to a can of beer. And I want to hear all about Cataract." They followed me up the bank, all talking at once.

Charles stopped suddenly and looked around. "You certainly picked a glamorous spot to meet us in."

Then for the first time I saw that I had rushed in my hurry through a veritable village of small outhouses, each with its door open showing the board seat with two holes.

We had quite a little celebration at Mr. Free's, sitting on the bench that ran against the wall, ginger ale and beer cans piling up on the one board table the place provided. The going had been tough in more than one spot in Cataract, they told me, and one night they had to sleep on a steep rocky slope, the only space between river and sheer walls three thousand feet high. "I could have slept in the boat," I said rather wistfully.

"Yes, yes, you could have made it, as it turned out. There was just one time when you might have had trouble. But how could we know that in advance?"

"You couldn't, of course, so never mind. I saw Cataract from the sky."

When I went to pay my bill which was very small—the fourteen dollars was the weekly rate—Mr. Free led me aside. He seemed rather embarrassed. "I heard you all planning to go to the café for dinner. Well, it's closed."

"Closed on the Fourth of July?"

He nodded. "Don't mention it, but my help over there started celebrating too early in the day. They're in no shape to cook— so I had to close."

I broke the news to the rest of them, but I said I had a little stove in my trailer and all the supplies were right in the middle of the floor so we could have dinner there. Then I remembered there were no pots and pans, not enough plates. So there was nothing to do but to load up and go to Hite. As we set out, Eloise called after me, "Do you mean you are going off on the river with all this bunch of wild men?"

"Yes," I said.

She shook her head. "You're a brave woman, a brave woman."

But I was glad to be back in a boat again, to feel the river under me once more. Hite turned out to be, at first glance, nothing more than a sandbar, a clump of small trees and bushes, and an open place beyond them where other campers had built a table with benches. A road came in from over the hill and Don said there was one family who lived just a little distance away, the Neilsons who ran the ferry. Then after dinner when I was exploring a bit, enjoying the sunset, I came upon four Boy Scout cabins tucked away under some giant old willow trees. They were not locked, so I went in and looked around. Each had one or two beds, all made up with clean sheets, a washstand and wardrobe, chairs and tables. Real luxury for the Boy Scouts, I thought. Or for me. So at bedtime without a word to anyone except Fred—lest they miss me and take alarm—I stole away to one of the cabins, spread my light blanket all over the bed so as not to have the Boy Scouts come and say like the Three Bears, "Who's been sleeping in my bed?" But it was a mistake. The night was hot and in here it was as breathless and stuffy as my trailer had been. The moon shone in across the bed and kept me awake, and the sun woke me with its first light.

I dressed and went on down the road to the Neilsons', for I could hear hammering off that way and I knew they must be up. They welcomed me with that very special cordiality of those who live in lonely places. One may find that same sort of welcome anywhere, however, by taking the trouble now and then to seek out someone who leads a lonely life, no matter if it be in the middle of a city. Mrs. Neilson took me all through her house, which was very nice indeed, comfortable and plenty big for the two of them; she showed me her garden and the orchard they had set out when they first came in '49, settling here because they liked the scenery. She gave me a drink of cool water from their well. It had a queer, mineral taste, but not unpleasant. She said they preferred the river water.

Camp was awake when I got back, Don just turning a beautiful pancake which I snatched on the grounds that I had not had any for such a long time. It was delicious. We were late getting away that morning. Mr. Neilson came down to see us off, and two bearded men in scant shorts and nothing more appeared out of nowhere. They looked brown and gaunt and hungry, but breakfast was over, all our supplies stowed away in the *Bronto-saur*. Perhaps they were only hungry for talk—or for uranium. They had a camp a few miles back in the hills, they said, and were prospecting. I did not talk with them but went and got in the boat, eager to be off. Only now, out in the sun and air, did I realize what a really rather dreadful little spot it was, back there in what I still think of as Hite where I had spent four days.

We were off at last; we rounded a bend and began to enter Glen Canyon. This is the longest of the canyons, the distance from Hite to Lee's Ferry, where it ends, being nearly 150 miles. The river was wide here with no rapids, but many cross-currents and whirls. Don in the small boat, towing us, kept moving from one side of the river to the other in order to avoid the back currents which looked almost as swift as the proper down-flowing one. Almost at once the buttes began to take on interesting shapes; great mounds were topped by formations that resembled ancient buildings. One, known as Castle Butte, over forty-four hundred feet above sea level, was an imposing sight, and yet not as castlelike as some others.

I heard more of Cataract now, from Charles and Tony, of how the rapids were almost continuous all one day, giving them no respite, of how the waves were sometimes as much as twelve or fifteen feet high. "Don't tell me any more," I said. "I can't bear it, that I missed all that." And yet, I thought, maybe it had not been a bad idea to let this group of men be off to themselves for a bit with no woman along. They would be freer, in deed, in speech. For last night for the first time on this trip I had heard a few damnits and oh hells, quickly hushed with an apologetic glance in my direction. As if I did not on occasion use a few such words! Indeed, since working in a munition plant during the war, I have had a vocabulary—did I care to use it— which would be banned in Boston. But they did not know this, and I was a little touched that they felt such words as they had used were not proper in my presence. Respect is a bit out of fashion nowadays, we are all too busy trying to be the same age, so I was pleased to be treated thus. Yet I think they were not any of them men much given to profanity or to talk that they would not consider fit for a lady's ears. And I thought too that my being there, to be told about the hazards of Cataract, was perhaps a satisfaction to them. For surely one of the great pleasures in going away or accomplishing anything is having someone to come back to and to tell about it.

So with such thoughts as these I comforted myself for not having been allowed to run Cataract. Everyone was relaxed and rather lazy this morning, probably feeling a bit let down after the excitements of the past few days. Al was reading another of his murders. We had nothing to worry about, save the fact that our canteens were about empty. Don had thought the Neilsons' well water not really fit to drink—and I had had a large cup of it! But he said there was good water at the old Hite ranch ahead, and we could fill up there.

I noticed that Charles was taking pictures of the marks left by different water levels on the rocks. Or when we came to a place where there were small steps in the muddy sand along the edge of the river where it had withdrawn he took pictures of them. "What's the idea?" I asked. "There's perfectly good scenery on both sides. Not spectacular, but interesting—those turrets and mounds and what looks like a cave that isn't finished yet."

"It's the river," Charles said. "It's falling so fast that we may not be able to go on after Lee's Ferry. So I want a record of it, just in case."

This was a new and disturbing thought. What a pity, if we could not get through Marble Canyon and on down the Grand, which was to have been the cilmax of the trip. And yet, with 140 more miles to go through this benign and gentle Glen, maybe we would have had enough by the time we got to Lee's Ferry. "But surely," I said now, "surely when all those other rivers come in, there'll be plenty of water. There is the Escalante, the San Juan, Navaho Creek, the Paria"—for I had studied a map while I was waiting in my hot tin trailer—"and I don't know how many more."

"Could be," Charles said. "We'll read the gages as we go on down. The one at Lee's Ferry will tell us yes or no."

In the middle of the morning we stopped on the left bank and walked across an open field to where on the face of the cliff there were remains of an Indian dwelling. It was hot, crossing the field, and I followed the others slowly, my little plaid parasol of not much help, for the heat was reflected up from the almost bare earth as if the ground were breathing hot breaths, blowing them into my face. It was here in the middle of this bleak bare field that I almost stepped on a small green plant much like a potato plant, with a trumpet-shaped white blossom of exquisite purity. It was the sacred datura or moonflower, so Don told me later. But when I broke the stem the evil smell of it reminded me of the Jimson weed, a pest in Mississippi, and I remembered walking through a patch of it barefooted once on my way to the little stream back of our house that my father had named, for some unknown reason, the Ganymede. There is nothing like a smell for translating one to other scenes. But evil-smelling or no, it was a wonder, this pure white flower, blooming in such a place.

The Indian dwelling was a ruin. At each side of a concave place in the cliff, there were the remains of the two lateral walls, built up of small flat stones. We came upon some bits of broken pottery and Don found an arrowhead. I found some pieces of flint, but left them. Soon every trace of that life would have disappeared, I thought, as we came back across the field. Yet once here the Indians had defended themselves from their enemies, the women had cultivated this field over which we walked, children had played. Nothing lasted but the earth itself, and that, with the wind and water and blowing sand, was ever-changing. I felt as transient as a butterfly.

We stopped for lunch at a sandbar on the right bank where the canyon widened out into a wooded valley. On the opposite side was a sheer high cliff, curtained with streamers of dark blue and purple that hung down over its face, the marks left by small streams of water running across it. As soon as he had eaten Don set off with some canteens in search of water. For on the map there was a stream somewhere near here and the site of the old Hite ranch where Mr. Hite, a solitary rancher of many years ago, had made welcome those voyagers who survived Cataract. Some of them had arrived at his door half-clad and starving, with tales of horror about that passage.

The sun beat down on us; we kept wondering why Don did not return. At last Fred said he would go look for him—maybe he had run into a rattlesnake, maybe he had fallen. So off Fred went. After what seemed like hours, Charles and Bruce went looking for them both. Al read his murder, Tony and I sat and worried. We distracted ourselves somewhat by composing limericks; I wish I had written down some of his. They were very clever. Now and then I got out of the boat and in my sock feet waded, fully clothed, into the water, to stand there up to my chin, cooling off.

Fred got back at last, calling, "They're all right—but wait, wait!"

"Wait?" I was coming up out of the water.

But he wanted to get a picture of me in dark glasses and cap and veil, just a head above the brown current of the river, so I waded in again. Then he told us that Don had hiked all the long six miles back to the ruins of the Hite place, had visited Hite's lonely grave. They were all on their way, would soon be here. Tony and I were quite cross to think how we had worried. And it was nearly five o'clock when they came limping toward us. "Wasn't worth it," Charles said.

"Any water?"

Don had two canteens full. The others in their worry had gone off without their canteens. Bruce said, "River water isn't bad. I've been drinking it all day." But I thought we were still too close to White Canyon.

We stopped that evening where the river seemed to end. For there was a sharp turn ahead with a great wall of tapestried rock blocking its way. I set my tent low on the sand close to the water, the others mounted the first of a series of shelves on the receding cliff wall. There was a full moon that night, so bright it kept me awake for a long time, but I lay there, quite content, the river purring gently beside me.

I was up at dawn. The water was strangely blue in this early light, as if it were a clear stream, and the reflection of Tapestry Rock turned the shadowy stretches to gold. I started a fire and had the coffee boiling before the others rolled out. We had a slow, lazy breakfast that morning, and when we were ready to set out again Charles and Tony with their cameras mounted the high steps, the ledges of the cliff, in order to shoot the big boat as it moved slowly down the river toward Tapestry Rock with Al and Bruce rowing. I looked back and watched them as long as I could, so small and lost they seemed up there on the heights. The river twisted and turned and it was some time before the small boat caught up with us, for Bruce said, "Let's lose them," and he and Al pulled away at the oars with what seemed to me like superhuman energy. But in the end, the motor prevailed and we were overtaken and attached to the small boat by a towline, the motor chugging away cheerfully.

Little by little walls of the canyon mounted higher; they

held buffs and yellows as well as red now, and there were many
arches set high on the walls, places where someday perhaps there
would be a natural bridge, or a cave. We stopped once to walk
back a way to see some petroglyphs, strange Indian carvings on
the face of the rock. What did they mean? I wondered, standing
before them with my parasol resting on my shoulder while the
others took pictures. There were queer geometrical signs, con-
centric circles, animals—mountain sheep perhaps, a big bird
with outstretched wings—and a number of shapes that were like
footprints. Some showed five toes, others were just flat, perhaps
moccasined prints cut there on the perpendicular wall. Was
someone trying to say, "See, see. I have passed by here, I have
left my footprints on the rock." An early Kilroy? Someone
anyway, hacking away at the hard stone with the urgency of his
mortality upon him. To leave some sign, to leave something that
will last when we are gone—it is an almost universal human
wish.

I went back to the boat while the others were exploring
farther down a side canyon looking for more petroglyphs. I
was thirsty and I thought the blue can with a spout felt heavy
enough to spare me a drink. I tilted it up—and got a mouthful
of white gas! Luckily I discovered my mistake before I had
swallowed any, but it left a fearful taste in my mouth. I rinsed
with river water. It tasted good in spite of the mud and, from
then on, I drank it freely. Later this cost me a week in the
hospital in Denver when I was sick with a virus, but suspected
of typhoid, amoebic dysentery and other odd diseases and kept
in solitary confinement—they called it isolation—while tests,
all negative, were made. But I thought of no such possibility
now. Indeed I felt utterly removed from the world, immune in
every way to all its trouble. It was a singularly restful, remote
and untroubled time, those days in Glen Canyon. The river
itself, after the wild torments of Cataract, seemed to be resting
from its turmoil. Now and then Al sang a snatch of song, never

more than a line or two—"I get ideas"—a most provocative
beginning with no end. Or "The higher up the cherry tree"—
and I will never know what was there. I only speculated idly
and did not ask.

It was late that afternoon when we came upon one of the
wonders of this canyon. On our right, where the red-and-black-
streaked wall rose some thousand feet above the river, there was
hollowed out a circular niche, from water level to sky, as if
planned for a giant statue that had not yet arrived. Small trees
were set in against the wall and they had a new, an almost tropical luxuriance. Here and there where water dripped through,
there was maidenhair fern hanging down from a precarious
footing on the wall.

We ran ashore and got out on the small strip of yellow sand
that formed the boundary of a circular, somewhat shrunken
pool. It was an enchanting spot. Tony shouted and the echo came
back quickly. "I've got to get a record of this," Charles said.
So he dug his recorder from the luggage, Tony brought out his
horn and they, with Don and Al and Fred helping, carried the
equipment around the edge of the pool, for Charles thought that
would be the best spot from which to catch the echo of horn and
voices. I stood on the ridge of sand and watched them flounder
along the wall, sinking into quicksand, pulling out by the trees
and bushes and making their difficult way, trailing yards of wire
cord till they were directly opposite me. "All right, play, Tony,
play," Charles shouted.

Tony lifted his horn, blew three notes that echoed and re-
echoed—and were followed at once by a fearful rumble, loud as
thunder. I think we all had the same thought at once, that the
horn had struck that fatal note of just the proper pitch to find
response in the rock overhead—as the violin may make a glass
ring—and that the rock was going to tumble down upon us.
"Let's get out of here!" Don shouted. I sprang backward toward
the boat, the others came leaping and plunging through the

bushes. Another roar came from the rocks just as I reached the water's edge, and then I saw that Bruce was sitting on the gunwale barefooted, kicking his heels back and forth in the water, banging the side of the boat. "Do that again," I said.

He struck his heels hard against the inflated side of the boat and again came that ominous roar from the rocky circular walls above. "It's all right! Just an echo!" I shouted.

But by this time they were almost out. Tony had gotten stuck in quicksand and been quickly rescued, hauled out by his arms, and they had gotten up such speed in their flight and fright that I do not think they heard, or at least understood me till they were all the way around to the boat.

Bruce hit his heels once more against the side of the boat so they could see for themselves what it was. But Charles said, "I don't like it even when I know what caused it." And to tell the truth none of us did. I have seldom heard a more ominous sound. So he set up his recorder on the brim of sand and got a few other sound effects—Al making a speech and me reciting a few lines of "Lycidas"—once I knew it all by heart.

Then we were off again, to stop that night just below a deserted cabin. There was a small wooded stretch, then behind us the cliff rose, ruddy and bare in the late-afternoon light. We went alongshore to have a look at the cabin. It was built of stone, cleverly set, like the Indian dwelling, in the concavity of the cliff, using that as one wall. The door was unlocked and we looked into the dark interior. Everything was in good order, neat but thick with dust of disuse. Bed and table and stove were tidy; there were cans on the shelves. Someone had been there though not very recently and perhaps would return.

Beside the door was a fig tree, well loaded with ripe figs. I fell upon them with a whoop of delight. "Haven't had any ripe figs in thirty years," I said between bites. The others took one or two but they had not my enthusiasm. I peeled back the skin, using the stem for a handle, bit into the lovely pink center, which is really the flower, sucked out the heart and tossed the rest of the skin away. Delicious! And how the flavor "took me back," as the saying goes. I was in Mississippi, a child again, leaning against the gray trunk of the tree by the garden gate, reaching up, peeling, biting, tossing away the skin and reaching up for another. And again I could see my father sitting reading on the front gallery, near his favorite fig tree, the purple fig, we called it, a string around his finger. The other end ran out to the fig tree and now and then he gave a tug which shook a branch and rattled a can and frightened the birds away. For they love the ripe figs as much as humans do.

Charles said, rather hesitantly, "Do you think you'd better be eating so many?"

I said, "Listen, I used to eat figs by the water bucket before you were born." So he said no more.

I gathered all I could carry and took them back to camp, had them for dessert that night and for breakfast next morning.

chapter

〜〜〜

17

This day, as the one before, we passed high tapestried walls that gradually became more gold than red. The sand was salmon-colored. At noon the others went in search of water while I found a spot between two rocks and let the cool river pour over me for the two hours they were gone. And it was that afternoon that we came to the site of the Mormon Crossing. We got out there and read the plaque that had been placed upon the cliff to commemorate their passage. How could they have come down here, I wondered, looking up at this great cliff, broken by a few faults, a few far-apart ledges.

There was no road across the Slick Rock Desert when they came seventy-five years ago. They were two months on the trail and by the time they got here there was snow falling, and few supplies were left. Two hundred and fifty men, women and children with a notion in their heads, a "call" to cross over and settle in the San Juan Desert, beyond this river and the canyon. Looking up from the cleft in the rock where they had blasted crude sloping steps, now washed and worn away, I could imagine the wagons held back by ropes, the wheels locked against the 25-degree descent, the wild-eyed horses, plunging—nine went over and were lost. There was no tape recorder there to make a record of their screams, but those who heard could never have forgotten all their lives the sound, echoed as it must have been from sheer cliff on the other side of the "hole in the rock." How could they have done this? And then by means of crude rafts passed over this wide muddy stream to the other, level side?

Well, perhaps, as they no doubt believed, the Lord was with them. I could think of no other way to accuont for such a feat. Beside it, what we had accomplished on this voyage down the canyon seemed small and easy. We all left that spot subdued, awed and full of wonder. Maybe a notion in a human mind was after all the most powerful thing in the universe.

Soon we passed an open space through which we saw Navaho Mountain, wooded and round. We went by the mouth of the Escalante River that day, too, and passed the San Juan. And yet the Colorado ran lower and lower. We could see the still fresh marks along the side where it had but recently lowered its level by visible inches. Don said when we stopped for the night, that we had traveled 643 miles from Green River, Wyoming. We had 76 miles more to go before Lee's Ferry. Would there be enough water to get us there? And what would we do if we got stuck? Climb the cliff and hike across the desert? Do a Mormon hole-in-the-rock in reverse? No one spoke of such a possibility, yet it was in all our minds.

This night, of the 7th of July, we stopped at one of the most dramatic of all our campsites. Where a slender side canyon cut back through the thousand-foot walls, there was a series of red rock ledges above the narrow strip of muddy sand at the river's edge. Here, on different levels, the others spread their sleeping bags. I began to set up my cot bed on a lower shelf; then it seemed to me that the rock still held too much the heat of the sun. It radiated toward me in waves of warmth. So I dragged my things down to the mouth of the small side canyon where a tiny stream of water trickled down and out to join the muddy river. I jumped across it easily and tossed my duffel over. There on the sand I made my camp. A cool breeze blew down the small canyon, a draft of air that seemed to come from another world.

We had stopped early this time, and immediately after supper Charles and Fred set out on an exploring expedition. Charles had studied the map and decided that beyond the sheer cliff below which I was settled the great boulders must block yet another canyon, one some earlier explorer had found and called Hidden Passage and so marked it on the map. So off they went while the others climbed up the ledges back of camp, Bruce and Al and Tony chasing each other as if playing a game of tag high against the rocky wall. I set up my cot—I had given up using the tent as the nights had grown warmer—and stretched out with my hands clasped behind my head, watching the changing light on the water as the sun sank behind the cliff. In shadow the river was gold, dimpled with small whirlpools, and it seemed swifter now that the San Juan had joined it. Across on the other side, the rounding, domed cliffs caught the last rays of the sun and the blue sky above them was reflected in the water below giving again the illusion that the water was clear. From the narrow slit of a canyon beside me, the breeze blew colder and colder. I had to get out a blanket. Then from back in its darker depths beyond the cluster of willows that shaded and overhung the small stream, dozens of bats came flying in the twilight.

They circled round my head, darting this way and that as if they sensed the alien presence of a human being. I covered myself to the eyes with my blanket and watched them, wondering at their manner of flight and their radar sense of objects in their path. There must have been a colony of them back in the narrow canyon. Was it true that they liked to settle in a woman's hair? I covered my head with the blanket as one almost brushed my face and swooped away beyond the small green willows that guarded the mouth of the brook. Then suddenly, as if with one accord, they all disappeared. And I began to wonder about Charles and Fred. Why were they staying so late? Had something happened to them?

It was almost dark when they came from the far side of the great rocks below camp. They arrived breathless, both talking at once: "You must see this—we'll spend all day tomorrow there—the most incredible place—the inside of a conch shell—

I've got to get pictures—enough for a whole short-short—"

I sat up and stared at them in amazement. If ever faces were transfigured, these were. They shone, with excitement and wonder. It was the way they looked, rather than any words they spoke, that made me know they had come upon a moving, a truly marvelous sight. "You must see it," they kept repeating. "It isn't a hard walk, once you get past the rocks."

"I'll go if it kills me," I said. "I've got to see anything that makes you look like this."

It did nearly kill me. Though perhaps I should rather blame those figs that kept me awake half the night. The moon, almost full, struck the top of the high sheer cliff over my head and its light there on the pale rock, with organ-pipe stripes of black where water had once run down, seemed to make it lean out, over me. Each time I awoke I found the level of moonlight lower, the apparent tilt of the rock more ominous. I kept looking up to see that it was not really coming down on top of me. When morning came at last, I was weak and dizzy, and as soon as I heard sounds of life, Tony starting the fire, Don rattling pans and tin plates, I went, more or less staggering, across the stream and along the riverbank to find Charles. "Charles," I said, "those figs—I wish I had listened to you and left them alone!"

He gave me one glance—no doubt I looked as pale and far-gone as I felt—and rushed for the medicine box. "Here you are," he said, and handed me a bottle of paregoric. "A small swig of this every few hours."

I could take nothing but crackers and a little black coffee for breakfast. How was I ever going to make it through Hidden Passage? Yet I was determined to go. I let them all go ahead of me except Tony and Charles and Fred who were still getting their photographic equipment in order, the film packed for carrying. So I could go at my own pace. I moved slowly up the path, circled the two great rocks that almost blocked the entrance and stopped to lean against the sheer wall on my left while I got my breath. Across from me, here where the canyon was perhaps thirty feet wide, a great hunk of the opposite wall had fallen, and quite recently, for some of the small trees it had struck were still partly alive, and the place where it had broken from the wall was a brighter yellow than the rest. Was there more that was just waiting for a jolt or jar to come crashing down? But I must not think of that—and I gave my attention to the luxuriant growth around me. I was amazed to recognize the leaf of the redbud or Judas tree. All the bushes and small trees here had a wild, fresh look, utterly unlike those that sparsely bordered the river. Here by the stream, so small that at times it was little more than a pool with a trickle at each end, there was a tropical richness. Of course we had been coming south all the time, I reminded myself, as I moved slowly along the narrow ledge against the wall of rock, pushing aside bush and branch, hoping snakes did not lie in my way. But it was cool in here.

Then I came to an end of my little shelf and had to descend to the level of the stream. Before me was a rounded rock that left no room on either side for passage. I could see that by hanging to a tree branch I might gain a first foothold. But after that, smooth curving stone stretched up to the top. The thing looked as big as a house. What was I going to do? Ignominiously give up? Or wait for somebody to come and boost and hoist me? No, that too, was a humiliating prospect. If the Mormons by faith could descend a canyon wall, I could by self-hypnosis mount this little private Gibraltar. I tossed my Cellophane bag up—and it slid right back at me. I tried again and it caught and stayed. Then I mounted to that first uneven foothold, saying to myself, "I am a fly, I can walk upside down, I can do anything, I am a fly, a fly, four-legged, sticky fly, I can't slip—" And up I went on all fours, catching up my bag and dragging it along with me as I mounted. And I did mount. Luckily the far side of the rock was less precipitous and I could simply slide down on my seat. So I made it. I looked around. The walls had drawn closer. Now there was no place to walk but beside the shallow trickle of water.

I moved forward slowly. The air was deliciously cool; no sunlight at all reached me. I looked up and grew dizzy. Over my head the walls came nearer and nearer to each other, leaving only a jagged narrow strip of blue sky. My head reeled and I sat down on my heels, leaning my back against the wall. Ahead there was another curve. I felt as if I were inside a giant helical shell, immense, terrible, beautiful. I took a sip of paregoric, removed my shoes, tying the strings together and slinging them over my shoulder, then I went on, splashing the clear cold water as I followed the stream. I rounded the curve and the ground-space between the walls widened out. Here it was like an ornate Empire theater and high on the wall was a carved-out balcony where kings and queens might sit. Lower down ran a horizontal window box of delicate green maidenhair fern. The colors of the rock were incredible—low down here they were purply-black and mauve and, as I looked up and up, they turned to red and gold, and enclosed at the top a weird new-moon-shaped scrap of sky. I had to blink and rub my eyes. No wonder Fred and Charles had come from their first sight of this with faces alight, with words that fell from their lips, inadequate and broken. It was not only the singular beauty of this canyon but its remoteness that was so staggering. It was so wholly new to human eyes. One came upon it as if walking alone in a new-made, a virgin world. Then too there was a stillness here, as if infinity itself had moved in, pervading, surrounding one. Even the small stream moved lightly without sound. I walked beside it now in the noiseless sand.

I have been at Pompeii, at Stonehenge; I have been where countless generations of man have lived and died and left their mark. Such historic scenes give one a very special feeling of the continuity of human existence, of kinship with all ages of

man, and a wonder at the alterations of time. But here in Hidden
Passage, where so few had ever come, was a new kind of wonder
for me, related less to time than to eternity, akin to something
greater than mankind. I saw now why Charles and Fred had had
no words, could speak in no more than broken phrases. I could
not do much better myself. No simple prose was adequate.
Poetry, perhaps? I got out my notebook and pencil and tried:

> To Hidden Canyon come with reverence.
> It is a holy place, this nautilus,
> This mighty, spiral-chambered carven shell.
> Step softly here where seldom man has trod—
> So Adam walked in Eden's virgin dell
> That lay still dewy from the hand of God.

But what good were such words as these, telling those who would
never come the proper manner of their coming?

Hidden Passage—it was well-named. I could not make it
stand forth to be seen. Nor could Charles with all his fine
cameras capture its essence or its meaning. I could hear him
beyond that last curve, saying, "Let's try it from here now—
no, the light—we'll go back a way." Their steps were muted to
silence that spread tangibly around me, that set me apart, afar
and alone. I looked ahead to where both walls drew in upon each
other, curving away into what must be yet another mighty coil
beyond my sight, and walked slowly on.

On one side above me the red and gold wall was streaked
with organ pipes of black and rose and taupe, and on the other,
a drift of fringed veil hung delicately purple across its topaz
face. Around me now on both walls, within my reach, ran an
even band some six feet wide of maidenhair and ribbon fern,
moist, brilliantly green and trailing downward as if from a
window box. Below it were powder-blue spears where water had
left its mark. Both green and blue were reflected in the stream
that lay mirror still right here. I walked beside it on a cool border
of yellow sand that narrowed more and more as I went on. Then

before me there was only a sheer wall on the left, on the right a slippery, steeply-rounding mass of rock, and before me a dug-out oval pool little bigger than a bathtub, but deep. A shaft of sunlight spotlighted it with gold. Small waterbugs rested motionless on the clear surface of the water, their shadows black, immense, below them. Polliwogs zigzagged among them as madly as live spermatozoa in the field of a microscope. Nosy little things, I thought, and it amused me to think how man with all his pride and self-esteem, his importance and achievement, had been through the ages dependent for his creation on just such small nosiness as this.

I sat down and leaned against the wall with fern fronds tickling my neck and had another drop of paregoric—believing in many small doses rather than one large one—and waited for the others to come and give me a steadying hand over the slippery rock beside the pool. From here we went on together, coming on a long straight stretch where the sun, directly overhead, laid its hot weight upon us, and left no escape from it.

"There's the end of the line," Charles said, as we rounded another curve, and he pointed to where the stream deepened and narrowed and seemed to be wholly blocked by a great round boulder some twenty feet in height and offering no foothold. Impossible for anyone with a camera in hand. But the three boatmen had managed somehow to brace themselves against the wall and scramble up. We could hear their voices above and beyond the boulder and now all at once, like heralds from a tribe of savages, they appeared on top of it.

"What's on beyond?" Tony shouted.

"More of the same," Don said, and sliding on the seat of his bathing trunks he came down to where he could jump off into the deep water. Bruce and Al followed him down. I peeled out of blue jeans and shirt, for I had worn a bathing suit underneath that morning, and walked into the pool. It sloped quickly downward so I had to swim. At the foot of the boulder, I turned on my back and lay there, arms outstretched, fingers just touching the sides, and looked up at the sheer straight walls of rock, wondering that this small stream could have cut through the hard upper layers and then hollowed out the softer ones to shape this fearful depth. Why didn't exploring man dig deep deep into what lay underfoot instead of setting off for interstellar space?

The walk back seemed endless, and I was glad when I could climb into the boat once more, open my small parasol and lean back against the duffel bags, which were like home to me. It was after noon by now and we went only a little way farther downstream before stopping for lunch on a hot shadeless bit of shore. A dry wash led away through an open field to where, according to the map, we could find another and far more enormous hollowed-out space, the one Powell named Music Temple. I started, went part way and gave it up. The others came back excited over the size and magnificence of that hollow ampitheater, where they found traces of names set there by Powell's party. But I felt I had really seen enough that day and that size was not everything after all.

Nor did I later that afternoon leave the boat to go with the rest looking for petroglyphs on a cliff beyond a park sparsely dotted with box elders and stunted willow trees. Instead I hung over the side and let the water pour over me, cooling and delightful. This was the one day when I did not feel up to doing all the things I wanted to do—or maybe the paregoric and sun together combined to make me too sleepy for effort.

The boats too had a hard time that afternoon. For the wind grew stronger as the hot hours passed; it kicked up waves the motors had to fight their way through. My parasol was whipped wrongside out. As often as possible Don steered us into the narrow shade of an overhanging cliff, and how welcome was that small moment's relief! So we came to camp not far from the mouth of Aztec Creek. Here there was a stretch of flat sand, a wide flat shelf of rock where the table was set up and the camp-fire built. I went upstream a little way to the mouth of a narrow dry wash and unpacked there, hoping its banks would protect me somewhat from the blowing sand. On the other side of the river was a great sheer cliff behind which the sun dropped all too slowly, the shadow creeping across the water to spread over us. But still the wind blew. We ate sand along with our canned chicken and sweet potatoes and breathed it, and when I went to bed that night I spread my veil across my face.

chapter

18

That was the night the field mice came. "Hundreds of them," Charles said at breakfast. But perched high on my army cot, I had not seen or heard or felt a single one, and I was rather sorry to have missed this one adventure with wild life— for we had seen little more than a crow or two for many a day, and I have always been fond of field mice. They seem so much more noble that the ordinary mouse. While my house was being built and I was camping in the shell of it, one came in and lived with me, quite unafraid, and I became quite devoted to him. When I took off my slippers to toast my feet at the fire before going to bed, he would slip inside one of them and sit there most companionably, bright eyes fixed upon mine in such a fashion that my humanity and his mousehood seemed to dissolve, leaving two living creatures communing amicably. But I do not know that I could have established so personal a relationship with droves of Arizona mice.

Don said persuasively, looking up from his study of the maps spread out on the half-cleared breakfast table. "It's only seven miles. How about it?"

"And seven miles back?"

He nodded, putting the maps away in their plastic container.

"Too much. I might make it there, but you all would have to carry me back."

Bruce, washing dishes, gave me a grin. "We'll do our best. If the going is hard we may stay overnight."

Don was not looking at me; he was bent over watching some

ants crawl across the sand, gathering up crumbs that had dropped from the table.

"That's all right. I'll just wait here for you," I said, "and you you can tell me all about Rainbow Bridge when you get back."

He looked thoughtful and, without seeming to notice what he was doing, scooped up a handful of sand and buried the ants under it. They burrowed out, found more crumbs and again set out in the direction they had been taking. He took up more sand.

"No, no, let them go," I said.

He stood up, crushed the ants under his feet. Then he gave me his quick reassuring smile, "There's nothing here to bother you, so—okay."

"It isn't nature, it's human beings one has to be afraid of," I said, "and there'll be none of them here."

"Let's go," Charles called from the lower ledge.

Fred stopped to ask, "What will you do all day?"

"Have a little peace and quiet for a change," I smiled. "But you might leave me your Stegner—I'll finish that."

They stuffed their pockets with sandwiches, a few odd cans of food, Tony and Charles shouldered their heavy photographic equipment and I stood and watched them trail off down the sandy shore toward the low green cottonwoods and elders that clustered around the mouth of the side canyon of Aztec Creek. Quickly they passed out of sight and hearing. I was quite alone, more alone than I had ever been in all my life, more so than I would perhaps ever be again. In a physical sense, at least. Beyond the rim of the canyon stretched mile on mile of rock and sand, empty of man, bare of all but the sparsest stunted growth of desert plant. Above was the deep blue cloudless sky and at my feet the river. The boats no longer tugged at their moorings, for the water had gone down overnight and they lay flat on the sand as if washed up by some storm of which I was the sole survivor. Oddly, I felt no hint of loneliness. Indeed I was rather pleased to have this day of solitude ahead of me. I thought of

Marvell's line, "Two paradises 'twere in one, To live in Paradise alone," and this was really a beautiful spot. "Well," I said aloud to rock and river, "Here I am. Well?" I said again. "So what?" they seemed to answer.

With that I got to work building up the embers of the breakfast fire, setting a pail of water to boil. I did my washing and had spread it out on the ledge to dry before the morning sun got high enough to hit me. Then I looked about for shade. The dry wash, where I had set my cot for the night, was no refuge— the sun came straight down into it and was reflected from its bare mud-and-rock banks. So I went beyond it to where I could creep in behind a tamarisk. There I spread my sleeping bag on the sloping ground and settled down to read.

Almost at once the wind began to rise. I had to dash to save my washing from blowing away. The sand cut my face and hands. From the turn of the river downstream a bar of sand projected, lapped by the water, but close to the canyon wall where it was dry the wind caught it up in clouds and whipped it toward me. The tin plates and cups left to dry on the table were caught by the wind and sent spinning. I had a frantic time chasing them, weighing them down with stones. My cot bed blew over and lay, legs in midair, like something crazy. Don's washboard he had bought in Greenriver went end over end. I ran about tucking things away, setting rocks on top of them, then came back again to my small retreat. But the sun meanwhile had shifted and the thin spindly branches of the tamarisk gave me little shelter. It was really hellish hot.

At last I rigged up a blanket that kept out sun and sand to some extent, and tied it in place with string, pinning it over with safety pins—for in my plastic bag I carried almost as many small useful things as had Mrs. Lecks and Mrs. Aleshine in their famous casting away. Again I settled myself to read and the hot hours passed. Without taking my eyes from the page, I peeled out of my garments, one by one. There were certain advantages in being alone, I thought, and I might as well enjoy them.

But the sun was relentless, the heat increasing as noon came on. Even this most fascinating book could no longer distract my mind. I laid Wallace Stegner face down in the sand and went to the water's edge. How queer it was, standing there in sun and wind. Did our savage ancestors feel like this, I wondered, raw and helpless against the elements? Vulnerable? Maybe they were tougher and more accustomed to it. I remembered reading once that if we thought of our fellow humans beings, even our bitterest enemies, as the skeletons to which they would eventually be reduced, we would feel pity for them, and being thus more aware of our mortal transience and fragility, we would find it easier to be kind. But bone was strong and enduring. It was the flesh that could bleed and suffer. Perhaps we should all go bathing together—Russians, Chinese and all the people who are strange and terrifying to each other when clad and armed. Then our common humanity might loom larger in our minds. Maybe the nudists had something, after all. It amused me to imagine a meeting of the heads of state, a top-level conference, a gathering of diplomats without benefit of so much as a top hat. It would not be a pretty sight but it might have a salutary effect.

I leaned down and felt the water. It was heavenly cool. So in I waded, stirring up clouds of silt. I lay down in it, stretched out, eyes closed against the sun, hands clasped behind my head, one elbow tilted downward to anchor me in the mud. For the first time since the sun had come up I was comfortable. I would just spend the rest of the day right here—why hadn't I thought of it sooner?

Did I doze? I do not know. I only know that all at once I no longer felt the water pouring over me; I was moving with it. I reached for bottom and it was not there. I whirled over, struck out for shore—only a few feet away. But the current had me, I could make no headway against it and the roar of swifter water down below came louder to my ears. I fought till I had no breath left, then turned helpless on my back, yet afloat. Did my whole life pass before me in that moment? It did not. Instead all in an instant I seemed to see the others returning, searching for me, finding me below the bend, caught on a rock, not only drowned but—like this! Dear me, that would never do. There was nothing unseemly about getting drowned, but to be discovered naked as a jaybird! Then, in a curiously detached flash of amusement the very fact that I could think at such a moment of so incongruous, so ridiculous a thing as propriety brought me to the brink of laughter. I relaxed and new strength came to me, or perhaps it was only a kindly counter-current that caught me. But I like to think that a bit of mirth in the face of near disaster was the saving factor. At any rate, almost at once my feet struck bottom and I staggered ashore.

Now let the sun shine hot as it liked, let the wind-blown sand cut me as it carved the cliffs to fantastic shape, and grate my face to gargoyle features—no matter. I would not complain, and I would never tell my campanions what a simple-minded idiot I had been, to get caught in the current. So I made myself a sandwich and went back to my book and the thin shade of the tamarisk tree. When the high jagged peak on the western wall pointed a narrow bit of shade across the river to make a cool triangle on the sand, I put on my clothes and went to sit in it. I was there when Fred and Bruce came into sight and shouted hello! They looked quite beautiful to me. The others followed soon after and had tales to tell of how wonderful Rainbow Bridge was and how Al, climbing up by Moki steps, got rimrocked on the side of a cliff, and how long and hot the tramp had been. I listened and said nothing of how I had spent the day except to thank Fred for his *Beyond the Hundredth Meridian* and say how much I had enjoyed reading it. I did not even complain of sun and sand.

During dinner, Charles, humping himself around his plate

to keep out the blowing sand, said, "Has it been like this all day?"

"Yes," I said.

And the sand blew half the night, too. I lay awake for a long time, till the wind went down and all I could hear was the sound of the river. The stars were brilliant till the moon set them at a distance and dazzled the edge of the cliff with white fire.

Next morning while we ate breakfast here came the wind again. So it was good to get in the boats and escape the sand. The heat was with us, the wind against us. But even so, it seemed to me a day of great peace and beauty. Fred in the small boat with Don made sketches, Tony read *Moby Dick,* the engines chugged away. Charles's camera buzzed as he turned it on the high red and buff walls of Tower Butte that loomed up ahead of us. Al read a murder and now and then sang a line from the song he never finished—"The higher up the cherry tree—" So I shall never know what hung higher up the cherry tree. Another line—surely from another song—was more complete in itself—"Leave your worries on the doorstep," he sang, reading on. I had left mine far, far behind. In space and time. And, though I knew that with the falling river we might not be able to go beyond Lee's Ferry, I still felt as if it would be ages before I would have to do anything more than float down the swift brown river and balance my shattered parasol against the wind and hear Al's other line of song. He was like a three-noted bird—"I get ideas, I get ideas—" What were they? I shall never know.

But I did find out a little more about him that day, for when he finished his murder I moved across the duffel to sit beside him. "Al," I said, "in that book of Stegner's I've been reading I came across the name of Galloway, a man way back yonder who figured out a new kind of boat for the rivers and got up the idea of running the rapids stern first. Was he any kin to you?"

"My great-uncle. Nate Galloway. He built a boat on the Duchesne River and came down this way clear to Needles back in the nineties. Then he was on the Stone expedition later. Used to hunt and trap through all this country." He himself had done a lot of camping, mostly in the Uintas, he said, but this was his first summer on the rivers. He had been in the Signal Corps during the war driving transports, he had worked in Roosevelt where he was born and here and there as an electrician. He had driven trucks for a while, had been in twenty-seven states. "But," he added, "I'm entering the dental school in Provo in the fall. I'm settling down now."

"I guess that competent-looking Virginia of yours has seen to that," I said.

He grinned, his teeth very white in contrast to that black beard of his. "And it's not too bad, either," he admitted.

At this moment a shout from Don made us all look where he was pointing. "Crossing of the Fathers," he called back to us.

I had just been reading about it—that this was where Father Escalante had crossed the river on his way back to New Mexico in 1776. It had been an Indian crossing before that, and later the Navajos had used it in wintertime, when the river was frozen, to pass on their marauding raids on the Mormons. Until the Mormons blasted off a great rock that blocked their exit from the canyon.

We lunched here on a strip of sand under the shade of some box elders. "I don't see how they got across the river here unless they swam," I said, looking out over the brown swirling surface of the water and remembering how it felt to be caught in that current.

"They swam their horses," Don told me. "Part way, at least. There is a shoal in the center out there and with low water they could follow it downstream for quite a way till they came to another one that leads across to the far side."

"Let's try it, Al," Bruce said.

So they put on life preservers, blew up their air mattresses, and jumping into the water, floated away downstream, shouting, rolling off now and then, and having such fun that I quite envied them. But I contented myself with swinging my feet over the side and splashing in a mild and dignified manner. We overtook them a mile or so downstream and hauled them aboard, much refreshed and cooled off for the rest of the afternoon.

We made several stops before we found a good campsite that evening. At one, Fred, leaping out, rope in hand, sank at once to his knees in quicksand, so that would not do. At the next, Don and Bruce fought their way through the thick growth at the water's edge to come back and report that there was no clearing where we could set up camp. The next stop was at the mouth of a narrow canyon half blocked by small trees and boulders. Charles jumped out to investigate, disappeared into the canyon. Don, looking ahead, said there was a better landing spot a few hundred yards further downshore, so we floated on alongside a level stretch of sand perhaps thirty feet wide with a thousand-foot sheer cliff rising behind it. The small beach ended where the canyon wall came out in wooded tiers and broken rock to the water's edge. There we tied up the boats and I jumped ashore. "Look out for that spot," I shouted, skirting a queer-looking place that gave under my weight. But Don jumped up and down on it and did not break through. He and Fred hauled down some large stones which they laid on top of it so that the others could bring the boxes and duffel across.

I had never seen such a weird-looking sinkhole, filmed over as it was by a toughened layer that resembled an elephant's hide in color and texture. It wavered up and down as they stepped on it, but seemed at first too tough to break. I was quite fascinated by it, and setting up my cot directly beyond it in the angle of the cliff, I kept watching, for I had a feeling that if the hide broke, it would reveal a bottomless pit below. There was something evil, ugly, about the place.

Charles came back from his little exploring trip. "You must go up that canyon. It's marked on my map—Guardian Pool—it's not far."

I looked up at the sky, gold and rosy with a sunset that was mirrored in the wide sweep and turn of the river before us. "It's too late now."

Charles nodded. "I'll take you there after breakfast in the morning. I'm going to cook dinner tonight."

"Any snakes there?" Tony asked.

"Hundreds, all over the place," Charles laughed, for Tony was always on the lookout for snakes, though the only time he had seen one, back at McPherson's ranch, he had just remarked in a very conversational tone, "Why, there's a rattlesnake."

I sat on the edge of my cot and watched the fading sky and listened to the gentle murmur of the river. When I looked down at the sinkhole, I saw that the stones had cut through the elephant-hide surface. Little streams of water were trickling around them as they sank, and here and there on the surface small fountains of water bubbled out to run down and join the river. Suddenly I was reminded of the pictures in the Doré-illustrated "Inferno" that I used to get from the bottom shelf of the whatnot in the parlor on Sunday afternoons when I was a child and lying on my stomach on the rug, examine with horrified fascination. It showed people buried alive, head first, their legs sticking out of holes from which smoke arose. Here was no smoke from eternal fires, only water, but the effect was curiously similar. I hoped I would not walk in my sleep that night and tumble head first into this evil hole.

"Come and get it," Charles shouted.

He had been stirring and tasting and mixing things in the big pot over the fire while Fred set up his tent a little way beyond and the others carried their sleeping bags down toward the mouth of the side canyon. It was a queer mixture, for he had added canned fish to the chicken-and-spaghetti. But we were hungry and it tasted good, if unusual, and when we had finished, we sat on in the light of the fire, talking.

Charles asked Al—apropos of what I do not remember—if he had been married in the Temple.

"Oh, no." He looked quite shocked at the suggestion. "I'm not good enough." Then as we all waited for some explanation, he added, "You see, I'd been married before, my wife too. And I smoke—and—there were other things."

After this we got him to tell us more about his church, its way of taking care of the poor and how everyone worked for the general good. When he was only ten or twelve, he said, he, like others of his age, had gone about after school collecting what people could spare in the way of food and clothing, delivering his bundles to a distribution point. He explained the system of elders and the organization of the church, its history and early struggles. He told us how in church anyone in the congregation at any moment might be called on to take over the service, and how in childhood they were taught and prepared for this. It sounded to me like excellent training. I looked across at Bruce, who had just been listening all this while. "Did you have this sort of bringing-up too?" I asked.

"Well," said Bruce rather apologetically, "it just happens that I am an Episcopalian."

I don't know why I was so astounded. Except that I had taken it for granted that, since he lived in Utah, he must be a Mormon. Or maybe I had just begun to attribute all virtues to the Mormon Church.

Well, I thought, this only went to prove—what I knew already —that the sect or kind of religion does not matter, it is the individual that counts, it is having some religion that is important —or having a reasonable facsimile thereof. For I have know confirmed unbelievers who were kind and honest, and above all courageous. For surely it takes even greater courage to face life—and death—nobly, lacking expectation of immortality or reward.

It was still hot when I went to my cot and a little later I heard the others shouting and splashing up by the mouth of the side canyon, having a swim before turning in. I rolled over and went to sleep while they were still at it. I woke from sound sleep to a nightmare of wind and flying fire and thunder that rolled and echoed down the canyon. For a befuddled moment I thought I had gotten trapped in that Doré picture of my childhood; then I realized that the wind had whipped the campfire into life again, was blowing the live embers toward me, along with all the tin cups and plates from the supper table. "Fred! Fred!" I shouted and scrambled frantically for my flashlight.

"Coming, coming," he called. I gave him my light and he ran about, barelegged, collecting what he could, pouring water on the fire. Then Charles and Don, Bruce and Al and Tony came. By a flash of brilliant lightning, I saw them dragging their sleeping bags behind them as they ran toward me, for all the world like a flock of chicks frightened by a hawk's shadow, Don shouting, "Mamma, mamma, let us in your room! Oh mamma, mamma!" and Charles laughing and yet breathless calling "I want my mamma!"

"Come in, come in," I shouted back. "You'll be safe here." For we all had read of how in a cloudburst all in a moment a ten- or twenty-foot wall of water could come tearing down a side canyon, washing all before it.

They settled down close to me in the protection of the high cliff that curled around us. I spread my poncho over me and lay down again. Black clouds went flying across the sky, the wind made a wild rushing sound in the trees on the rocky ledges above me, little waves flapped at the shore at my feet. Big raindrops tapped my cheeks like cold wet finger tips, thunder rolled, but farther away now. Then abruptly the rain stopped, and as I watched, the clouds broke and the stars were there.

After a while the wind died down and a stillness came. There was only the persistent sweet sound of the river, a rustle as someone nearby turned in his sleeping bag. They were all wrapped in slumber now, each in his little cocoon. In all our camping nights I had never been so surrounded, and it was strange that now, lying wakeful far into the night, a great loneliness came over me. They were all so young, I thought, so damnably young, so deep in fresh young sleep. I felt as if I were the only living creature in the world. I wished for some companionable presence, a kindred contemporary in this great dark isolation of my spirit, some human warmth within reach of my hand.

"Peace, old woman, be still," I whispered in the night. "Let the sleeping dogs of longing lie. Rest now on your narrow cot under the starry sky."

chapter

19

The next morning, Monday, July 11, as soon as I had finished my second cup of coffee, I asked Charles if that side canyon was really worth going to see. He and Don were spreading out their maps on the table and he gave me a vague, somewhat distracted glance. "Yes, yes, you ought to see it—only I—"

"Just tell me how to find that pool—and there weren't really any snakes there, were there?"

He laughed. "Of course not. You take a left turn after a bit—"

Tony spoke up, "I'll go with you."

So we set out along the sandy strip of shore and arrived shortly at the tree- and boulder-choked entrance to the canyon. There was a ledge on the right, not too high, which we were able to follow for some distance, then by sliding down and leaping the tiny stream we found passage on the other side. There were reeds and grasses here where the earth was spongy and, as I planted my feet in Tony's footprints, I could not help thinking of those "hundreds of snakes" of Charles's, imaginary though they were, and I half expected every stick to rise up and rattle at me.

It was cool and fresh-smelling here at the bottom of this narrow cleft in the rock. High above us the sun had laid a yellow band, a bright border below its rim, and the light was reflected in a paler yellow on the opposite side. The slender strip of sky was deep blue and cloudless.

"Charles said it was not far." I paused to get my breath, for Tony's long legs were carrying him at a pace which now began to be too brisk for me.

"I'll go ahead and shout back to you," he said.

I followed more slowly, but close enough to see which side of boulder or bush he found best. He was a small figure, dwarfed by the height of the canyon walls, when I saw him pause. He gave a shout that echoed from wall to wall, then disappeared. When I neared that spot I saw there was yet another fissure branching off to the left and it was into this that Tony had vanished. There was no running stream here, only hard sand, a clear pathway at most some twenty feet wide, with sheer walls, slightly concave, rising from lower shadows to rose and gold, to shoulder the sky a thousand feet above. At a crook of this small canyon, Tony was standing motionless. I moved to his side.

Before us was a hollowed-out niche where the walls curled inward to shape a ragged quarter moon of deep blue sky that was not at the zenith, but off-center, giving the place a devil-may-care aspect, like a man with his hat on the side of his head. Here at our feet lay a still small pool, an emerald cut to a perfect circle, a jewel framed in a ring of amber sand. Low on the walls was a band of maidenhair fern, its rich deep green giving color to the pool. There was no sound here, no rush of waters such as had filled my ears for so many days and nights. There was not a ripple on the pool, not a breath of stirring air to move the trailing delicate fronds of fern. I felt as if I had strayed by chance into the golden, glowing heart of the world and found it good.

Tony and I looked at each other briefly, then in silence we circled the pool. Our feet, noiseless on the hard-packed sand, left no mark of our passage. We might have been disembodied spirits. And who knows, I thought, what choice invisible shades might walk beside us with sandaled, silent feet? Some sages of the ages, strayed from Elysian fields, could hold converse in such a spot as this—"solemn troops and sweet societies." And if only my ear were properly attuned I might catch a phrase, a word that would be the key to wisdom.

Again at the entrance we stopped and looked. "Gosh!" Tony said in a whisper. Then we turned and made our way back to camp.

"Did you find it?" Charles asked.

"Yes. But tell me, why do they call it Guardian Pool?"

"I don't know. Somebody found it and named it. That's how it is down on the map."

Most of the duffel was aboard, but no one seemed ready to leave just yet. Al had decided to shave off his beard and Charles had to have a shot of this complicated process. I did some washing, and everyone spruced up a bit so we would make a good impression on the population of Lee's Ferry, where we would probably arrive late in the afternoon. Then the motor gave us trouble. Don was determined to repair it. He seemed to feel that he should be able to control a mechanical thing in the same manner in which he might discipline one of his fourth-grade pupils. And so, after we had shoved off, for almost two hours we just drifted with the current, Bruce and Al putting in an occasional stroke of the oars to guide us, till at last he gave up and got out the spare motor.

Charles was doing his washing this morning. He was up to his elbows in a pail of soapsuds, various garments were spread around him on the platform, all washed and smoothed out and drying in the sun. He was getting ready for civilization. I said, "Now if you could just wash what you have on and take a swim with a cake of soap, you and your entire wardrobe would be as clean as the day you left home."

"We-ell," said Charles with a longing look at the water, "I might, only—"

"Don't mind me," I said with decision, getting to my feet. "I know how to keep my eyes front, and I will. You must remem-

ber that I once dissected the entire male form and I assure you
that I have neither curiosity nor interest in turning my head."
With that and the sound of Charles's laughter in my ears, I
went back to my heap of duffel and sat down with such emphasis
that I broke the spout off the water can that had gotten mixed
with the duffel that morning. By this time I was so callused that
only the can was injured. A little later, I heard shouts and
splashings, for Bruce and Al had quickly joined Charles, hanging on to the rope at the stern of the boat.

The sun blazed down without mercy. I moved forward, took
off my shoes and dangled my feet in the water. We stopped
once to mount a high bank and explore a cave. It looked
scarcely worth the effort, but I scrambled up after the others
lest I miss something. The cave proved to be far larger than it
looked from the water; it was shallow but wide with a high
curving roof. On the wall there were names and dates cut in the
pale yellow stone and Al found his great-uncle's name among
them, half worn away, but still legible, with the date, 1894.
We lunched for the first time this day in the boat, having lost so
much time getting started. And we lost still more time as we went
on down the river, for every now and then, in spite of Don's
watchfulness, we ran aground on sandbars and all hands—but
me—had to get out and haul and drag to get the boats into
deeper water.

The significance of this was all too plain. The river was too
low here for comfort, but with only sandbars to contend with
it was still possible to get through. Below Lee's Ferry where
Marble Canyon began with its rocks and rapids there would be
no chance of passage. "But we'll see when we get to Lee's
Ferry," Charles said. "We'll read the gage there and know just
what is ahead."

In the middle of the afternoon the scene around us changed,
became more dramatic and exciting. Cliffs rose some two thousand feet on each side, there were sharp twists and turns in the

course of the river, and my neck began to ache from tilting my head up to look. This was just a sample of what we would meet with if we went on down toward the Grand Canyon, and I felt sad to think we might not be able to make it. On the other hand, I had seen a good deal. Perhaps I had seen enough.

In the midst of all this grandeur we came upon Sentinel Rock. It was curiously disappointing, far less impressive and poetic than the drawing in the Stegner book. Indeed we might not have noticed it particularly had it not been marked on the map. It did not rise from a small island as in the picture, and from only one angle did it present the appearance of a sentinel. This set me to thinking about the difference between fact and facts touched and altered by imagination and personality, and I wondered how it would be with my words when I came to describe these scenes through which we had passed. Would they tell it true? Well, there would be the photographic record for reality. My account would have to be just the way it seemed to me.

So the afternoon passed, the walls moved back, their height diminished. We passed a great glacier of salmon-colored sand, blown over from the Painted Desert, Charles said, and came upon a water gage. We drew up alongshore and stared at it with chagrin. It was not even in the water, but stood high and dry on the bank. Al got out with a spade and dug down to water level in order to read it. "Seventy-eight hundred," he called to us.

Seventy-eight hundred what, I wondered, but I did not have the heart to ask, everyone looked so downcast. We couldn't go on with less that twelve thousand, Don had said.

So we came into Lee's Ferry. Here were a few trees, some scattered small houses and a dirt road that came right to the water's edge and stopped. Don turned in and tied up the boats. We sat there in the hot afternoon sun and we seemed to have come to a place of the dead. Such buildings as there were had a closed deserted look and there was not one human in sight. "Maybe the town is further down," I suggested.

Just then we heard the sound of a motor and from downstream there came a small boat with one man in it. He tied up beside us, cut the engine. Yes, this was Lee's Ferry, all right, and he was Dean Tidball, in charge of the government survey station here. And no, there was nobody else here. We all stared at him in dismay. He was a lean, sun-browned man with an easy, amiable air, but no, he never let anybody use his car and of course the truck belonged to the government and he could not rent that out to anyone. The nearest phone was about forty miles off.

It looked as if we had come 31 days and nights and traveled 719 river miles in order to land at the end of nowhere.

chapter

~~~~~~

20

"Of course," said Mr. Tidball a little later, "There's a kind of motel lodge up on the highway."

"How far?" Fred demanded.

"About seven miles. It's a bus stop."

Seven miles! I could never walk that far—and what about my luggage? I felt as if I would be spending the rest of my life right here in this deserted, shadeless spot.

"I go in three days a week, to pick up supplies and mail," Mr. Tidball went on.

"When will you be going next?" Charles asked.

"In about half an hour," he said.

"Will you take me?" I asked.

"Yes, ma'm, be glad to."

"Will you have room for me?" Fred asked.

"Sure thing. If you don't mind the truck."

Half an hour to shake out my two duffel bags, find my civilization clothes—if there was a bus stop, there would be a rest room where I could change—repack and make sure I was leaving nothing behind! And say good-by. But I had no time now to think of that. I set to work there in the broiling sun and I had just gotten my toilet things, my crumpled black suit and squashed hat, street shoes and nylons into a small cloth handbag when Mr. Tidball blew his horn and I saw the truck at the top of the slope, waiting for us. For the last time Tony and Bruce shouldered my duffel bags and the others came with Fred and me up the slope to the truck.

"Now as soon as you get to a phone, you'll be sure to call Vernal and have them send the truck for us?" Don said for the third time.

"Yes, yes," Fred and I said together.

Bruce gave Fred a slip of paper. "Just call my mother, would you? Here's her number. Tell her I'm okay and I'll be home sometime."

"Sometime's right," Tony groaned. "We'll be stuck here for two days at least."

Al gave me a phone number. "Would you please call Virginia? Tell her to get forty dollars out of the bank and bring me some clothes and come on here and we'll have a trip to Las Vegas."

"All right, all right," I promised.

Mr. Tidball had the motor going. Charles was cranking his movie camera. I gave them all a quick hug and quicker good-by, good luck, and climbed up into the high front seat, Fred right after me. They all shouted good-bys. Al came close alongside us, saying, "Tell her if she doesn't come in a hurry, I'll be gone in the truck, to Vernal."

"All right, I'll tell her." I leaned out the truck window. "Good-by, good-by and thank you all for everything! And—oh, Charles, I hope they won't cover it all up with mud and water! Just for electricity—"

"You see now what I'm trying to do with this." He tapped his camera.

"Yes, yes, and I'm right with you—good-by!"

The truck gathered speed and we were off. I turned to Fred. "It all happened so fast, I'm in a daze. I can't realize we are actually leaving them."

"I know," Fred said. "It's like leaving part of your life."

We jolted on down the road, stopping at the Piave Creek for Mr. Tidball to take a sample of the water—it was part of his day's job to do that, he said. Then again he stopped farther along and left us sitting on a rock by the roadside while he walked a mile or so down to the Colorado to take a sample or a measurement or something. Fred and I smoked and watched the sunset fade and Fred made a sketch of the two of us—how he got himself in, I don't know—in the back of his Stegner book, the truck in the background and the smoke of my cigarette curling up in a kind of question mark over my head.

Then we were off again, passing through a region of great standing rocks, passing a great cathedral-like formation, and abruptly we came out into the world. It was bare and flat and the far horizon put a rim all around it. Just at dusk we drew up at the side of a long low building that faced a paved highway.

"There's a restaurant here; you can get your supper and wait for the bus," Mr. Tidball said as he helped Fred with our luggage.

"Where does the bus go?" Oddly enough, this was the first time either of us had thought to ask.

"Flagstaff. It'll be along sometime toward morning."

Flagstaff, Arizona. That was all right. Any place that was a place would be all right. I could take off from there for California, Fred for the East.

We went into a fair-sized room with a bar and small tables. A man and two women sat on the high stools at the bar. Three young Indians in tight jeans, plaid shirts and wide hats with rolled-up brims lounged at the other end. There was no one eating. A man was behind the bar and Fred went up to him. No, he said, the restaurant was closed—they'd run out of water.

"But can't we get anything to eat?" Fred asked.

The man beckoned to one of the women and she came over. "Sure, I can give you crackers and cheese—and you can have some beer before we close the bar."

First of all Fred, always thinking of others, got a box of cold beer for Mr. Tidball to take back to the river and he did not forget to put in some packages of powdered grape for any of them who did not want beer. Mr. Tidball, his arms full of papers and packages, told us good-by, said, "Oh, it was nothing," when we thanked him—and there we were, with half the night to wait out.

There were rooms, the woman said, but we could use no water. The little they had must be saved in case of fire. Her price seemed too high for the little sleep we would get, and when she told us there was a sitting room across the road at the motel where we could wait, we decided to sit it out. The restaurant would close soon, she said, but we could stay there, if we liked, for our beer and crackers and cheese.

While we were eating, still in something of a daze at being out in the world again, it occurred to Fred that there might be some mail for us here. I did not expect any, for we had arrived nearly a week sooner than planned, and even had anyone written, there was no post office here or at Lee's Ferry.

He came back from the bar with several letters for me, a big fat one for himself. I tore mine open, and as I read, my own small world came round me with a bang. The impact was almost more than I could take. I could eat no more. I looked across at Fred, chuckling over his long typewritten pages and I wondered if he knew how lucky he was, to have letters he could laugh over. Lucky? We get what we deserve, or so they say, and certainly Fred deserved all that was good. As for me, well, I was probably getting my deserts, and—well, there it was.

Fred, as if feeling my eyes on him, looked up. "Listen, Esther says—" and he read me a few lines, to which I paid scant heed.

Then the lights overhead blinked. The restaurant was about to close. So we said good night and carried our luggage across the road to the lodge. The sitting room with empty chairs and Indian rugs was utterly deserted. Indeed the whole place had an air of desolation, as if a plague had struck and all the human beings had taken flight. "This air is terrible," I said and went back to the porch. But it was wide, low-roofed and no coolness was here, either. I sat down on the stone steps and, after Fred had finished writing a letter, he came and joined me.

Down the road, all the lights had gone out; there was only darkness on the flat level earth, and the stars. We watched Orion slide lower and lower on the horizon, and the slow hours passed. We talked a little, I smoked and Fred had his pipe going. "There seem to be awfully few of us, all of a sudden," I said after a while.

"Yes, I miss them too," Fred said.

"You know, Robert Louis Stevenson says somewhere that the best we find in our travels is an honest friend and that he is a fortunate voyager who finds more than one."

"It's in his preface to the *Travels with a Donkey*."

"I feel as if I had been very lucky that way on this trip."

"Yes," he agreed. "Same here."

"Well, Fred," I said after a long silence, "we've seen some sights, haven't we?" Even as I was speaking, I seemed to hear, as I often do, for childhood impressions go deep, my father's voice reading from the Bible, as he did every morning—"The kingdom of God cometh not with observation . . . for, behold, the kingdom of God is within you."

Fred nodded. "And we've had some experiences that will be a part of us for as long as we live."

"That makes us kind of kin—having shared all this." For different as we all were, the experience had drawn us together in a remarkable way. But then, my thoughts ran on, wasn't every human being a fellow traveler with the next one in what John Bunyan called the wilderness of this world? So why couldn't all the peoples of the earth feel akin, knowing that we are all embarked upon the fearful and wonderful journey of life on this planet—living, breathing, having children, eating and drinking, loving, laughing, dying, enduring under the great sky? "We take our common humanity too much for granted,"

I said aloud, "and we are too blind to the wonders of the world. It takes such a journey as this to make us see."

"These canyons would shock the most callous into wonder," Fred said.

"Yet I suppose each of us will remember them differently. What's sharp and vivid to me may have been overlooked by you. You know," I went on, "I wish everyone would write his own account of the Expedition, and tell it true. That would be like a half-dozen searchlights turned on the whole reality that is too much for one to illuminate alone." Suddenly I remembered an old Mississippi friend, Susie Neill—Susie Ridgway, that was. She used to look at me with a twinkle and say, "I wish I knew what you were thinking in the back of your head." I chuckled to myself. That was what I really wanted to know about these companions of mine.

"Of course," Fred said, "Charles will have the physical reality on that film of his—and as he goes around the country giving his lecture, he will tell it as it seemed to him."

"Yes, I'm looking forward to that."

"Will you write what you really thought?"

"I'll try. Though the hardest thing in the world is to be completely and truly oneself." Then after a while I asked, "What does it mean, Fred? All that we saw and did."

He puffed on his pipe in silence for a bit. "The meaning— it's always so damned elusive."

Yes, I thought, how often reading a book I had said to myself, "Now here's a man who really *knows*. He will tell me. In the last chapter, maybe." Then when I got there I saw that, for all his learning, he knew no more than I. And science, too, all too often just bogged down in fact.

Fred said, "Maybe we each have to seek it alone, face it. Not forgetting we are all a part of the same mystery, and so not alone."

"But at least we got a *feel* of something, didn't we?" I per-

sisted. As when Bob was telling me about his research, I did
not understand the detail, yet I got a glimmer of its essence.
And suddenly I remembered the old man on Tangier Island, the
oyster man. He said, "Sometimes when I'm on my boat alone
at night, I lie on the deck and look up at the stars and I get
a feeling." So now, looking up at the wide sky I repeated,
"We got a feeling."

"Um-m," Fred agreed. "Of time, of having been where past
and present meet. Those rocks. The history of the earth is in
them. And coming up here on top again, there's the feel of this
world, revolving in space."

"Makes me small, diminished. And yet bigger too, more
important. Because I can see and wonder, because my mind can
leap from the marshes of the dinosaur's day to this. Oh Fred,
we see more than those coral bugs at Jones Creek! That's something." Then I quoted another stanza of the poem I started that
day in Hidden Passage:

> All things hidden lead us on and on.
> The root and end of man are secret things,
> But in this rocky heart of solitude
> The fearful, deep, primeval silence brings
> A kind of answer to our WHITHER? WHENCE?
> A whisper that can almost tell us WHY.

Fred said little, but I think he liked those lines. Anyway,
after a while I was emboldened to ask, "Did you get what you
came for, Fred?"

"Um-m—yes, I think I did."

Then, feeling as if we were the only two left living on this
wide dark circle of the earth, I told him what I had imagined
about him on that first night of our meeting, back in Green
River, Wyoming. "Was I right?"

He turned in the semidarkness and gave me a rather amazed
look. "That was—some of it." For always there is more, deep
down, where none can see. "What about you? Did you get what

you came for?"

I was silent for a long time. In our talk, in the feeling of warmth and companionship that Fred always gave me, I had found a brief oblivion from my own personal problems that had come down upon me as I sat with him in the café across the street. Now I was again assailed. I searched my mind, I asked myself what there was, in all I had seen and done on this voyage down the canyons, that was the answer to what I sought. What was there I could carry out with me into my world that would sustain me in time of grief and dismay? Then strangely enough after all the more dramatic places I had been, it was as if I were walking again, silent and trackless on the amber sand around the still green pool. Guardian Pool. My Guardian Pool, my keeper. A place of peace and reassurance to which I could always withdraw, as now. Reassurance, yes. For no matter how old we get, or even how wise, we all long to hear a voice saying, as to a child, "It's all right, little one, it's all right." And as I saw again the trailing fern that ringed it round, the scrap of deep blue sky overhead, small enough to be my own personal, intimate and bearable section of time, space and eternity, I felt a quietness come over the tumult of my spirit, and fresh courage came to me. I would manage somehow. Maybe everything was not as bad as it had looked at first glance. I'd make out. Anyway, I would try.

I turned to Fred. "Yes, yes, I think I got what I came for."

He looked at his watch. "We'd better get over on the highway," he said. "The bus will be here soon."